MINNESOTA'S HEADLINE MURDERS! 1900-1919

MINNESOTA'S HEADLINE MURDERS! 1900-1919

Patrick L. Shannon

— Beaver's Pond Press —
Minneapolis, MN

Edited by Beth Wright

ISBN: 978-1-59298-777-1
Library of Congress Catalog Number: 2017917026
Printed in the United States of America
First Printing: 2018
22 21 20 19 18 5 4 3 2 1

Book design by Athena Currier

Beaver's Pond Press, Inc.
7108 Ohms Lane
Edina, MN 55439–2129

(952) 829-8818
www.BeaversPondPress.com

To order, visit www.ItascaBooks.com or call
1-800-901-3480 ext. 118. Reseller discounts available.

In Memorandum

Michael J. Conley, a shooting guard

Wally M. Hinz, a first-class guy

Dawn Murphy Davidson and Judi Murphy Helmer—
kindness, love, and laughter is their remembrance.

Contents

Preface

A HUNDRED YEARS AGO, there were no crime-scene technicians. No one systematically collected and catalogued evidence. There were no forensic laboratories to make comparative analysis of blood, DNA, body fluids, entrance and exit wounds, fingerprints, gunpowder residue, ballistics—or any of the types of processing evidence law-enforcement officials have at their disposal today.

There were no police academies or trainings, only on-the-job learning. If a murder happened in their jurisdiction, the local authorities were responsible for the entire investigation. Their goal was simply to find answers to the most fundamental questions of who, what, where, when, why, and how.

I can appreciate the challenges those early-twentieth-century investigators faced. I am a retired agent with the Minnesota Bureau of Criminal Apprehension and spent seven of my eighteen years working homicide cases. While in my time we had access to the latest investigative techniques and advanced forensic science, the motives for murder and the emotions involved were no different from what they were a hundred years ago: money, humiliation, jealousy, fear, resentment, anger. Moreover, like today, some investigations were satisfactorily concluded, and some were not.

For this book I researched murders that occurred in Minnesota from 1900 to 1919 (the beginning of Prohibition) and chose ten that grabbed all the headlines. The murders, subsequent investigations, and trials were the front-page news of their day. The courtrooms where the trials took place were always standing room only, and deputies turned many people away.

Most of the sources I used came from the Minnesota Historical Society Library. My research involved reading prison files, trial transcripts, death certificates, and newspaper accounts, including obituaries. I also visited cemeteries to obtain family data. I visited pertinent county historical societies to gather more information: Ramsey, Traverse, Hennepin, Brown, and Beltrami. I researched and found descendants of the victims and defendants and interviewed those willing to speak to me. I tried to be as thorough as the investigators were a hundred years ago.

For each chapter I created a narrator based on a historical person who played a role in the events described. Each raconteur, from the juror to the small-town chief of police to the defense attorney, offers a different perspective on the case.

The chapter narrators offer details of the crime, the circumstances that led up to it, the ensuing investigation, and the arrests, trials, and outcomes. At the end of each chapter, I've explained, based on my research, what happened to the key figures after the narrative.

The following chapters provide a glimpse of daily life in the early twentieth century as well as a portrait of the hard-working police officers, attorneys, judges, and others who aimed to provide justice for the people of the young state of Minnesota.

P. Leo
Minneapolis
December 2017

CHAPTER 1

A Woman to Die For

1900

"In the eyes of the law, it is as great a crime to murder a bad man as a good man, as an intoxicated man as a sober man."

—Hennepin County District Court Judge
Frank C. Brooks, February 18, 1901

The West Hotel of Minneapolis, one of the nation's most eminent hotels, was an unlikely location for the November 1900 murder of the young millionaire Leonard R. Day. The crime, its investigation, and the trial that followed were consistently the leading story in the local newspapers as well as many others throughout the country. The case read like a best-selling novel, with elements of mystery, wealth, sex, and violence.

Twenty-five-year-old Day inherited his wealth from his father, the owner of the Day Lumber Company of Minneapolis. At the time of his death, he lived with his mother at the West Hotel. His life became entangled with that of another young man, twenty-four-year-old Franklin H.

Hamilton, a sports reporter who also had a wealthy family (he was directly descended from Alexander Hamilton). Their connection was their mutual interest in a young woman, Caroline Slagle. Added to the mix were a billiard room, some unsavory characters, and an excess of alcohol.

The narrator for our story is Ezra Fitch Pabody (pronounced "Peabody"), a thirty-two-year-old bachelor who served on the jury in Hamilton's murder trial. His family moved from Indiana in the early 1880s, when his father became the pastor at Riverside Presbyterian Church in Minneapolis. Pabody was a draughtsman for the American Bridge Company who ordinarily enjoyed a quiet life at home with his parents and sister at 28 South Thirteenth Street in Minneapolis.

I first read about the murder of Leonard Day in the papers. The story caught my attention in part because I knew his nephew, Gene Day. I got curious after reading several articles, so after work one day, I walked over to the West Hotel, on Fifth and Hennepin, to learn more about where the crime took place. I first stopped to talk with the concierge, who told me the West is Minnesota's first world-class hotel with 407 luxurious furnished rooms, 140 baths, and the largest and most opulent lobby in the nation. The hotel advertises that it is 100 percent fireproof. I was amazed by the lobby, constructed of massive marble walls and pillars, flowing white marble stairs, glimmering hardwood floors, and glorious stained-glass windows. I learned the hotel was

E. F. PABODY, JR., FIRST JUROR.
Courtroom drawing of E.F. Pabody. Source: *Minneapolis Tribune*, February 5, 1901.

built by John West and opened in November of 1884. It is the most lavish and expensive residence this side of Chicago.

The concierge told me that the West employs more people than the largest flour mill in Minnesota. The residents use the bellhops for communication with other rooms or outside businesses. Each room has a speaking tube, which connects it to the business office. The concierge boasted about the hotel's posh silverware, English chinaware, and Irish linen from Belfast. It is too expensive for my budget: some rooms cost five dollars a night!

The newspaper articles I read recounted the murder, and the events preceding and following it, in detail. The night of Saturday, November 24, was windy and cold. Frank Hamilton spent the day covering a high school football game between Minneapolis Central and Elgin. He had supper at Scott Blake's bar and restaurant, then went to the *Minneapolis Times* building to write a summary of the game. At 8:30 he left his office to go on the "hotel run." This part of his job involved going to various hotels and checking their registries to see whether any celebrities were in town and available for an interview. That evening's hotel run began at the Vendome, moved to the West, and then on to the Nicollet Hotel and later the Golden West. He apparently did some drinking on his journey. He returned to the *Times* office, located 47-49 South Fourth Street, about 10:00, worked on a couple of stories, and visited with colleagues. At 11:00, he and another employee went across the street to George Starr's saloon. When his colleague had to leave, Hamilton telephoned his roommate, *Tribune* reporter Guy Canfield, and invited him to join him at the bar. They were already drinking heavily by the time two of their friends, Ralph Gary and Ray Evans, arrived and ordered their own drinks. When the saloon closed at 1:00, they headed to the West Hotel.

Meanwhile, Leonard Day had spent the evening with two friends at the Variety Theatre. After the show, they went to a restaurant and met up with two women. Apparently Day had set up the appointment ahead of time. They socialized for a short time and proceeded to the West Hotel. There the men assisted the two women into a hack[1] and sent them home.

1 A one-horse carriage that was the taxi service of the day.

West Hotel—500-514 Hennepin Avenue, Minneapolis.

Day entered the hotel by himself and went to the billiards room at 12:30. Fred George and Charles Force were playing billiards on one of the twelve tables in the room, and Day asked if he could join them. The billiards room was officially closed, but the men insisted on playing one more game. Charlie Ferris, the room attendant, gave in and allowed them to play longer. The hotel turns off the electricity in the building at midnight, so the only illumination in the room was from two gaslights above the table the men were playing on.

About 1:30 Sunday morning, in that dim, smoke-filled room, the pool game was still going when the thunderous, drunken crowd of Hamilton and his friends barged in from the bar. Fred George made the introductions. When Day realized he was meeting Hamilton, their conversation got heated. "You're the man I have been looking for!" Day yelled at Hamilton. "I told Miss Slagle that I was going to call you out." Day then asked Hamilton if he was the one who told Miss Caroline Slagle, a woman he'd been seeing, that Day had syphilis. Hamilton admitted that he had, and the two men exchanged heated words and then fell to the floor, wrestling. George separated them, and Day complained that Hamilton didn't fight fairly: he had pulled Day's hair. Day and Hamilton both decided they were going to settle the matter in a fistfight. Hamilton, however, was so drunk that Day felt it would not be a fair fight. Ray Evans stepped in and told Day he would fight for Hamilton. Day ignored him. Day and Hamilton agreed to postpone the fight, and Hamilton asked Day if they could shake on it. The two shook hands.

About the time this dispute was settled, another one broke out between Charles Force and Ray Evans. It seems Force had called Evans a vulgar name, and Evans kept pestering Force about it. Finally Force dropped his billiards stick, walked over to where Evans was sitting, and grabbed his head, slamming it back into the wall. The blow was so forceful it split open the back of Evans's head, and blood began to flow from the wound. Evans began to act like an insane man and attacked Force. The men were separated, and security was summoned. Night watchman Stephen O'Malley arrived and escorted Evans out of the room. Evans, while departing, screamed at Force that he would return and cut out his "g-- d--- heart."

Unexpectedly, Day and Hamilton again began exchanging punches—their momentary truce apparently at an end. George once more attempted to be the peacemaker and tried to separate the two combatants. He quickly realized that his right thumb and index finger were cut and bleeding profusely, so he left for the water closet to clean himself up. Moments later, Leonard Day staggered out of the shadows and collapsed into the arms of one of the men, who lowered him to the floor. Only a few men stayed behind in the room, including Hamilton and his roommate, Canfield. Night watchman O'Malley summoned the police.

I can imagine the confusion and panic that reigned as the men shouted orders to the bar employees for brandy and hot water. They took off Day's shoes and socks and poured hot water on his feet, trying to get him to drink some of the brandy. The men worked his arms up and down, and rubbed his hands. He was laid on a pool table with coats underneath his head. Hamilton rubbed Day's hands and, in his groggy state, prayed. All eyes were on Day as he labored to breathe. George Bennett, a hotel resident, observed the large amounts of blood coming from Day's chest. Putting his mouth next to Day's ear, he whispered, "You're dying." Why he said that, I will never know. Day's lips moved as if he wanted to respond. The men in the room watched as his lips stopped moving and he slipped into unconsciousness.

Now at Minneapolis police headquarters, Lieutenant Mealey dispatched officers Frank Cederburg and Thomas Rooney to the scene. Upon arrival they found Hamilton next to Day, in obvious grief and praying. Officer Rooney asked O'Malley what happened. He pointed to Hamilton and said, "He did it." Hamilton replied something to the

Leonard R. Day. Source: *Minneapolis Tribune*, February 18, 1901.

Franklin H. Hamilton. Source: *Minneapolis Tribune*, February 5, 1901.

effect that it was self-defense. Rooney took Hamilton over to the hotel bar and waited for Detective Joseph Lawrence to arrive and interview the witnesses.

Dr. William B. Murray finally arrived at 2:35 a.m. He immediately took off Day's jacket, vest, shirt, collar, and undershirt, and noticed a severe wound on the lower left area of Day's neck and markings on his head from a wicked beating. The doctor informed the men that because he couldn't stop the internal bleeding, Day would probably not survive. And in fact, Leonard Day never regained consciousness. He stopped breathing around 3:00 on Sunday morning as he lay on the pool table at the West Hotel.

Coroner Dr. Hugh J. Nelson arrived and ordered that the deceased be taken to the morgue for an immediate inquest. By this time, Day's family doctor, Dr. H. H. Kimball, and family attorney, John B. Atwater, had arrived. They insisted that Day's body be brought to an undertaking establishment. An argument followed, and it is my understanding that the coroner won.[2]

Officer Rooney and *Times* City Editor Charles R. Francis walked Hamilton down Hennepin Avenue to the police station. He was put in the superintendent's office—not a cell—for comfort's sake. Once at the station, Chief Doyle asked him to make a statement. Hamilton replied, "I refuse to talk about this matter. I have been advised by my attorney."

A coroner's inquest was held that Sunday afternoon. Witnesses must have been hurriedly gathered to testify. "There wasn't a man in the room that wasn't drunk," one observer stated. Hungover witnesses tried to recall and testify about the confusing and drunken brawl that had occurred in the billiards room twelve hours earlier. The majority of witnesses testified that Hamilton was the only one involved in an encounter with Day.

---

2 Back at the hotel, the question was who would tell the victim's mother, Laura Day, that her only child was gone. When no one came forward, Dr. Kimball went to her hotel room, woke her, and told her that her son was dead. Overwhelming grief struck Mrs. Day. Fourteen years earlier, she had lost her husband. Now she had lost her son, and perhaps her reason for living.

Deputy Coroner Dr. Charles A. Erdman described the fatal wound as a "gaping cut," an inch long at the junction of the collarbone and the breastbone. A knife had cut through the artery that lies directly underneath the collarbone, causing internal hemorrhaging. He was convinced that two knives or two blades had been used in the attack on Day.

The coroner's jury sorted out the witness statements as best they could. They rendered a verdict later that afternoon, stating Frank Hamilton was the person who killed Day. Hamilton was led to the county jail to await his trial.

The funeral for Leonard Day was held in the West Hotel parlor the following afternoon. The service was private, with only a few family members and friends attending. Day's body was then transported by a horse-drawn hearse south on Hennepin Avenue to Lakewood Cemetery in Minneapolis. I think he was buried before most of his friends and associates knew he was even dead.

The murder caused serious trouble for the West Hotel. The newspapers reported that the Sons of Old Harvard, one of the largest and most notable organizations in the northwestern United States, was scheduled

Hennepin County Courthouse, 1901.

to hold their annual convention at the renowned West starting on December 1. The cities of Minneapolis and St. Paul had been making arrangements for this convention for nearly a year. Four days after the murder, Minneapolis Mayor James Gray issued an order revoking the license for the sale of liquor at the West Hotel. The city blamed alcohol for the fights and the West Hotel for supplying it. Nevertheless, the mayor eventually gave into pressure from local businessmen, the liquor license was reinstated, and the convention was held at the West.

Little did I know that I would have a front-row seat for the murder trial I was reading about in the papers every day. I received a notice from a deputy to appear for jury duty, instructing me to be at the courthouse on the morning of February 4, 1901.

That Monday morning was cold and windy. I arrived at the brand-new courthouse on Fourth Avenue and went directly to courtroom number one on the third floor.[3] Hennepin County District Court Judge Frank C. Brooks was the presiding judge. Hamilton was represented by two prominent attorneys, former prosecutor Frank Nye and Robert L. Penny. Hennepin County Attorney Fred H. Boardman and his assistant Al J. Smith represented the prosecutor's office. Huge crowds crammed into the courthouse to see the defendant.

Potential jurors were asked to sit near the front, and I was one of the first to be called for questioning. Mr. Boardman and Mr. Penny asked me what I knew about the case and if I had an opinion of the defendant's innocence or guilt. I told them I had no opinion. I did tell them that I knew the deceased's nephew, Gene Day, but I had not seen him since the death of his uncle. I informed them of my age and where I worked and lived. The daily newspaper referred to me as "a neatly attired young man of refined appearance" and said that my "conscientious replies and demeanor commended me on both sides." Hence, I was picked juror number one. I was excited and also honored to serve.

---

3 The east half of the courthouse was in use by Hennepin County employees. The west side was assigned to the City of Minneapolis for various offices, but they were still moving in at the time of the trial.

The next day, the front page of the *Minneapolis Tribune* was dominated by news of the trial:

> *The most sensational trial of recent years was begun yesterday in the criminal courtroom of Judge Frank C. Brooks. Frank H. Hamilton, journalist and society man, is on trial charged with the murder of Leonard R. Day, son of late millionaire Leonard Day. The case is one that had excited the widest interest all over the United States and abroad. In Paris, where Day was a well-known habitué of the American Quarter, there is almost as keen a following of the affair as that observable in Minneapolis.*

We jury members were assigned to a fourth-floor dormitory which was on the same floor as the jail. We all had single beds, which were lined up in a row. We could not speak of the case, so many of the men played cards; some read; others visited or walked around for exercise. I found a quiet place just outside our dormitory where I chose to be alone and read.

On Friday, February 8, the last juror was selected, and the prosecutors began presenting their case. I did not know this until the trial, but the prosecutors were referred to as the "State" because they were enforcing state law. The crowds, packing the courthouse, increased daily. The lift became so busy with the public that its use was restricted to the lawyers and court officials only. Members of the public were forced to climb three flights of stairs to get to the courtroom, only to find out they had to have a reserved seat to be admitted. The women usually tried to get to the first row. I noticed they were often asked by other spectators to remove their hats so those sitting behind them could see. People who could not get into the courtroom tried to listen in the stairwells and the halls; I think many just wanted to see the accused in person. Hennepin County deputies were extremely busy managing the crowd, with several additional deputies assigned to the courthouse for the duration of the trial. I enjoyed my location in the jury box because I could see and hear testimony so well, but this also made me feel anxious because I have never enjoyed crowds or the feeling of being hemmed in.

A disturbing aspect to the crime's investigation is that on January 1, 1901, a new mayor, A. A. Ames, took office. He quickly fired Chief Doyle and many of the police officers. The investigators for the Day murder were released just over a month after the crime and less than a month before the trial. Ames released the officers who did not support him during the campaign, choosing instead to promote and hire only officers and people who had. I wondered if Ames cared about the case. Mayor Ames has long been known for his drinking problem, and now I feel he has lost his grip on reality in his inebriated old age.

I had not spent much time in a courthouse before, and as a draughtsman, I found the entire building an excellent piece of architecture. I truly enjoyed my leisurely walks through the courthouse after everyone went home. I admired the beautiful marble walls, the unique lighting

Crowded courtroom during Hamilton trial. Source: *Minneapolis Times*, February 14, 1901. Notice the drawing of the billiards room by witness stand.

fixtures, the huge stained-glass windows, and the iron-wrapped lifts. The courtroom we were in was mostly hardwood oak: columns, furniture, wall panels, and the judges' elevated desk, which they referred to as the bench. Electric lights hung from the high ceilings and vast windows let in light and fresh air.

I worried that the smoking would get to me. Lots of men smoked pipes or cigars or chewed tobacco while in the courtroom. The smell of tobacco was a constant, and ultimately soaked into my clothes. I do not smoke, and neither does anyone in my family, so it was difficult for me to get used to.

The first witness was Dr. J. W. Little, who explained the cause of death. He was followed by John Walsh, the former morgue keeper, who produced the clothing worn by Day at the time of his death: a white necktie, white shirt, vest, and white undershirt. All the items were saturated with dried blood that now appeared as a rusty dye. I was shocked and horrified by the amount of blood. It was hard to look, and hard to look away.

Newspaper reporter Joseph Mannix testified that while he was having lunch with Hamilton a few days prior to the murder, Hamilton had asked him about Day. Mannix told Hamilton that Day was the child of a mother who could see nothing in her son's actions that would warrant any criticism. He also described Day as a lively, high-spirited but unbridled kid, who, although indiscreet, did not have a vicious nature. Mannix then asked Hamilton why he wanted to know, and Hamilton replied that he had made a remark about Day to someone who had then repeated that statement to Day. Hamilton went on to say that Day now wanted to meet with him. Mannix responded, "Why Ham, don't bother with him. He is an indiscreet and harmless kid."

The drunks, as I like to call them, testified that they were drinking heavily, a fight broke out, and they did not see anything. They said Evans's head got pushed into the wall and shortly afterward he was kicked out of the room. They seemed to want to protect themselves from any involvement in the affair. Ray Evans was the worst. Evans, a bookkeeper at the Flour Exchange, seemed nervous and hungover when he testified. He stated he was drinking heavily that evening, but was not "intoxicated." He got into it with a guy, and his head was injured. He said that he was escorted out of the room and came back just for his coat, not to fight. Evans denied saying that he would cut out the man's heart, and he continually denied that he was drunk. Yes, he owned a small knife, but did not use it against Day, and yes, he did have blood on him, but it came from his own head wound.

It was becoming apparent to me that no one had a clear vision of the struggle between Day and Hamilton. They were all consistent with their recollections that there was loud profanity, yelling, and screaming, and that there was a struggle involving Evans. Besides all the drunkenness, I think witnesses couldn't describe the struggle in detail because the room had been so dark.[4] The only lighting was from the two gaslights that hung over the pool table. It would be very hard to see much in that room aside from the billiards game.

On Monday, February 11, the state announced that it was going to call its featured witness: Caroline Slagle. From newspaper reports before the trial I knew a little about her. The press pestered her from the time of Day's death until the beginning of the trial. She said nothing. Finally on February 7, during jury selection, she met a *Minneapolis Journal* reporter at her home. The reporter found her intensely nervous and very weary of the whole situation. He wrote that she wore a morning gown, and reclined on a fashionable oriental couch with a large crimson poppy in her raven hair. Two expensive vases filled with red roses were centered on the table, and sheets of the latest music were open at the piano. A dish of fruit was positioned on an artistic little stand, giving the room an air of great care and refinement—it was the home of an educated woman. She gave the reporter the following prepared statement:

> *The newspapers have bothered me incessantly since this trouble. Reporters from Cleveland, Chicago, Omaha,*

4 The billiards room measured approximately sixty feet by forty-five feet and had a fifteen-foot ceiling.

> *Kansas City, St. Louis, and I know from not where else, have persecuted me for interviews and photographs. One was here the other day and called through the door that if I did not give him a picture he would trust to his imagination and make one of me and label it 'The Woman in the Case.' I protest that I do not desire this notoriety. If the press must have a statement, here it is: I was a friend of both of the boys. I did repeat a remark, which Hamilton made of Day. I carried Hamilton's remark to Day because Hamilton requested me to do so. There was no cause for jealousy. Neither of the boys were in love with me. I never flattered myself for a moment that such was the case. Neither of them was engaged to me. Each one knew that the other came to see me. I kept company with both of them, and they both knew it.*[5]

Many women attended the trial (some for the first time)—I think they just wanted to see what Miss Slagle looked like and to hear what she had to say. It would certainly give them a lot of fodder for speculation and gossip. I admit, though, that I was anxious to see her myself.

When Boardman stridently called her name as his next witness, the courtroom was still and uncomfortably quiet. I was surprised to see a young woman appear from a side room and not the back of the courtroom. She walked directly up to the clerk to be sworn in. The only noise in the entire room was Miss Slagle's French shoes clicking on the floor as she went up to be sworn in. *Tick tack, tick tack, tick tack.* People craned their heads to see her, and those who could not see her quietly rose to their feet in a crouched position. A reporter wrote that she reminded "one of an Egyptian princess with her long, narrow eyes, in a tight fitting black velvet gown, with a wide silver girdle, the lovely pallor of her face which was enhanced by her large, black, Gainsborough

5 *Minneapolis Journal*, February 7, 1901.

hat . . . with her peculiar cast of countenance and extraordinary composure."[6] All eyes were upon her in the quiet room. My first impression was that she was attractive and expensively dressed and that she looked calm yet stern. Upon taking her seat, she looked at Hamilton and gave him a slight nod and then looked over at the prosecutor, Boardman.

Caroline Slagle. Source: *Minneapolis Journal*, February 7, 1901.

I took notes all during the trial to help me keep track of the testimony. I wrote that Miss Slagle lives at 307 Plymouth Avenue North, Minneapolis, with her father, who is a physician.

Miss Slagle testified that she had known Day and Hamilton for about three months before Day died. She denied that she knew them "very intimately" but said she knew them "fairly well"; she had visited Hamilton in jail more than once. Boardman then asked her if she had any conversations with Hamilton about Day before the murder. Out of nowhere she said that she had been advised that that was privileged.

An argument between the opposing lawyers arose. Penny told the court that a witness does not have to testify to anything that might incriminate her and so the answer to the question should remain privileged. Boardman stated the witness did not know where he would be going with his questioning and continued by saying that he would not ask her any questions that would embarrass her. Judge Brooks agreed, saying he did not feel the answer was privileged and that he could

6 Arthur James Pegler, *Minneapolis Tribune*, February 12, 1901.

not see how this would incriminate her. The judge added that he was unable to see what the defendant may have said to the witness that could be in any way privileged. This resulted in a private whispered discussion between Judge Brooks, Boardman, and Penny; the lawyers huddled at the right side of the judge's desk. The discussion was fairly close to the juror's box, but I was disappointed, because I could not hear what they were saying.

I watched Miss Slagle during this off-the-record meeting. She sat composed, looking first at us, then at the curious crowd, and finally at the disputing lawyers. She remained stoic during the attorneys' private discussion. Like the boys at work would say, she was easy to look at. Well, whatever Penny told the judge during the meeting caused him to change his mind. Judge Brooks told Miss Slagle that if she was prepared to say that answering the question might in any degree tend to incriminate her, then it was her privilege to refuse to answer the question.[7]

Miss Slagle bowed her head, looked into her lap, and softly answered, "It would incriminate me."[8] I was stunned. I think I knew what she meant, but not for sure.

Boardman said he was finished with the witness. Penny then continued with a few routine questions about the fact that she was not a special friend—he meant a girlfriend—to either of the boys. The last question to her that I noted was: "Then you were not very intimately acquainted with either one of them?" She replied, "Not very intimate." The words *not very intimate* would stick in my brain for a long time. I concluded that she had sexual relations with these two men, but not "very" often.

Miss Slagle left the stand flushed with color, but erect, and with perhaps a bit of defiance. She stared at the crowd full-faced; she was bold and slightly aloof as she emerged from the room. The Minneapolis newspapers stated that the defense had scored in keeping out some of the testimony, but the state had also made its point—that the

7 Ibid.

8 Ibid.

conversation was something a woman would not tell about herself. She left me with questions to discuss with the other men on the jury.

Courtroom drawing of Caroline Slagle. Source: *Minneapolis Journal*, February 12, 1901.

The next day, Tuesday, February 12, former police officer Thomas Rooney testified that he was one of the first officers on the scene. He was a stocky man, a little on the short side, and to me looked more like a laborer than a policeman. Rooney had been on the force for ten months at the time of the murder. He had been terminated at the first of the year by the new mayor and was now employed as a machinist at a furniture factory. Rooney told the court he arrived at the scene at about 2:45 a.m. and immediately went over to the victim, who was lying on the billiards table. Hamilton was sitting in a chair next to Day's body. Night watchman O'Malley told Rooney, "He [Hamilton] did it. Lock him up." Rooney asked, "What did he do?" O'Malley pointed to the victim and replied, "He killed this man." Rooney said that he then grabbed Hamilton from his chair and escorted him out of the billiards room and into the bar. In an emotionless voice, Rooney testified that while he was lifting Hamilton out of his chair, Hamilton said to him, "Officer, I will go with you. I am prepared to take the consequences. Let the law take its course. I killed him, but it was in self-defense." That statement was delivered in a cold and direct manner that left all of us in the courtroom in a frozen silence. "Officer, I'll tell you how this whole trouble started," Hamilton then said. "I will tell you how this trouble started."

Everyone in court was on the edge of their seats, and we all listened to him as one would listen to a mystery story read aloud. No one in the courtroom showed any sign of emotion as Rooney related how Hamilton explained his reasons behind the fight. To me, Hamilton's exact words, at least as Rooney quoted him, were unprintably frank.[9] Here is Rooney's testimony as to what Hamilton told him, which I copied from the *Journal.*

> *"There is a girl by the name of [giving the girl's name] living at [giving the street and number];[10] we both had been intimate[11] with her. I heard that Day had the syphilis. I told her that he had it; she told him what I said, he got sore, and has had it in for me ever since." The next thing of importance that I recollect was, he said, "This is terrible; I wish it had been the other way." I said, "What other way?" He said, "That he had killed me, instead of the way it is." Then later on he said again, "Officer, place your hand there." I did so. He said, "I had to do it. Do you suppose I would stand up and let him pound me? I should say no." After that a gentleman came in and shook hands with Mr. Hamilton. He told me his name was Francis; he was the city editor of the* Minneapolis Times. *He asked Mr. Hamilton if he had a knife, or to let him see his knife, and Mr. Hamilton*

9 *Minneapolis Journal*, February 13, 1901. The newspaper would not print the exact words of Rooney's testimony. The newspaper chose the word intimate, and the actual trial transcript left it blank.

10 The trial transcriber would not put down the actual woman's name or address, for whatever reason, although it was a known fact that Miss Slagle was the woman in the case. Trial transcript, Minnesota Historical Society collections. Public version, *Minneapolis Tribune*, February 13, 1901.

11 The court transcript is blank at this word, and someone wrote in "screwing."

> *took out a small pocketknife. He said, "Is that the only knife you have?" And Mr. Hamilton said, yes. He said, "Did you have a larger knife?" Mr. Hamilton said yes. He asked me if he might have an interview with Mr. Hamilton. I said, "Yes, but I must hear it." Then we went—we moved from where Mr. Hamilton had been seated, when Mr. Francis entered, but I think it was either in the chairs here in the barroom, or here, (pointing on the drawing of billiard room) and I am not positive which place it was. And we moved to another place where there was no one around and Mr. Francis asked him some questions about an attorney, if he had an attorney, and he said he had sent for one. Mr. Francis said then, "Keep your mouth shut, don't say a word until you see your attorney."*[12]

When asked if there was any more conversation regarding the second knife or its size, Rooney said there was not, to his knowledge.

On cross-examination, Rooney, the state's primary witness, explained that his beat was from Third Street to Sixth Street and from Hennepin Avenue to First Avenue North. He admitted that he memorized his testimony and practiced before appearing in court. He strongly denied, with the exception of the knife question, that the county attorney suggested to him any of the answers. The defense attacked Officer Rooney by saying that the entire testimony is the result of all the state's witnesses gathering together prior to court to get their story straight. Rooney did not budge.

The state prosecutor, Boardman, rested his case. It was a difficult case to start with, because most of us on the jury had more sympathy for Hamilton than for the deceased Leonard R. Day. Maybe it was because all we knew before the trial was from the newspaper, and Hamilton is a popular newspaperman. The prosecutors did turn that feeling around for me, however. What they did not prove to me was who owned the

12 Ibid.

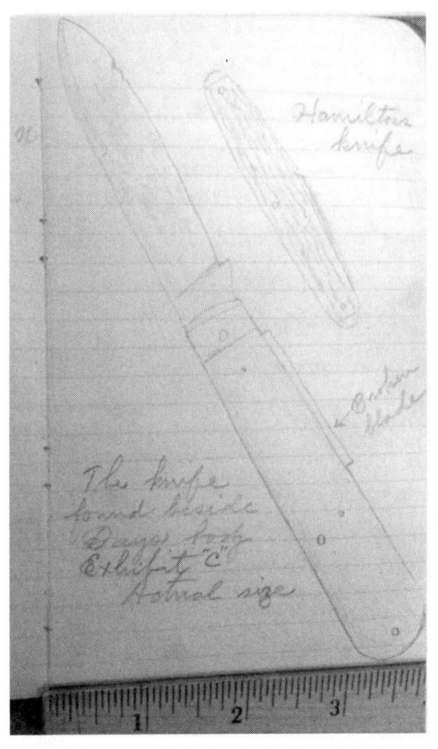

Actual drawing of the knife in Pabody's diary, which he wrote in throughout the trial. The knife he sketched was Exhibit C in the case, and the alleged murder weapon. Source: Hennepin County Historical Society.

knife—the murder weapon. Also, they did not show that Hamilton acted alone. I kept wondering about Evans.

On Thursday, February 14, Penny aggressively initiated the defense portion of the trial. His introductory speech listed facts of which he wanted to make sure the jury knew. From my notes:

- Shortly after his father's death, Hamilton moved to Denver because traces of tuberculosis were found in his lungs. Hamilton had acquired the "liquor habit" because at age sixteen he was prescribed whiskey and the Colorado air to cure his tuberculosis.
- Day was a spoiled son of a doting mother; he had large wealth; he traveled wherever he wanted and at any time he wanted; he associated with immoral men and women; he had a tarnished reputation wherever he went. He was drunk the previous two evenings and stayed out until the early morning hours on each of these evenings—so much so that the "fire" of alcohol was "pent up, ready to burst forth in a fury whenever a slight occasion might occur that would bring it out."
- Hamilton was a respected and loved member of the community.
- Hamilton did not go to the West Hotel to look for Day. Day had asked to meet him.

- Everyone was intoxicated.
- The cuts on Day were not all from a knife.
- Day carried a knife.
- Hamilton was knocked out cold and thus could not have inflicted these wounds.
- Ray Evans was escorted out of the billiards room, but may have been in the fight because he returned for his coat. He was covered with blood when he departed the hotel on the night of the murder. He had his pants repaired the next day for a cut or a rip in them.

The first witness for the defense was S. K. Jackson, a former room clerk at the West who was now working at the Pfister Hotel in Milwaukee. Jackson said he worked at the West for four years and knew Day during that time because Day was a resident there. Jackson knew Day carried a knife with him. Jackson testified that Day got acquainted with a chorus girl from the Burgomaster Company, while the company was performing in Minneapolis. He said that Day followed her to Milwaukee, and Jackson spoke with Day at the Pfister. The company was in Milwaukee for a week and then went to New York, where Day followed. On November 21, 1900, Jackson was in Minneapolis. He met Day as he was walking across the rotunda at the West. Day asked Jackson to come to the bar with him and have a drink. While they were drinking, Day told Jackson that Hamilton got next to his girl when he was traveling. Day told Jackson, "The son of a bitch, when I see him, I am going to do him up."

The next witness was the defendant. Frank Hamilton looked to me as if he had all the weight of the world on his shoulders. He was of medium height, with combed-back black hair, and was clean-shaven. I would guess that he had lost weight, because his clothes hung somewhat loosely on him. He also appeared pale—I suppose from sitting in his cell since the murder.

Now referring to my notes, I will summarize his testimony. Hamilton described himself as being very intoxicated at the time of Day's death. He remembered parts of the evening and remembered talking with Day. He did not recall being introduced to Day, but he recalled having words with him. Day called Hamilton a cad. Hamilton asked Day if he would fight, and Day said no because he thought Hamilton was too drunk. Ray Evans then came up to Day and said he would fight if he wanted to fight. Hamilton believed that he and Day ignored Evans; he then said that Day told him something offensive, and Hamilton threw him down on the floor. Someone separated them, and they got up and shook hands. He testified that he was positive about that.

During his testimony Hamilton went over to where the case exhibits were on display. He stood next to a drawing of the billiards room and pointed to the upper right corner of the top table of the middle row. He said that was the table he'd been standing by before he talked to Day. His next recollection was that there was a general fight going on, and that he was surrounded by a whole bunch of legs and arms. He recalled that someone—he did not know who—hit him in the head with either a club, a billiard cue, or a piece of iron. He then turned around looking to clinch someone—anyone—he didn't care whom, so they couldn't strike him. That was the last thing he could remember up to the moment when he was rubbing Day's hands and someone else was pouring hot water over them.[13]

Hamilton's next recollection was when he was sitting in the barroom with a police officer. He said he became very chilled and nervous while there. The *Times* newspaper editor arrived and told Hamilton to say nothing until he obtained legal advice. The three men then walked to the police station. Hamilton was asked if he came to the West to fight, and he said, "Not in the slightest." He said that he did not stab Day: he did not feel it was physically possible for him to do that. He also denied owning the knife found at the scene.

Penny asked him about the statement he gave Officer Rooney, in particular the part where he admitted that both he and Day were

13 *Minneapolis Tribune*, February 14, 1901.

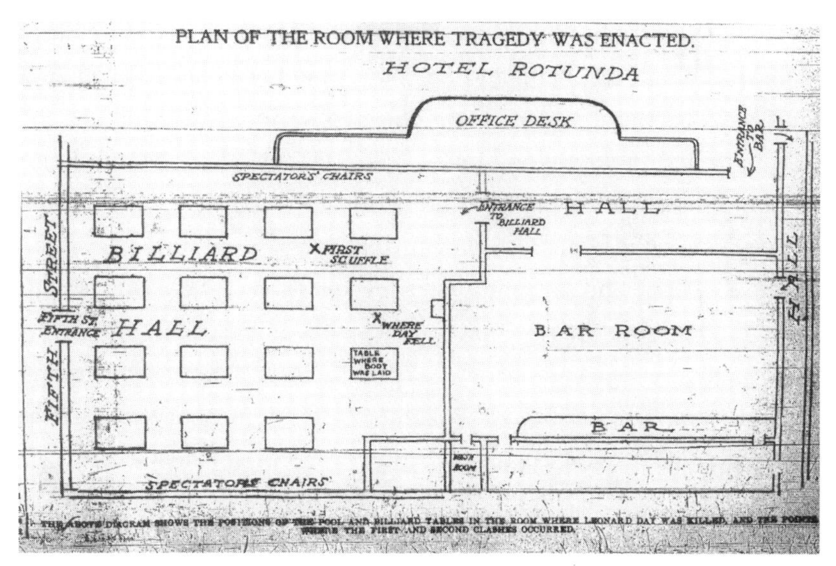

Drawing of the West Hotel's billiards room. Source: *Minneapolis Tribune*, November 26, 1900.

intimate with the same girl. With anger starting to redden his face, Hamilton replied that Rooney's testimony was a lie and "made out of cloth. Nothing of the kind was said." Penny then asked him if he recalled telling Rooney the girl's name and address. Again Hamilton denied that he said that and answered, "It is all made out of cloth. I know." Penny's last question was if Hamilton remembered saying to anyone "that you were up against it," that you were "in for it," or words of similar import. Hamilton replied that he did not.

That afternoon the cross-examination began with Boardman asking the questions for the prosecution. Hamilton answered most of the questions with "I don't know." According to my notes, Boardman asked Hamilton if he could explain why it was that he could remember nothing after he and Day had shaken hands. Hamilton answered, "No, sir, I can't. I was very drunk." The final question from the prosecutor was if Hamilton could recall if he had killed Day. Hamilton responded: "As far as I—I can't remember."

The next defense witness was Ulysses G. Gilbert, who stated he was a bushman[14] and a pressman on clothing. He explained that he

14 A bushman was one who repaired clothing.

had repaired Evans's clothes after the murder. He described the clothes as having blood on them, and he found a bloody handkerchief in a pants pocket. The state prosecutor objected, saying something like the testimony was irrelevant and immaterial. The objection was upheld, so I did not hear much more from the bushman. I was very disappointed because I thought Evans was more involved than he admitted. I wanted to raise my hand and say that I had a few questions for the witness, but I did not dare. Too many people would be looking at me.

Finally, the state and the defense gave their summations. Boardman, for the state, summarized the testimony of the men in the billiards room and showed the jury where they were when the murder happened. He eliminated them all except Hamilton. Boardman pointed at Hamilton and said, "Hamilton killed an innocent man, a man who declined to fight. Hamilton killed him in a rage of jealousy." The county attorney reminded us that on the walk to the police station Hamilton refused to answer any more questions. He asked the jury whether that sounded like an innocent man.

Frank Nye, for the defense, said Hamilton carried only one knife, which he produced for the police. Every man carries a pocketknife; no gentleman carries two. Nye went to great lengths to exhibit Hamilton's strong character. He told us that several of the men in the billiards room could have been suspects. "Everyone was intoxicated and thus their accounts were less than reliable, yet the state is making their case of such witnesses. Hamilton did not kill Day, for he was incapable of doing it," the defense attorney concluded.

Judge Brooks gave us on the jury a choice of four possible verdicts: murder in the first or second degree, manslaughter, or acquittal (that is, not guilty). In his final instructions to us, he read from a typed document that was passed around the jury:

> *Now as I have said before, any one of four possible verdicts may be returned in this case. You may find the defendant not guilty, and will do so if you entertain a reasonable doubt whether*

> *or not he unlawfully killed the deceased. If you find beyond a reasonable doubt that the defendant killed Leonard Day, and did so with premeditated design to effect his death, your verdict will be that you find the defendant killed as charged in the indictment. If you find the defendant intentionally killed Leonard Day, but without any premeditated design to do so, your verdict will be that you find the defendant guilty of murder in the second degree. If you find the defendant unlawfully killed the deceased, but did so without any design to effect his death, then your verdict will be that you find the defendant guilty of manslaughter in the first degree.*[15]

In reference to the defects of character alleged by the defense against Day, Judge Brooks said, "In the eyes of the law, it is as great a crime to murder a bad man as it is a good man, an intoxicated man as a sober man."[16] I have always tried to keep in mind what my father told me a long time ago: never talk poorly about a deceased person, because they cannot defend themselves.

The judge dismissed us, and we walked to the jury room, which was located next to the courtroom on the third floor. A large mahogany table sat in the center surrounded by chairs; and there was an indoor washroom on one side. We took a vote right away and found most of us had not made up our minds. We took turns talking, and when it came to me, I said that I thought Evans was more implicated than he said he was.

I had a lot of questions about the case that I knew I could never get answers to. How did all that blood get on Evans's clothes? Why were his pants ripped? He was out of his mind screaming shortly before the murder. No one had seen Hamilton stab Day. Could Evans have been involved in the group fighting? I think he could have been. I was suspicious and thought he knew more than he was admitting. I wanted

15 *Minneapolis Tribune*, February 19, 1901.

16 Ibid.

Officers of the court. Left to right: Fred H. Boardman, county attorney in charge of the prosecution; Al J. Smith, assistant to the county attorney; Judge F. C. Brooks; Frank M. Nye, counsel for the defense; Robert L. Penney, counsel for the defense. Source: *Minneapolis Journal*, February 2, 1901.

to know more about his whereabouts from the other witnesses. Evans even testified as if he were the defendant. Hamilton was so drunk that he could not fight, so where did he come up with the strength to make a full-blown attack on a sober Leonard Day? And meanwhile, Evans yelled at Force that he was going to cut out his "g-- d--- heart."

At the beginning of the next day, eight of us, including me, voted for acquittal, and four were for murder. We deliberated all day.[17] No one was moving either way. One member was informed that he had a sick family member, so he was in a hurry to go home. We all thought we had to compromise. If we did not, there could be another trial, and Hamilton could possibly be found guilty of murder. A vote for a compromise was decided on. I insisted that we recommend some sort of leniency to the sentencing, and everyone agreed.

At 9:15 a.m. on Wednesday, February 20—forty hours after we received our instructions—we informed the deputies that we had reached a verdict. The elevator brought Hamilton down from his cell. A huge crowd had waited for a verdict the day before, but only a handful had returned the next morning.

Once everyone was seated, the judge asked, "Gentlemen of the jury, have you reached a verdict?"

"Yes!" replied the foreman.

The judge was handed the verdict and then gave it to the clerk.

---

17 The jury ate a bushel of oranges and apples over the course of the trial.

"Gentlemen, you will listen to the reading of the verdict," the clerk declared in a monotone voice.

The foreman read, "We, the jury, find the defendant Frank H. Hamilton guilty of the crime of manslaughter in the first degree and recommend him to the mercy of the court."

Silence greeted the verdict. There were no cheers, backslappings, or handshakings in a joyous victory. No tears or shouts of despair. Judge Brooks briefly thanked us and released us from our obligation and duty. Hamilton looked dazed but said nothing. The *Minneapolis Journal* said that he seemed almost in a trance when his attorneys whispered a word of comfort to him. Assistant County Attorney Al J. Smith asked the court to keep Hamilton in jail as he awaited his sentence. Hamilton told his attorneys that he did not want to talk to his friends at that time. He returned to his cell and met with the supervisor of the jail, Captain Alexander, who later quoted him in the *Journal*: "Captain, I have been convicted, but I did not deserve it. My God, I did not deserve it."[18]

The county attorney, Fred Boardman, almost apologized in his statement to reporters, which I read later in the same paper: "Had I not believed Hamilton guilty, I certainly should not have prosecuted the case against him. I liked the young man's looks from the outset and it was positively a painful duty, in a sense, to be forced to proceed against him."[19]

Judge Brooks, after a long deliberation, sentenced Hamilton to seven years of hard labor. The sentence was to be served at the Stillwater Prison.[20]

I went back to the jury's sleeping quarters, picked up my personal belongings, and shook hands with my cojurors. I grabbed the books I read and returned them to the library.[21] Well, it was over, and I prayed we did the right thing. I missed my quiet life.

---

18 *Minneapolis Journal*, February 20, 1901.

19 Ibid.

20 The Board of Corrections later commuted the sentence to five years.

21 *Tom Sawyer*, *Three Men in a Boat*, *Tom Grogan*, *Michael Strogoff*, and *She*.

On the street, the newspapers reported that the verdict and sentence were not popular, but Hamilton himself still was. His relatives, friends, and associates were concerned about his health because his stomach was constantly nervous and he had developed a cough.

I felt somewhat responsible, but there did not seem to be an easy resolution. Poor Hamilton and poor Day. Heartrending. I believe if the young men were not drinking alcohol, a life would have been saved and the other not ruined. I don't drink, and the actions of those men, that cold November night, are a good example of why. Alcohol takes away your discipline and your good judgment, as it did for Hamilton and Evans. Mr. Penny was right when he told us that the fire was ready to burst forth in a fury.

Whatever happened to . . . ?

Leonard R. Day rests with his parents in Lot 249 in Lakewood Cemetery, Minneapolis.

Franklin H. Hamilton was incarcerated at Stillwater Prison on March 11, 1901. He was assigned inmate number 5585. He worked on the *Prison Mirror*, a newspaper that was established in 1867.[22] He was eligible for parole on August 20, 1903. Parole was denied twice in 1904—on January 8 and March 8. Hamilton was released on October 7, 1904. Prison records show that he suffered from depression, insomnia, and loss of weight while incarcerated.

Hamilton went to work for the *St. Paul Globe* for a short time, then moved to San Francisco for his health. There he took a position as an editorial writer for the *San Francisco Examiner*. His fiancée Pauline Krueger followed him. Miss Krueger was a prominent photographer in Minneapolis. They were married on November 13, 1905. The earthquake

22 In July 1903, the *Mirror* advertised that it had a circulation of 2,500 and cost one dollar per year.

Franklin H. Hamilton's 1901 Stillwater Prison mug shot. Source: Minnesota Historical Society.

of April 2, 1906, destroyed much of the city of San Francisco, including the Hamiltons' home. With direly fragile lungs and the stress of being homeless, Frank Hamilton became vulnerable to bouts of pneumonia. On Christmas Day 1906, while visiting friends in Alameda, across the bay, he suffered a severe asthmatic attack and died four days later. He is buried next to his wife at Sleepy Hollow Cemetery in Tarrytown, New York.

Laura A. Day died in 1935 at her mansion on 104 West Franklin, Minneapolis, at the age of eighty-one.

Caroline Slagle continued to live at her Plymouth address after the trial, according to the 1905 census. She was still listed in the Minneapolis directory when her father died in 1906. Otherwise there seems to be no further trace of her.

Ezra Fitch Pabody worked his entire career—thirty-five years—for the American Bridge Company, located on Second Street between Sixth and Seventh Avenues in Minneapolis. He was their contract manager at the time of his retirement. He and his widow sister, Eleanor, resided at 1920 Colfax Avenue in south Minneapolis. Ezra was an avid reader and writer, and he enjoyed the tranquility of his bachelor life. He was a member of Westminster Presbyterian Church and the Minneapolis Athletic Club. He died on December 17, 1940, at the age of seventy-two as the result of a heart condition, after a long stay in Franklin Hospital, located on Franklin Street off Lyndale Avenue in Minneapolis. He is buried with his sister and parents in Lot 236 at Lakewood Cemetery.

His teenage diary and his journal recording his experiences during the Hamilton trial can be read online via the Hennepin History Museum collections. The physical diary is available for review at the Hennepin History Museum (Reference B33.1).

The **West Hotel** opened in 1884. It was built by John West, the former manager of the Nicollet House, with the financial backing of his uncle Charles W. West. The glamorous hotel was designed by LeRoy Buffington in a Queen Anne style that was quite popular in the last decades of the nineteenth century. The West had gable roofs, projecting bay windows, towers, and dormer windows.

The West had the honor of hosting many of the delegates to the 1892 Republican National Convention held at the Industrial Exposition Building from June 7 to June 10. The party nominated President Benjamin Harrison for reelection. This was the first convention where women were allowed as delegates. Harrison lost in the November election to Grover Cleveland.

The hotel advertised that it was fireproof, but on January 10, 1906, at 7:15 a.m., a large fire swept through the hotel, killing nine people. When it reopened, it did not return to its previous active occupancy. The area around the hotel became more industrialized, and not having bathrooms in all its rooms, its appeal dwindled. After changing owners several times, the historic building was demolished in 1940.

CHAPTER 2

Did the Dentist Do It?

1904

"Under such conditions as these, it should be forever understood that the courts of this country are competent to bring to justice the lawbreakers and are a safe refuge for the innocent."

—Blue Earth County District Court Judge
Lorin Cray, August 1, 1905

THE 1900 UNITED STATES CENSUS counted 5,403 people living in New Ulm, Minnesota. The Brown County seat was a rural community whose residents were proud of their strong German heritage and valued self-reliance. German and English were the common languages spoken in most homes, but children were only allowed to speak English at school.[23]

23 In New Ulm in 1904, 3,265 of the 5,720 residents reported German parents. There were 2,913 female residents and 2,807 male residents. See Minnesota Secretary of State, *Fifth Decennial of Minnesota*, 1905.

In 1904 the town was shocked by the murder of the dentist Louis A. Gebhardt. He was one of nine children in his family and grew up in Black River Falls, Wisconsin. He had graduated with the 1898 class of the College of Dental Surgery of Chicago, where he was a popular student and secretary of his class. He moved to New Ulm in the fall of that year and established a practice in a rented office on Minnesota Street, off of Center Street, above a barbershop and newspaper-printing company.

On the evening of Tuesday, November 1, 1904, people walking in downtown New Ulm may have noticed lights burning in the office of the dentist. A passerby on Minnesota Street, on the Ottomeyer block, may have heard the buzzing of a polishing machine coming from the dentist's second-floor operating room. It had been an unusually mild day, with a high of sixty degrees, and some people had their windows open.

About 9:30, Asa P. Brooks, the editor of the *New Ulm Review*, was looking through some mail in his office when he heard some scuffling in Dr. Gebhardt's office, directly above his own. His first thought was that the dentist was wrestling with some of the boys who occasionally stopped by to visit him and test his agility. The commotion continued, and then Brooks heard screaming coming from the dentist's office. He ran up the stairs, only to find that the office door was locked. Standing on the rail of the stairs and looking through the transom, he could see someone lying in blood on the floor near the safe and another man kneeling over him. The man kneeling was moving his right arm up and down until he heard Brooks and looked toward the door. The two men made eye contact.

Brooks was stunned by what he had seen and ran down the stairs for help. He saw William Cavenaugh, a plumber, across the street and yelled for him to come over. Together the two men ran up the stairs and simultaneously looked over the transom. They saw a bloodied and mutilated man lying on the floor of the operating room. They did not see anyone else, yet they felt that someone else was in the room and sensed he was walking close to the wall to stay out of their vision. Then they fled outside and started telling people what they saw. Cavenaugh called a doctor, while others looked for a police officer.

Withn five minutes, grocer F. H. Behnke and patrol officer Joseph Weisenborn ran up the twenty-five steps to the dentist's office with an excited crowd following them. Officer Weisenborn looked over the transom and yelled, "Oh Jesus!" The two men kicked in the door and entered Gebhardt's operating room; two lights in the office were still on. They found a dead man lying face down on a large rug in a pool of blood. His head and neck were covered with blood from several apparent knife wounds. The waiting room was lit, but the adjoining doctor's office was pitch black.

Sherriff William J. Julius. Source: Brown County Historical Society.

Our narrator for this story is thirty-year-old William (Bill) J. Julius, a first-term Brown County sheriff in 1904. He was previously with the New Ulm police department for five years, yet the truth be told, he had never received any formal police training. He lived with his wife and four children in the residential part of the county jail. Sheriff was an unusual job for a person like William, who liked to be liked and was uncomfortable with conflict. His backbone would be tested when he was in charge of the murder investigation of the popular young dentist. The peaceful community demanded an arrest quickly, and if they did not get one, they would investigate the murder themselves.

The investigation I am going to share with you almost caused me to lose my sanity. The case wore heavily on my family, my associates, and me.

During this investigation, I often asked myself why I had ever wanted a job like this.

I kept a weekly diary about my investigation and how the pressure constantly increased on me to solve this murder. I had never worked on a murder case in my life. I found some comfort in documenting what I did and the trials that followed, tracking the evidence, the case we tried to build, and the testimony both sides presented in court.

Week One: November 1–5, 1904

Tues. Nov. 1: Tonight Klause[24] told me there'd been a murder, asked me to go with him to the scene. Arrived at Dr. Gebhardt's dentist office[25] 10:15.

Could tell there'd been a terrible struggle. Rug pushed aside, scuffed up, chair turned over. Map hanging on wall with large smear of blood, as if someone's head had been pushed against it. Blood spatters on walls. Safe also spattered with blood, open, $50 inside.

Turned body over, couldn't recognize who it was. Multiple stab wounds on neck and head, which was smashed in by heavy object. I removed papers from victim's pockets: identified him as Dr. Louis Gebhardt. I was shocked—have never seen anything like this before.

Talked briefly to Dr. Reineke, who shared his reception area with Gebhardt. Doctor said he didn't even recognize the features of the man he worked next to every day.[26]

Examined crime scene. New pencil lying in blood near body: "Vogel and Co. Lumber Dealers." On floor of next room, hammer with bloody handle—homemade, battered face. One claw missing. Handle looked as if murderer had tried to wipe blood off. Handkerchief lying next to hammer, partially soaked in blood. No knife.

---

24 Adolph Klause was chief of police in New Ulm.

25 5 1/2 Minnesota Street.

26 It was common, in that era, for dentists and medical doctors to share a waiting

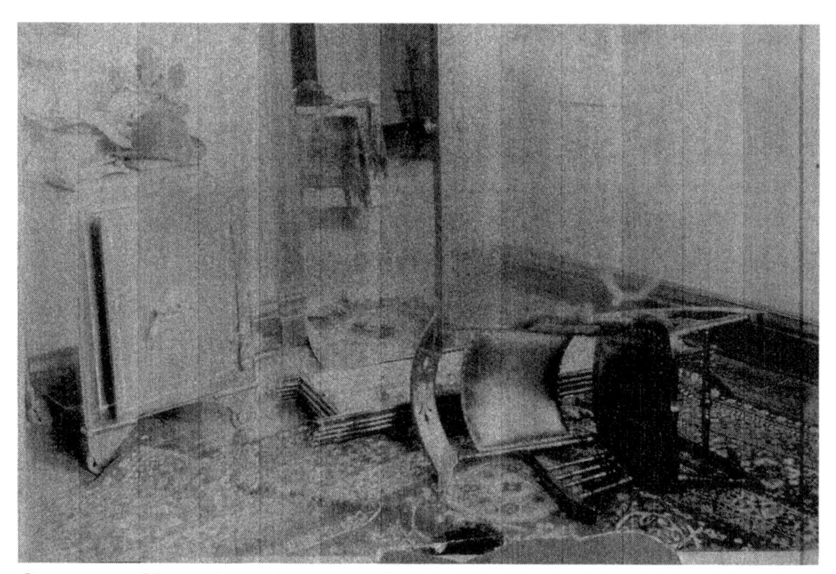

Crime scene. Victim lay on lower right hand corner of photo where an 'x' is marked.
Source: *Brown County Journal*, November 5, 1904.

Noted blood on window frame in office of Reineke, also on curtains. Screen busted out. Murderer must've grabbed telephone wires below window, lowered himself to alley.

Sent several men to guard all exits from New Ulm and search town for suspects. Had them check trains. Wanted to prevent murderer from leaving town. Didn't catch anyone.

Body taken to Buenger's.[27] Dr. Weiser performed autopsy, determined blows to head came first. Total of eight stab wounds to neck and face.

Wed. Nov. 2: Coroner[28] notified Gebhardt's relatives in Wisconsin. Brother wants victim's eyeballs photographed—thinks eyes could have image of murderer on them. Meyer took photo at Buenger's. *Brown County Journal* wrote, "This

---

room located between their offices. Dr. Reineke advertised that he specialized in eye, ear, nose, and throat and gave his location as the Ottomeyer block in New Ulm.

27 Buenger's Undertaking Parlor.

28 Dr. L. A. Fritsche.

is reasonable, for if he was looking at the murderer when he breathed his last, the retina will have the last scene that he saw recorded upon its surface." I thought this was a good idea—we need more evidence. But didn't work.

The window in Dr. Reineke's office that the murderer jumped out of to the alley below. Source: *Brown County Journal*, November 12, 1904.

Coroner conducted inquest at crime scene.[29] Determined newspaper man Asa Brooks was only one who saw murderer. Here is what Asa said:

> *He was on his knees of course. I cannot tell, on that account, how tall he was, but from the features, his general features, I should judge him to be a man of less than average stature. He had a small face and it was free from any beard, though he may have had a slight mustache. I would not swear that he did not have a mustache. I think he had a little thin black mustache. He had black hair and at that time I am quite sure that he had a slouch hat on the back of his head; he had on a black suit of clothes; his coat, and as much of the rest as I could see, was black; he wore a collar and tie—I do not know if I can describe the tie—and was to all appearances a well-dressed young man.*[30]

---

29 Today, the building's address is 5 North Minnesota Street.

30 *Brown County Journal*, November 5, 1904. The *Journal* was a weekly newspaper

Brooks thought man no older than twenty-five, pale looking, as if worked inside all day. Inquest's conclusion: Gebhardt murdered by person or persons unknown.

Gebhardt had busy practice, reputation for being kind, caring, competent. Unmarried man active in church, civic affairs. As far as I can tell, no enemies. Considered best of five dentists in town.

I believe he knew his assailant. Gebhardt always courteous, so when man entered office, he took rocking chair from next room for guest to sit on. Talked for a few minutes, fight broke out. Eventually murderer took heavy instrument, maybe hammer, hit dentist on head. Proceeded to stab him with knife until dead. Looked out the door around outside edges of frosted glass and saw Brooks watching him. Ran into Reineke's office, leaving blood on door. Grabbed wires, climbed out window, leaving blood on window and sash. Telephone wires broke fall to ground, so probably not injured. No footprints in the alley.

THURS. NOV. 3: Services held for Gebhardt at Congregational church.[31] E. R. Dow preached. Short service also held at residence[32] of C. A. Zelle, where Gebhardt once lived. Brother Robert attended. Body transported by train back to Black River Falls, Wisc.[33] Service there at mother's house.

Me, my deputies, the police, & county attorney are all working together on this tragic case. We're overwhelmed, decided to approach Brown Co. commissioners for help. They hired six private detectives, two from Pinkerton to assist us.[34] More private detectives from the Cities heading down here,

---

distributed on Saturdays.

31 3rd and Minnesota, New Ulm.

32 408 South Broadway, New Ulm.

33 Herman Held and Adolf Meile escorted the body back to Wisconsin. Both were brother Masons and Woodmen.

34 A. E. Rydell and J. G. Callihan of Pinkerton, St. Paul; H. F. Cheney of Theil Detective Service, St. Paul; Wm. Baxter, Baxter Detective Service, Minneapolis.

probably because of $1,500 reward.[35] Anyone who solves this case will get lots of praise, free advertising from press.

Louis A. Gebhardt. Source: Brown County Historical Society.

People are always asking me, "What was the motive?" "Who would've wanted to kill the dentist?" "Was it revenge, robbery, jealousy?" "Could it've been the crime of a morphine addict, cocaine fiend, insane man?" Detectives think a woman involved, but no one mentioned a woman Gebhardt was friendly with.

Citizens of New Ulm very uneasy—a brutal murderer at large in our community. Business during eve hours very slow, no one wanting to come into town after dark. Merchants never work by themselves. Lots of men walking around armed, in case of another attack. Children kept inside. Men stand around in little groups talking about the murder.

Everyone I see asks me about case wants to talk about their theory, but I have no time. Feeling lots of pressure to make an arrest. People say they'd feel better if someone locked up. I'd feel better too, getting them off my back.

The exact number of detectives (or investigators) assigned was not made public because it was thought that some of them could work more effectively if they were not identified.

35 The State of Minnesota contributed five hundred dollars, the City of New Ulm three hundred dollars, Mrs. Susan Gebhardt four hundred dollars, the Masons two hundred dollars, and the Woodmen one hundred dollars.

Fri. Nov. 4: A group of the locals called a town meeting. People frustrated, wanting to take things into their own hands. Held at opera house.[36] *New Ulm Review* called it "monster meeting" with more than a thousand men. Phillip Liesch[37] called meeting to order, wanted citizens' committee appointed to assist co. attorney, police, my office. I stood off to side, said nothing. Felt relieved when Judge Webber elected chairman—I knew meeting would run properly, not become hysterical event.

Hoidale[38] spoke to crowd, mentioned bloodhounds he had out looking for murderer on Nov. 1. Also asked private detectives to use all means possible to track down known narcotic fiends in town that night. Said he could not share all evidence obtained so far, could tip off suspect—he hinted it was Dr. Koch, another dentist in town. Hoidale asked for more time and for people to have faith in investigators. Said he'd resign if town felt investigation wasn't progressing satisfactorily. Got big round of applause.

Sat. Nov. 5: Word has gotten out initials G.R.K. were on bloody handkerchief found at scene. Everyone knows only person here with those initials is dentist George R. Koch. Rumor has it he's been staying home, not going to work. I've heard two dentists were good friends, used to work on each other's teeth for free.

Took Krause & another officer to Koch's home[39] to search it for clues. Koch & his sister cooperative, showed us all of Koch's handkerchiefs, marked "G.R.K." All looked like one at crime scene. Ida Koch told us she prints brother's initials with indelible ink.

---

36 26 North Broadway, New Ulm. This turned out to be the largest public meeting in the county's history.

37 Liesch was one of New Ulm's newspaper publishers.

38 Einar Hoidale was Brown County attorney.

39 Located on the bluff, west side of city, near Hermann Park.

George R. Koch and sister Ida Koch. Source: Brown County Historical Society.

Looked at clothes he wore on Nov. 1 but found no blood, rips. Looked at hands, noticed burns on back of one. I said, "Don't go downtown with those hands, George. The people will kill you." He explained he had small cuts on hand, told by doctor to clean them with alcohol. He did, then put piece of wood into furnace, which ignited alcohol, causing blisters.

Searched Koch's office, found nothing to link to murder. Hoidale told us not to give up—says we're on right track.

Week Two: November 6–12, 1904

Tues. Nov. 8: Election Day. I ran unopposed, so reelected. If any idea of this case coming, I don't think would've run again. Getting ton of criticism about not sending men around to back of building in time to catch murderer, who must've climbed out window. But no footprints below window, no witnesses who saw murderer leave.

Wed. Nov. 9: Learned someone leaked information about case, making my job harder. Recently Gebhardt rec'd sample bottle of headache medicine in mail. Showed medicine to Reineke, who told him it looked like poison, not to take it. We found powder in Gebhardt's cupboard, turns out to be strychnine. Mailed from Minneapolis & St. Louis train, route of Winthrop & Storm Lake. Don't know exactly where sent from—Twin Cities or any point along the line. Or here in New Ulm, taken to the Cities, and returned here. Now people know about it, some say it was intentional, premeditated murder.

My friend Sheriff John McMillan[40] helping me with the investigation, wants to arrest Koch soon as possible. Convinced Koch is murderer, even went to co. attorney and demanded warrant for Koch's arrest. John accused Hoidale of not doing anything against Koch because law partner is Henry Somsen, Koch's brother-in-law. Hoidale jumped out of his chair, told John that Brown Co. doesn't need his help and when enough evidence, warrant will be issued. Some insults exchanged, John walked out.

Thurs. Nov. 10: Really busy for Klause & me. Koch everyone's main suspect. Still, people keep talking about cocaine-fiend theory. We're trying to locate every addict in state. One just arrested in Rochester, so Klause & I went there. Turns out he had an alibi for night of murder. Another was arrested in Minneapolis, so I took Asa Brooks to help identify. Brooks said he was not man he saw killing Gebhardt. Took the train to Osceola to identify yet another man. Turned out he didn't fit description. I don't put much credence in fiend theory, but got to show citizens no stone unturned.

I think murderer had to be insane. Saw witness looking at him through glass in door, continued to stab his victim. Had to be pretty young and able—escaped quickly. Brooks told me

40 John McMillan, sheriff of neighboring Nicollet County.

he'd never forget those wild, dark, piercing eyes. Some people think murderer lived in town, familiar with streets & area, since made clean getaway. Maybe a Dr. Jekyll/Mr. Hyde.

Fri. Nov. 11: Pinkerton boys took hammer found at crime scene, asking people if they recognize it. No luck. Every detective wants to be 1st to solve this crime. Every day trail's colder. We're reacting to public opinion rather than conducting investigation—everyone knows everything about what we're doing. People in town tell me things private detectives are doing that I didn't know about. All of us police pretty worn down.

Sat. Nov. 12: Pinkerton boys have new idea. When murderer escaping, had to open a window. Pushed aside curtains, unlocked window, placed right hand underneath upper sash, lifted window few inches. Took his left hand, raised window as far as it would go. Shape of three fingers of his left hand on lower sash. Pinkertons cut fingerprints out of window sash to compare with suspect's fingerprints once arrest made. I've heard about this new kind of evidence, haven't used it before. I like idea. Hope it works.

Week Three: November 13–19, 1904

Wed. Nov. 16: Public pressure keeps getting worse. People look at me different, as if I'm deliberately not making arrest. They want co. attorney to step down. He's refused, told them he's still running investigation. Everyone yelling, "Why isn't Koch in jail?" No secrets in investigation. Everyone knows what we're doing. Sometimes they make up things. Full of suggestions of what we should've done, what we should do. I worry people will take law into own hands.

Sat. Nov. 19: All over town people handing out posters for another mass mtg. Opera House. Told every farmer in area.

Everyone is excited for the citizen committee to investigate the murder.

About a thousand came. Everyone complained about how scared they were of cold-blooded maniac killer running loose and nothing done about it. Picked committee of five local men to conduct investigation, hire detectives & attorneys, spend allocated funds. They say won't interfere with my investigation. If my office checking out same lead, they'll discontinue efforts—so they say.

Committee asked Chicago attorney George Popham, classmate of victim, to speak. In his spiel he reviewed evidence, thought committee should be close to arrest of Koch. Also said not to fear slander, that if anyone knew anything, should come forward.

Secretary read resolution—who would be in charge, how money would be handled. Apparently they're accountable to no one for security reasons. The mayor, who's chairman, asked anyone who knows something about murder to come forward, protection given. Mayor asked for pledges to start committee investigation. He donated $150. Total raised = more than $1,000.[41]

Week Four: November 20–26, 1904

Sun. Nov. 20: Last night's meeting in the paper. Read it just to see they got everything right. Here's full resolution:

It is hereby resolved by the people of New Ulm, Minnesota, in a mass meeting assembled on this 19th day of November,

---

41 Shell Brewing Co. and Gebhardt brothers gave one hundred dollars each. Hauenstein Brewing Co., not to be outdone by Shell, pledged one hundred and five. The city council pledged sixty, and fifty dollars came from F. H. Retzlaff and Dr. O. C. Strickler. At the end of the meeting $1,115 had been committed for their budget.

> *1904, that a committee to consist of not more than five citizens of this city be appointed and organized for the purpose of conducting a thorough investigation of said crime in order that the person or persons guilty thereof may be detected, arrested and dealt with according to law; and it is further resolved that the Honorable Charles Silverson, mayor of the city of New Ulm, be and hereby appointed, at this meeting, to be chairman of said committee, and that he be authorized and empowered to forthwith appoint the other four members of said committee and given the power to act.*[42]

Paper listed all donors to fund. Shell Brewing & Gebhardt brothers $100 each. Hauenstein Brewing $105. City council $60. F. H. Retzlaff & Dr. O. C. Strickler $50. Total $1,115.[43]

Wed. Nov. 23: Committee started investigation. Interviewing same people we did. But private detectives sharing their work with committee, which is paying them. We don't know what new information they've uncovered. But they don't know what we have either. Rumors flying every which way. People starting to pick sides. Town divided over whether to arrest Koch or not. Don't have enough evidence to win at trial. Meanwhile I still have to run a jail plus all other law enforcement work.

Fri. Nov. 25: Committee hired Mrs. M. E. Holland, calls herself 2nd best fingerprint expert in world. She works in U.S., husband works in London—supposedly Scotland Yard. Committee took

---

42 *Brown County Journal*, November 26, 1904.

43 Others contributing at the meeting: Joseph Flor, Dr. J. H. Vogel, Karl Tastel, Ernest Pfeiffer, H. W. Engelbrandt, Charles Leohardt, John H. Siegel, Rev. Dallmann, S. D. Peterson, W. P. Hoy, Frank Nieman, A. J. Vogel, Frank Kretsch, W. G. Little, John G. Gronau, George Zickrick. Louis Sandau, W. B. Mather, Dr. G. B. Weiser, O. E. Kluegel, Ed Maltzahn, C. W. A. Krook, Wm. Stork, R. Higgs, R. Geisinger, E. Pfeafferle, Dr. L. A. Fritsche, B. Stockman.

her to crime scene, where she analyzed rooms for finger & palm prints. She recorded some prints. No prints of suspect to compare yet.

WEEK FIVE: NOVEMBER 27–DECEMBER 3, 1904

WED. NOV. 30: Just learned Hoidale & committee had secret mtg. Heard about it from Hoidale, before public knowledge.

Dr. Gebhardt's office windows on the second floor. Newspaper office on the lower right next to barbershop. Source: Brown County Historical Society.

Committee asked him for all investigators' reports. Hoidale said belong to county, and because it's an ongoing investigation, not going to hand them over. Reports not public information. Only grand jury could issue warrant for arrest, not him. Etc. Hoidale told committee if they wanted to arrest Koch, go ahead. Enough evidence to protect them from liability. All seemed to agree no more evidence to gather. Investigators exhausted all leads.

I wish citizens would remember Hoidale is part-time. Has own business to attend to, specializes in collections, for God's sake. Not a lot of murders around here, all of us scrambling to figure this out.

WEEK SIX: DECEMBER 4–10, 1904

FRI. DEC. 9: Got called into mayor's office this afternoon. He told Klause & me committee decided enough evidence, filed

General H.W. Childs. Source: Minnesota Historical Society.

complaint against Koch. Justice Henningsen issued warrant not long after, around 6:15.

Trying not to attract crowd, we waited until 8 to go to Koch's. Seemed to be expecting us. Didn't want to talk, just put on his coat, walked with us to jail. Already has his attorneys lined up: Brown & Abbott of Winona and Sommerville and Olson of Sleepy Eye. His father must be helping pay.

Small crowd gathered as we entered courthouse, giving us support, yelling derogatory names at Koch. (I wonder how they found out about arrest?) I took Koch's Bertillon[44] measurements, completed initial statement. Locked him up for night.

Met with mayor again, who said committee needed Koch's palm & fingerprints. Mrs. Holland to compare Koch's prints to ones at murder scene.

Returned to jail about 10, woke Koch, told him we had to fingerprint him. I explained he'd be first in county fingerprinted. He refused, said his attorneys told him not to say/do anything might incriminate him. Wouldn't do anything until his lawyer said OK. I called one of his attorneys, Abbott, at the Dakota Hotel. Abbott said no.

44 Bertillon is a system for identifying persons based on bodily measurements, photographs, and notation of data (as markings, color, and thumb line impressions).

Klause & I talked it over, agreed we're legally in charge and directed to get prints by committee & mayor. Went into Koch's cell again, but this time not asking—taking. Koch grabbed bars, wouldn't let go. Wrestled with him, got him away from bars, but unable to get him to open his hand. Decided to stop because probably have to do bodily harm to take prints. Going to try again tomorrow.

Sat. Dec. 10: You'd think I killed Gebhardt. Koch's attorneys & friends after my job. *Review* reporter came over for interview. Told him "no comment." Judge Webber, not one of my strongest allies, called our act "outrage." He said sheriff or policeman has no right to take evidence from defendant's hands, just like no right to force confession. *Brown County Journal* wrote:

> *The legal right of the sheriff and chief of police to force the prisoner to give his fingerprints had been questioned. The argument used in this case is the fact that no man can be forced to give evidence in any case that will in any way incriminate himself. Many affairs, even had he submitted to have his finger impressions taken, could not be introduced at the trial for this reason. The bearing this legal fact has upon the case is well defined and the attorneys for the defense affirm that the sheriff and the chief of police exceeded their authority in this matter.*[45]

But other lawyers say no breach of legal authority committed in attempt to secure fingerprints, state can make use of all methods to secure means for identification. At least some people on my side.[46]

---

45 *Brown County Journal*, December 17, 1904.

46 Ibid.

This afternoon took Koch in front of Justice Henningsen, who bound him over to me until grand jury meets. Koch didn't seem upset with us. Don't know why not—everyone else is.

Week Seven: December 11–17, 1904

Tues. Dec. 13: Grand jury in session. Deputies & I swamped all day Monday serving subpoenas. Governor Van Sant appointed Childs[47] as prosecutor. Hoidale stepped down from case because partner Koch's brother-in-law, but continues to gather evidence for presentation to jury.

Fri. Dec. 16: Koch indicted. 19 for indictment, 2 against. Gossip on the street: before his death Gebhardt's business increasing, Koch's wasn't. So motive's supposed to be professional jealousy. Also Koch & Gebhardt not such good friends as everyone thought.

Week Eight: December 18–24, 1904

Mon. Dec. 19: Trial date set for December 26. Childs in town reviewing testimony. Has distinguished legal record, prosecuted two murderers successfully. Assisted by Frederickson of Springfield and Pfaender of New Ulm. Koch represented by Sommerville[48] of Sleepy Eye, Somsen of New Ulm, and Abbott of Winona. Brown and Olson dropped from his original group. Webber[49] will preside.

Week Nine: December 25–31, 1904

Mon. Dec. 26: Jury selection started. Only two picked. Blizzard last night made traveling difficult, so fewer men showing up

---

47 Henry W. Childs was a former attorney general for Minnesota.

48 A state senator.

49 Webber was seventy years old and had twenty-one years as a ninth judicial district judge.

as candidates. Lawyers examined twenty-five of thirty eligible. We've served over 150 jury subpoenas. Koch wore black suit, looked like young professional, sat through all questioning of potential jurors.

Noticed neither side seemed concerned about fingerprints. Could be evidence proving Koch innocent or guilty. Read in the *Review* fingerprints "evidence which has been rarely used in criminal cases in this country, although it is coming more into use yearly, but in Great Britain and some other countries, fingerprints, and especially thumbprints, are accepted as conclusive evidence and where prints have corresponded a prisoner has been convicted with an absence of all other testimony."[50] But attorneys on both sides didn't push for fingerprints to be taken. Procedure too new, I guess.

Thurs. Dec. 29: Bill Baxter, of Baxter Detective Agency in Minneapolis, telling anyone who'll listen Koch may be innocent, or had someone else with him at time of murder. Baxter in New Ulm off and on for seven weeks, suspected man who moved out of New Ulm shortly after the murder. He said whoever sent poison to Gebhardt is probably man who killed him, if we could find typewriter used to print label of parcel containing poison, we could compare. Fact is we've already looked into that. Took typewriters from secretaries in office near Koch's.

Baxter's other theory is love triangle caused fight. Hasn't given any reports to defense or state because, he said, "You got to understand me. I am not hired by the defense or anybody. I came down here originally for the fifteen hundred dollars reward and that is what I have been working for all along and that is what I am working for now."[51]

---

50 *New Ulm Review*, December 21, 1904.

51 *New Ulm Review*, December 28, 1904.

Week Ten: January 1–7, 1905

Mon. Jan. 2: More than 200 interviewed for jury. At one time state & defense talking about allowing jury to be just ten men. Judge made them push on. Today last two chosen. Seven farmers, postmaster, saloon keeper, blacksmith, two merchants. Most would have difficult time convicting son of E. G. Koch. *Review* described father as "man whose personality can fasten itself so strongly upon his fellows and is one of a thousand."

Tues. Jan. 3: Childs opened trial today. Told jury two classes of murders: one is deliberate purpose, which murderer plots and usually does at night, when selects his victim & instruments, carries out purpose deliberately. This class always attempts to cover up their tracks, so evidence against them must be circumstantial.[52] Other kind of murder born of heated passion. Said murder of Gebhardt belongs to the first class; evidence of state purely circumstantial.

Weeks Eleven through Thirteen: January 8–28, 1905

Wed. Jan. 11: So far only the witnesses for the state have been testifying.

Dr. L. A. Fritsche: When first heard about murder, sometime between 10 & 11 at night, went directly to scene. Pencil found in pool of blood introduced. Stated body in operating room. Hammer introduced. On cross-exam, said hammer had not always been in his possession—lent it to Pinkerton detectives for investigation.

---

52 Circumstantial evidence is evidence not bearing directly on the fact in dispute, but on various attendant circumstances from which the judge or jury might infer the occurrence of the crime. Direct evidence would be a witness who actually saw the defendant commit the crime. Circumstantial evidence in this case would be, for example, the hammer.

Actual handkerchief left at the murder scene. Note the initials G.R.K. in the bottom right corner. Source: Courtesy of a private collection.

I was next. Told them about condition of room, stated my theory terrible fight occurred. Shown bloody handkerchief with "G. R. K." and identified it as one found at crime scene.

Herbert Baltrusch, age 18: He & his brother working at *Review*, below Gebhardt's office. Saw Koch walk out of barbershop, wearing black overcoat. Next heard loud footsteps going upstairs to Gebhardt's office and footsteps walking in office. Also heard buzzing sound like dentist polishing something. He & brother left office about 9:45. Asa Brooks had just walked in to check mail.

Alfred Heinz, age 18: Works at Stamm's barbershop next door to *Review*. Left about five min. past nine, went out, stood by Pfefferle's drugstore. Stood there about fifteen min., when Koch walked by, said hello. He observed Koch walking north until reached Fesenmaier's hardware store, where stopped, looked in, stood for about two mins. Came back to Alfred and asked who was still working at the barbershop. Had short conversation.

(But Koch told us he returned to office that night about 9:15, turned off light. When I heard Alfred's testimony, wondered, how could Koch be in two different places at same time?)

Anton Simmet & Mr. Pfefferle: Koch stopped by barbershop at 9:20, talked to them for few minutes. Simmet: Koch in earlier, had haircut. Pfefferle walked distance between murder scene & Koch house; took him 15 mins., 45 sec.

Cecilia Martinka, age 16: Speaks with strong German accent. Rode in with her two brothers & Francis Roesch from Nicollet County on night of murder. Arrived about 7. She & Francis went to visit her sister, who lives near Catholic church about eight blocks from Gebhardt's office. At about 9 walked downtown, met Joseph Polta in front of Amman's Harness Shop. Walked down Minnesota St. to Congregational Church, turned around. Walked back downtown, stopped in front of bank. Only man they saw standing in front of watering trough. Heard noise coming from Gebhardt's office. Polta said, "There's a fight." Went over to barbershop, looked up at Gebhardt's office. Miss M. asked to describe noise—puckered up, said, "Oh, oh!" made other gruesome sounds. Testified she heard church bell ring twice, meaning 9:30. Defense attorney Sommerville tried hard to trip her up, but she didn't bend a bit.

Francis Roesch: Recognized man by trough as Behnke, man who kicked in door at murder scene. Corroborated Miss M.'s testimony.

Alfred Keller, age 18, & his friend Herman Lindmeyer: Closed Pfefferle's drugstore, where Keller worked, at about 9:20, walked for a while. K. heard bus go down to meet train scheduled to arrive in New Ulm at 9:37. Train's usually early, so estimated time to be about 9:30 when heard cry & groans from dentist's office. They saw Brooks run out of his office, upstairs to dentist's office.

A. J. Vogel: Playing cards in law office of Hoidale & Somsen earlier that eve. The other players: Dr. Vogel, Hoidale,

Somsen, Higgs, & Koch. He handed out advertising pencils for his lumber company, gave one to Koch. Saw Koch in drugstore next day putting rubber cots on fingers. Koch told Vogel he'd injured middle joints of index & middle fingers with carbolic acid. Vogel described sores as red and size of eight-penny nail.

Klause: Also observed Koch's hands. Burns on left hand fresh, quarter-inch in diameter. Also saw scratches that looked fresh. Did not ask him about wounds. Told about Koch's sister showing us 20 handkerchiefs belonging to Koch with initials "G.R.K."

State also called witnesses who testified hammer found at scene belonged to Koch.

Reineke: Told about bottle of poison sent to Gebhardt. Told victim powder looked like poison to him & not to try it.

Strickler: Shares an office with Koch. Said he had strychnine missing from common chest, located in the waiting room, about the time Gebhardt rec'd strychnine. Saw scratches on hands of Koch shortly after murder & described Koch in state of "almost nervous shock."

I noticed Strickler had trouble testifying against close friend. Koch looked pale & lost self-assuredness during testimony.

Fri. Jan. 13: Asa Brooks causing problems for state prosecutors. First told people thought murderer looked like Koch, but needed to see Koch's eyes before could be certain. Now believes it wasn't Koch. State wasn't anxious to put him up as witness, but defense insisted only eyewitness of murder be called to stand. Judge ordered Brooks to testify.

Brooks: Heard fighting, ran upstairs, climbed up on stair rail & looked in transom window, made eye contact with murderer. When asked if man was Koch, he replied, "No sir, it was not."

At previous hearing, Brooks's description of murderer matched general description of Koch. On witness stand now firm wasn't Koch. Brooks says was close friend of victim & only acquaintance of Koch.

The defense called witnesses who described clothing Koch wearing night of murder. Clothes produced with no blood on them. (There's been argument he had two sets, one used to murder, other used for alibi.)

They called Koch's father, Ernest G. Koch, 72, prominent person & considered pioneer.[53] Very well liked & respected. Former president of Brown County Bank & treasurer of county for past ten years.

Ernest Koch: Son arrived home at 22 mins. to 10 that evening. Remembers because Sat. prior chided son for coming home late, so when son came home looked at clock. Son went out for couple mins., returned, read book next to father. About half hour later son went to cellar for apple, retired for eve.

Mon. Jan. 16: George Koch took stand today. Courtroom filled to capacity, with many having to stand. Room quiet as he described how injured hands: Sun. prior to murder, out on ride with young lady. Got out to practice shooting, horse became frightened. In attempt to grab horse, he fell & hurt hands.

Explained actions on Nov. 1: visited lady friend until 8, then visited law office of brother-in-law. Walked leisurely in business district, talking to people. Returned to office to turn off light he'd left on. Went to barbershop, where he talked politics. Arrived home about 9:45.

About strychnine: said he had poison of his own, so why steal from Strickler? Handkerchief: if his, probably stolen by drug fiend who committed murder. Pencil: still had one given to him. Hammer: didn't belong to him, but did have similar one. Answered no to every question asked by state prosecutor.

---

53 Settled in New Ulm in 1861.

Actual items of evidence left at the murder scene: handkerchief, bottle of poison, pencils, hammer. Ruler is used to illustrate the size of the items. Source: Courtesy of a private collection.

Did good job of testifying, seeming self-assured, confident. Well coached, I think.

Wed. Jan. 18: Final arguments to jury today. State's case summarized by Childs: Brooks's description similar to Koch, "G.R.K." initialed handkerchief, pencil, hammer, poison, injured hands, seen in area at time, timing, anatomy knowledge.

Summary from Brown for defense: good rep, no motive, father has money, at home at time of murder, Brooks says Koch not murderer, real murderer tried to frame Koch.

Fri. Jan. 20: Jury deliberated forty-one hours. 9:40 in the morning, foreman told Judge Webber unable to reach verdict. Vote was three for guilty, nine for acquittal. The night prior, vote five for guilty, seven for acquittal. Judge Webber asked jury if matter could possibly be resolved. Jurors said no. Thanked them, dismissed them. Jurors shook hands with defendant & lawyers.

Childs announced another trial. He & Brown argued over bail. Childs said proof was evident, presumption great, thus no bail. Brown produced affidavit signed by three physicians—Fritsche, Schoch, Weiser—stating Koch growing pale, losing flesh. Brown said Koch would not run. Judge agreed, asked Childs what bail should be. Agreed on $20,000.[54]

WED. JAN. 25: Read in paper today what one juror said after trial: "I never want to have such an experience again. It is awful to be imprisoned for three weeks and to feel that a man's life is in your hands."[55]

FRI. JAN. 27: Koch released on bail today after forty-nine days in jail.

WEEKS FOURTEEN THROUGH SEVENTEEN: APRIL 16–MAY 13, 1905

MON. APRIL 17: Next trial starts on Wed. The defense has been granted a change of venue, to Mankato, with Judge Cray.[56] Once released on bail, Koch went right back to work. You'd think his business ruined. But in fact had so much, started scheduling people days in advance. I'm sure picked up some of Gebhardt's clients. Some people say reason for killing—to help his business.

Koch has three lawyers, all from Mankato: Clark, Pfau Sr., Pfau Jr. Gives him advantage because they'll be playing on home field. Blue Earth attorney Wilson & Pfaender of New Ulm assisting Childs.

Defense attorney Sommerville filed affidavit of prejudice against Blue Earth Sheriff Williams, stating he was soliciting

54 Doctors L. A. Fritsche, Charles Stube, and Charles Wagner signed the bail bonds. The bond was also signed by Jacob Klossner, E G. Koch, and W. E. Koch.

55 *New Ulm Review*, January 25, 1905.

56 Defense attorney G. W. Sommerville was a state senator, and would have been in session if an earlier date was picked. Blue Earth County was picked over Watonwan because Watonwan County had a population of only 11,000 and Blue

jurors only from men not of German ancestry. Judge shown list of men Williams contacting. Judge agreed only a few German. County coroner, E. R. Kennedy, assigned in Williams's place.

Mon. April 24: Took five days to fill jury. All got asked tough question: could they find man guilty of murder on circumstantial evidence to result in capital punishment? Most said no. Defense wanted to know which newspapers they read. Majority said *Minneapolis Journal* or *Tribune*, *St. Paul Pioneer Press*, *Mankato Free Press*, or *New Ulm Review*. Defense wanted men not influenced by reading papers. Total of 157 men called. Opening presentations to jury started late this afternoon.

Judge Cray had bailiffs tell everyone no more smoking in courtroom, even before court in session. Said court smelling like spittoon. Court so crowded, ladies asked to take hats off so people could see. Not inch to spare.

Wed. May 3: Most witnesses same as at first trial. State eliminated some to avoid duplication.

Chief Klause: Went to Koch home four days after murder. Described Koch's sister Ida showing us handkerchiefs, Koch showing us his clothing.

Defense called Klause "fabricator." Looked as if Adolph going to come out of chair & pop him one, but didn't. Miss K. soundly denied telling us handkerchief was brother's.

Ole Ulen of Lake Hanska: New state witness. Has lived in Lake Hanska for 14 years, farms there. When Koch had part-time practice in Hanska, Ulen went to him to get tooth pulled, in June or July 1903. Koch asked him who pulled his teeth before, Ulen said Gebhardt. Koch said Gebhardt no better than rest of them, not be in town long. Ulen asked if Gebhardt sick or planning to move. Koch said someone going

---

Earth had a population of 32,000. The judge, Lorin Cray, also lived in Mankato.

to kill him. Then Koch asked Ulen if he would do it. Ulen said not even if he got whole of New Ulm. Defense went after Ulen because medicated for pain. Ulen said didn't take medicine because tasted terrible—spit it out.

Reinhold Dahms: Another new witness. Age 22, bricklayer, lived with Koch family winters 1897-1903. Cut wood, did chores. Identified hammer found at scene as belonging to Koch. Used it when doing some of his work. Didn't testify at first trial because liked George & family.

Mrs. Katherine Kasz: Cleans offices in Strickler block, including Koch's office once a week. About three weeks before murder used Koch's hammer to take out window to clean. But she said hammer at scene not one she used. Prosecutors surprised—own witness reneged.

Klause told me later Mrs. K. said hammer at the trial didn't look like Koch's because of evidence tag.[57]

Mrs. Willhemina Dahms: Only speaks German, so Dr. Leidoff sworn in as interpreter. Lives with family on 2nd St N., renters for past eight years from Kochs. Lives about four blocks away, only cow pasture between. Gate between two homes made of wood & wire, rope securing it. Mrs. D disturbed about 9:50 on night of murder by someone running west of house. She got up, saw no one. Dogs chased after person as far as gate. Next morning found blood on post. Klause few days later sawed off top part of post.

Defense attorney Abbott questioned her. She works land every day so familiar with what post looked like. Abbott asked her if they had hired man to help them. "No." "Have you a husband at home?" "Yes, where else should he stay?" Laughter in courtroom. Judge slammed down gavel several times. Judge told interpreter to remind Mrs. D. to answer questions, not ask them.

---

57 A rule of trial attorneys is to never ask a question of a witness unless you know the answer.

Tues. May 9: Asa Brooks testified today. Gave his background: born in Ill., moved to several places, didn't remember where or when. Lived in half a dozen places in Penn., on his own since age 12. Moved around in Minn., where he worked for newspapers. Has worked in New Ulm for past four years.

Some people disappointed with Asa because first said murderer looked like Koch. Now says definitely not Koch. Prosecuting attorneys challenging credibility. Said born in 1868, age 36. But at first trial said 34.

His testimony changed about murder, too. I got this from court reporter:

Childs: Did the noise upstairs indicate that there was trouble upstairs?

Brooks: I did not think so.

Childs: Didn't you testify before that you heard quite a hollowing and anguished outcry?

Brooks: Don't remember that I did.

Childs: You don't think there was trouble upstairs before you went up?

Brooks: No, sir.

Childs: Then why did you go up?

Brooks: To get into the game.

Childs: Did you think that there was a jollification going on up there?

Brooks: I thought there was a rough house.

Childs: How long had it been since there was a rough house before? Was it a common thing?

Brooks: It had been about a year.

Brooks criticized in papers by some citizens for not calling an alarm when he looked into Gebhardt's office. People thought might have chased, saved Gebhardt. I'd say maybe, maybe not.

CHILDS: Did you or did you not know the man who was above the prostrate form?

BROOKS: I did.

CHILDS: Didn't you feel that you were looking at something very extraordinary?

BROOKS: I thought it was something that I had no business to see.

CHILDS: Did you speak?

BROOKS: No, sir.

CHILDS: Why didn't you call out?

BROOKS: There was no excuse for it that I could see.

CHILDS: What impression did you have when you got down?

BROOKS: I thought an operation was going on.

CHILDS: How could you think that?

BROOKS: I am not a philosopher.

CHILDS: Did you ever see a dentist lying on the floor with the patient above him?

BROOKS: No, sir.

CHILDS: What were your feelings once you got down from the transom?

BROOKS: My feelings were so mixed up that it would be ridiculous for me to describe them.

Childs read from transcript from hearing where Brooks said didn't know if Koch or not. Childs went on to name several people and exact time & places where Brooks said wasn't sure if Koch murderer. Brooks denied conversations.

The door on the left is the entrance to the shared waiting room of Dr. Gebhardt and Dr. Reineke. Brooks stood on this railing and looked in the top transom to see the murder happening. Source: Author's collection.

Then onto T.W. Barnes: Has office across hall from Koch. Used to borrow hammer from Koch; hammer in evidence not same.

Defense called witnesses who saw Koch's hands after murder, said no major damage. Defense also tried to prove Koch didn't send poison—questioned several mail clerks.

Tues. May 9: Koch testified yesterday. Courtroom jam-packed. Judge Cray told bailiffs not to admit boys under 21, girls under 18. Anyone sitting had to arrive at least half hour early. No standing rule not enforced, but people still turned away.

Koch dressed in dark suit, with new haircut, generally clean & neat. Answered questions clearly, briefly, to the point.

On Nov. 1 left his home about 7:00 in the evening. Went to office, picked up box of perfumery, went to boarding house of Miss Fitzpatrick. Gave her the birthday present, left about

8:10 or 8:15. Went back to office, from there went to Hoidale & Somsen's office. Left to go home, remembered left light on at office. Walked back, greeting people. Turned off light, walked over to Stamm's barbershop, there between 9:15 & 9:20. Talked politics, then walked home, passing newspaper office. Went to bed not long after.

Morning after murder refilled carbolic acid bottle. Refills it regularly because degenerates; fills bottle from Dr. Vogel's. Making crown using blowpipe & gasoline blaze. Accidentally tipped over bottle, spilling on back of hand. Washed immediately, but left white spots on skin. Told Vogel about it, advised to clean with alcohol. Day or so later, treated hand with alcohol, shortly after put wood into furnace, caught fire, gave him blisters. Childs very aggressive on cross-exam, but Koch didn't change story.

Wed. May 10: Judge limited asst. attorneys' closing arguments to one hour, no time limit for lead attorneys.

Childs is smooth, organized, precise orator. Told jury:

> *If another man was brought in here [as defendant who tried to frame Koch], then the defense must know that this other man had known that Koch hated Gebhardt, that he knew that the defendant was going to be at his office, that he had one of the defendant's handkerchiefs, that the defendant's father had an old hammer, and the defendant received from Vogel that pencil and no one outside that card party knew that.*

L. L. Brown, for defense: about 45 years old, tall, pale. Wears glasses, chews the end of his cigar when speaking. Challenged witnesses' statements as he read from his notes. Reviewed various testimony, asked jury if convict based on it. A newspaper described statement: "He would quote their exact words and interpret and apply them with the effect of a shot between wind and water."[58]

WEEK EIGHTEEN: MAY 14–20, 1905

WED. MAY 17: Total of 45 hours of deliberation. Jury appeared before judge twice, told him no agreement. Today foreman said no one changing minds. Childs & Sommerville agreed to discharge jury, have another trial.

Votes from two trials: 16 for acquittal, 8 for conviction.

FRI. MAY 19: Koch's bail remains $20,000. Continues to practice dentistry in New Ulm. Recently moved to new office, located above Model Meat Market. Probably felt resentful of former office partner after testified for prosecution.

WEEK NINETEEN THROUGH TWENTY-THREE: JULY 2–AUGUST 5, 1905

THURS. JULY 6: Third trial began today in Mankato. Same judge & attorneys. Expecting same witnesses, too.

WED. JULY 12: State eliminated testimony about poison sent to Gebhardt. Childs believes not convincing.

WED. JULY 26: Yesterday defense called Miss Mary Fitzpatrick. Daughter of state senator from Winona. Was with Koch, a regular pursuer of her friendship, on Sun. prior to murder.

On that day, riding with Koch in buggy when he noticed some quail. Jumped from buggy, shot at one of them. Horse spooked, started to act up. Koch grabbed reins, dragged short way, fell to ground, scraped hands. Miss F. didn't notice scrapes on hands at time because it was dark.

---

58 *St. Paul Dispatch*, May 11, 1905. The phrase "wind and water" refers to that part of a ship's side or bottom that is frequently above water by the rolling of the ship or fluctuation of the water surface—i.e., the vulnerable part.

On Nov. 1, eve of her birthday, Koch came to her house about 7:15. Gave her perfume, left shortly after 8.

Wilson of co. attorney's office asked Miss F. if Koch was sitting in the parlor when she rec'd phone call on Nov. 1. July 26 *Mankato Free Press* wrote:

> *During the visit she had received a phone call and stepped from the parlor to the hall to answer it. She soon recognized the voice as Miss McCabe's and pronounced the words "It is Miss McCabe." The latter was trying to disguise her voice and succeeded at first. Miss Fitzpatrick had been in the habit of calling McCabe "sweetheart" or some other such word when telephoning her and she applied this term to her at this time. Koch was sitting where he could overhear everything that was said, and he had known that Fitzpatrick was talking to McCabe and had asked her afterwards whether it was or not. He had asked, "Is it Ida McCabe?" and Miss Fitzpatrick said it was.*
>
> *"Didn't he say that it was Dr. Gebhardt?" asked Mr. Wilson.*
>
> *"He said it would be a good joke on me if it had been Dr. Gebhardt instead of Miss McCabe. He said this because Miss McCabe's studio is located close to Dr. Gebhardt's office and she frequently used his telephone."*
>
> *"Did you ever go to any entertainment with Dr. Gebhardt?*
>
> *"Did I ever go with him?" asked Miss Fitzpatrick.*
>
> *"Yes."*
>
> *"Yes, sir."*[59]

Defense asked her about relations with Koch—friendly, no trouble, friends with his sister, etc. But state scored some points

59 *Mankato Daily Free Press*, July 26, 1905.

with phone story. I think Koch believed man calling for date with Miss F. Koch heard Miss F. say "sweetheart." Koch may have thought Gebhardt calling his girl. Prosecution pointing to jealousy as motive.

Fri. July 28: Yesterday Brooks, age 34 or 36? testified for fifth time. *Review* referred to him as man above reproach—never drinks or uses God's name in vain, best friend of victim, went to World's Fair in St. Louis with Gebhardt & sister. *Review* went on & on about integrity of Brooks who is their editor. I think he wrote it himself. He testified didn't see Koch in Gebhardt's office night of murder.

Childs tired but determined. Twenty-two witnesses called for second trial not called for this trial. He believes Koch killed Gebhardt, frustrated can't so far convince all jurors. Again explained to jury all circumstantial events & evidence involving Koch.

Abbott, for defense, discounted & cast doubt on testimony of state's witnesses.

Wed. Aug. 2: Yesterday morning at 11, nine months since eve of murder, third jury started deliberating. 1st trial jury deliberated 41 hours. Second trial, 45. This jury deliberated 2 hours. Court was quiet as Clerk Thorne read verdict: " . . . not guilty."

About 200 people applauded. For Koch, patting on back, handshakes, kiss from sister. Koch told *Free Press* he felt fine, would return to New Ulm next day. Hinted might look for different place to work.

I'll give some credit to Childs and his assistants and the defense lawyers. Those men fought a fair, rigorous, enduring legal contest that may never be matched again in Minnesota. I bet Koch will hold some type of record for being a defendant in three first-degree murder trials within an eight-month period. The pressure on these men and the courts was evident whenever you entered the courtrooms. And the trials got a lot of press here, around the state, even nationally.

The trials are now over, and everybody is tired of talking and reading about the murder case. Time to put it past us. The people of Brown County don't seem to be worried about a murderer running around loose any more. The citizens are split on whether Koch is innocent or not.[60] I hope time will tell.

Whatever happened to . . . ?

Einar Hoidale, the Brown County attorney, moved to Minneapolis. He practiced law out of the New York Life Building. He resided at the Hampshire Arms, Ninth Street and Fourth Avenue.

Sheriff William J. Julius was the sheriff of Brown County, Minnesota, from January 1, 1903, until his death on April 28, 1928, at the age of fifty-eight. He was in the printing business before joining the New Ulm police department in 1897. He married Charlotte Blass on November 23, 1891, and they had six children. Charlotte died in 1908. In 1920 he married Eva Schuster, who survived him, along with their two young children and four of his children from the first marriage.

He was a popular and well-respected man in Brown County and very active in civic and church affairs. He was remembered in this way: "As an officer, Mr. Julius was fearless and yet considerate at all times. He always responded promptly, when duty called."[61] He is buried at the New Ulm Catholic Cemetery.

Attorney General Henry W. Childs died in August 1906 of appendicitis. He was fifty-seven. He was a three-term Minnesota attorney general and was recognized as a prominent and successful attorney-at-law. He was remembered in legal circles for investigating the business

60 No one else was ever arrested for the murder.

61 *Brown County Journal*, April 6, 1928.

methods of several bond investment companies. These investigations resulted in the securing of the collection of taxes against several lumber companies. He successfully brought suits against several oil companies under the Inspection Act, and was "instrumental in securing the decision of the state supreme court making the state of Minnesota a preferred creditor in all cases of insolvency."[62]

District Court Judge B. F. Webber. Source: *Minneapolis Journal*, December 4, 1906.

His wife and a son survived him. The family resided at 1995 St. Anthony, St. Paul. His law firm of Childs, Edgerton, and Wickwire was located at 302 National G.A. Building, St. Paul.

District Court Judge B. F. Webber,[63] eight-year Brown County attorney, was elected District Court judge, ninth judicial district, and assumed his duties on January 1, 1883. He was an honored and respected member of the bench and bar of Minnesota. He retired for health reasons and to be more of an assistance to his ailing wife in 1905. Financial and health problems were a merciless burden to him in retirement. He sadly took his own life by hanging on December 4, 1906. He was seventy-three. The *Minneapolis Journal* stated that the strain of the long first trial "no doubt hastened the end that came today."

62 *St. Paul Dispatch*, August 30, 1906.

63 Resided at 324 South Broadway, New Ulm.

Dr. George R. Koch working on an abscessed tooth of a circus ape in Minneapolis, 1915. Source: Minnesota Historical Society.

Dr. George R. Koch stayed only a short time in New Ulm after the last trial. He moved to Minneapolis within the year and started a practice at office number 425 in the Medical Arts Building at 608 Nicollet. He resided for several years at 903 Third Avenue South in Minneapolis. He practiced dentistry for a total of sixty-one years. During those years, in Minneapolis, his offices were located at 502 Besse Bldg., 431 Syndicate Bldg., 519 Nicollet, 91 South Seventh Street, and 512 LaSalle Bldg.

On June 26, 1918, he married Elizabeth McGregor. They resided at 4324 Elliot Avenue South in Minneapolis. Koch retired in 1962. Elizabeth died on October 19, 1970. Koch moved back to New Ulm for his final days and lived there in a senior residence. He died on Saturday, November 22, 1975, at Fairview Hospital in Edina, of heart failure and pneumonia. He was ninety-five. He was buried at the New Ulm City Cemetery.

CHAPTER 3

The Mystery of the Murdered Butcher

1905

"It is to be regretted that no exceptional circumstances appear in this case, save the revolting acts, which reveal a foul and premeditated murder."

—Judge Olin B. Lewis, Ramsey County District Court, May 11, 1905

THE POPULATION OF ST. PAUL IN 1905 was 196,552, and the city had 205[64] police officers who walked or rode a horse in patrolling their beat. The walkers were subject to developing flat feet, and thus the police were often referred to as the "flatfoots." The department's chief was the fifty-five-year-old John J. O'Connor. He liked cigars, whiskey, gambling, and a good crook. He had a superior opinion of the city and also, as you will discover, of

64 Estimated. In 1900 there were 195 officers in St. Paul, with a population of 163,000. Police headquarters were at 85 W. 3rd; other stations included Central Substation (85 W. 3rd), Rondo Substation, Rondo and Western, Margaret Substation, 749 Marshall, Ducas Street Substation, Robert and Delos (southeast corner), Prior Ave. Substation, Prior near Oakley.

St. Paul Chief of Police John J. O'Connor. Source: Minnesota Historical Society.

himself. This chief explains how he and his detectives resolved a complicated "who done it."

I will recount for you the case of a murder that happened in broad daylight on a busy St. Paul street. This case illustrates some first-rate police work, if I don't mind saying so myself. Pay attention, for you're going to learn how the best police department in the country investigated a convoluted murder.

Saturday was the busiest day of the week at the Schindeldecker Meat Shop, located at 523 West Seventh Street in St. Paul. About 12:40 p.m., on February 18, young meat market driver Walter Gerenz returned to the shop after lunch. He was troubled to find the front door locked, so he went around to the back door. Upon entering he saw a horrifying sight. Christian H. Schindeldecker, the thirty-five-year-old owner of the shop, had been stabbed, and his body dismembered and hacked into pieces. The back room was saturated with blood. Gerenz told me later that he'd stood frozen in disbelief. Blood was still oozing out of the mangled body of his employer, and he felt sick as he ran out the door to summon the police.

The coroner and a few of my men arrived shortly thereafter. The scene looked as if Jack the Ripper had struck again. The front door was nailed shut from the inside. The cash from Schindeldecker's pockets was gone, as was the money in the cash drawer. The victim's wife estimated that he had about one hundred dollars on him when he was killed. Next to the body were two penknives, a handkerchief, a pencil, and a buckskin pouch. We later determined that

Schindeldecker Meat Shop. Source: *St. Paul Pioneer Press*, February 19, 1905.

those items belonged to the victim and had been taken from his pockets.

I surmised from the scene that the victim had put up a desperate fight. Several light brown hairs were discovered in the victim's hand. His own hair was dark. The coroner believed he was killed by several blows to his head with a blunt instrument. He was then dragged to the back room, where he was stabbed and hacked. A hammer, with the initials "C.H." stamped into the metal, was found in a basket in the back room. Gerenz said it did not belong to the meat market.

Coroner A. W. Miller discovered blood from the victim on a shelf in the rear shed about five feet from where he lay. The perpetrator must have been covered with blood when he left the murder scene. Dr. Judd Goodrich, who had been called to the scene, said the victim could not have been dead more than ten minutes before his arrival. He said in all probability the murderer had left the scene about five minutes before the body was found.[65]

65 *St. Paul Pioneer Press*, February 21, 1905.

The hammer used in the murder. Source: *St. Paul Dispatch*, February 21, 1905.

I theorized that the murderer was not alone. Someone had to carry another set of clothes because it would be highly unlikely that a blood-soaked man could go unnoticed at that time of day in such a busy area of town. Marin Witten, who had employed Schindeldecker four years earlier, said that the murder victim had been a tough man. He thought the murderer must have been "suffering with one of the most violent forms of insanity" because not many men could take him on in a fight.[66]

The murder was particularly bizarre because it happened at a frequented place of business, at midday, and on a busy street. If robbery was the motive, did the victim possibly recognize the assailant, who then killed him? People asked each other, "Why the overkill?" The extra stabbing extended the time the murderer remained in the meat market, taking a chance that a witness could see in the window or an employee would catch him exiting the rear door. Was there another motive besides robbery? Was there some type of message being delivered? Was the victim involved with some sort of cult or gang or knew something that brought on his murder?

66 Ibid.

The entire population of St. Paul was talking about the crime. People were locking doors that had previously remained open. People were afraid to stay home alone. Merchants shuddered when an unknown customer walked into their store. The city was obsessed with rumors. Tips about the identity of the murderer flooded my department.

Christian M. Schindeldecker. Source: *St. Paul Pioneer Press*, May 5, 1905.

I appointed myself the supervisor of this investigation, prioritized this case above all the others of my department and assigned all available personnel to follow up on all the leads. I am in the habit of leaking information to the *St. Paul Pioneer Press* and the *St. Paul Dispatch*, because I receive favorable press in return. (It's important to keep up my public image.) I appealed through the newspapers to anyone who was in the area of the meat market at the time of the murder to contact my department. I also made another good investigative decision by having my men go door knocking on every house in the immediate area. We interviewed over a hundred people in the first week about what they had seen on the day of the murder.

Walter Gerenz, the clerk and delivery boy for Schindeldecker, told us he had walked home to eat lunch that day at about 12:05 p.m., going up Seventh to Goodhue. As he turned up the street, he passed a man he knew as Ed near the schoolhouse on Western Avenue. He didn't know his last name, but they knew each other well enough to say hello. Ed was talking with another man when Gerenz walked by on his way to his room. He lived with the Schindeldeckers at 418 Superior.

I initially thought that Gerenz knew more about the crime than he was telling. My detectives and I wanted to locate this Ed in order to corroborate Gerenz's alibi. I assigned detectives Daly and Sweeney to search the fifth ward in an effort to locate Ed. During their canvass of the ward, the detectives spoke with beat patrolman Patrick Newcomer, who told them that he was aware of an Ed Gottschalk, who resided at the rooming house at 480 Goodhue. Newcomer also told the detectives he had heard Gottschalk's wife left him because he beat her and that he might be a former convict.[67]

On the evening of Friday, February 24, six days after the murder, Detectives Daly, Fraser, Moran, and Sweeney went to Gottschalk's room on Goodhue. Gottschalk was irritated but cooperative. The officers took him to headquarters for questioning. Gottschalk told them that he never left his room on the day of the murder. Although he seemed to be forthcoming, something just did not seem right. I sent the detectives back to search Gottschalk's room. They seized several items of potential evidence: twenty dollars and ninety-two cents' worth of silver coins from a teacup in a cupboard, a loaded .32-caliber pistol, and some recently washed clothes that were stained—possibly with blood. Mrs. Louis A. Nelson, who roomed at the same house, told the detectives that Gottschalk was not home during the time of the murder. She recalled that on that day, Gottschalk left with a young man before noon and returned about 1:30 p.m.

When the detectives interrogated Gottschalk at the station, he continued to claim that the stains were from cleaning fish. Previously he told them all the money he had to his name was what he had on him, one dollar and ninety-two cents. As the interrogation continued, Gottschalk gradually became less believable. I had a gut feeling that Gottschalk was hiding something. I have an inerrant instinct for things like this, so I decided to hold him in the stir until we had more information.[68] I know he would skedaddle if I didn't.

67 Beat officers would have been the best source of information about the residents in their district.

68 Actually O'Connor needed a body in jail to ease the pressure.

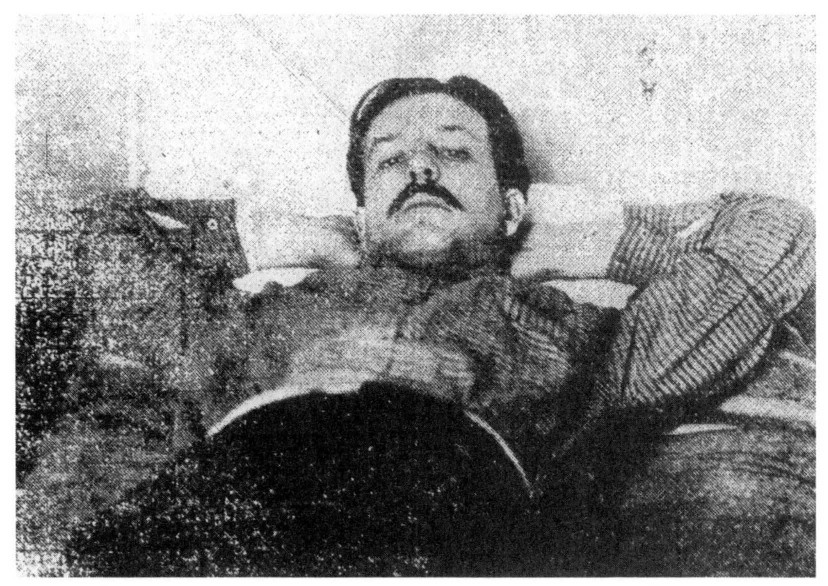
Edward Gottschalk in jail cell. Source: *St. Paul Pioneer Press*, May 9, 1905.

On the next morning, February 25, a week following the murder, St. Paul mayor Robert Smith offered a reward in the following proclamation:

> *Whereas, on Saturday, the 18th of February, 1905, at North 523 West Seventh street, a law abiding and peaceful citizen in the person of Christian H. Schindeldecker, while engaged in the conduct of his business, was in open day murdered under circumstances of exceptional brutality;*
>
> *And whereas, the efforts thus far made for the discovery of the author or authors of said crime have not resulted successfully;*
>
> *Now, I, Robert A. Smith, mayor of St. Paul, do hereby, by virtue of the authority vested in me by the laws and ordinance of this city, offer a reward of the sum of one thousand dollars [$1,000] for such information that will lead to the arrest and conviction of the murderer or murderers of the said Christian H. Schindeldecker.*[69]

69 *St. Paul Pioneer Press*, February 25, 1905.

I hoped the reward would loosen some tongues and obtain additional information on Gottschalk. And I thought some of the local private detectives might be interested in solving this case for the reward money.

Chemist Nicholas Lehnen was assigned the task of determining if the stains on Gottschalk's clothing were from blood, and if so, whether it was human blood. Lehnen gave us a written statement that the stains were from blood, but he couldn't tell right away if the bloodstains were human or animal. He didn't know how long it would take him to find out.

Joseph Hartman was rumored to be a friend of Gottschalk. We wanted to talk to him, but no one knew where he was. Hartman was last seen on the Monday after the murder. Hartman's parents told the police that Joseph had burned his picture and his clothing that morning. Then he asked his mother for a nickel to ride the trolley car. She refused, and Hartman left without saying where he was going. That was the last time they had seen him.

Hartman's father, Charles, came to my department and identified the hammer with the initials "C.H." on it, found at the crime scene, as his. I then sent the old man Hartman up to jail to visit with Gottschalk. I thought Hartman could loosen his lips a bit. When there he asked Gottschalk when he last saw Joseph. Gottschalk told him that it was the Wednesday of the previous week. They had gone fishing on Sunday and Monday, but he did not see him on Tuesday. On Wednesday, he said, they were fishing at Pickerel Lake. He told the father that they were spearing fish for a while. Joseph was still there when he left, but when Gottschalk looked back, he saw Hartman walking the trail some distance behind him. Gottschalk said that was the last time he saw him.

"Why do you ask me that?" Gottschalk asked. "Joe and I were best of friends."

"Did you have any trouble with Joe?"

"Never any trouble, except for this," Gottschalk nodded at the handcuffs. "God knows neither Joe or myself is implicated in that murder, but this suspicion that rests upon us is the only trouble he and I have ever had while we were companions."[70]

The fact remained that Hartman had disappeared on Monday afternoon, two days after the murder, and he had not been seen since. A railroad man told the police that he saw Hartman the day after the murder with a cut over his eye.

We discovered that after the murder, Ed Gottschalk paid his landlord, Adam Aydt, his February rent of five dollars and that he also paid off his six-dollar grocery bill to John Mascek. We were now interested in how he obtained the money. Gottschalk had no answers for us. We kept him in jail, and now he was under strict confinement with no one allowed to visit.

Although he had lived in St. Paul several years, he was a loner and appeared to have few friends other than Hartman. Gottschalk said he could account for the money found in his room even though he did not make much money cleaning gas burners and selling fish. He said nothing to the jailers about the crime, except that he was innocent.

On March 2 the chemist told me that it might take up to three more weeks for him to determine if the blood found on Gottschalk's clothing was human blood. He warned me that if it turned out there were more than one kind of blood in the fabric, he would not necessarily be able to do an accurate analysis.[71]

Gottschalk was consistent in his explanation of how the blood got on his clothing. He said it was from the fish he cleaned in his room or out in the back of the house.[72] The chemist told me that sometimes it could be difficult to tell the difference between fish and human blood.

On Friday, March 3, Edward Gottschalk was arraigned in St. Paul municipal court. I of course was the complainant, and I read the formal

70 *St. Paul Pioneer Press*, March 1, 1905.

71 *St. Paul Pioneer Press*, March 2, 1905.

72 *St. Paul Pioneer Press*, March 3, 1905.

complaint aloud. Municipal Court Judge Robert C. Hine told the suspect that he had the right to obtain an attorney and have a preliminary hearing to determine if he was in any way involved with the murder of Schindeldecker.

Gottschalk told the judge that he did not have any friends or money. He asked the judge if he could tell him the name of an attorney. Hine explained that a list of attorneys would be provided to him once he was back at the jail. The judge then informed him there would be a hearing the next morning at nine o'clock. While standing and speaking to the judge, Gottschalk leaned forward toward the cuspidor, and the two officers standing next to him grabbed him, apparently fearing he was going to try to run. Gottschalk seemed amused and said he would not run even if he had the chance. He just had to spit.

My men sent circulars to police departments throughout the country and interviewed relatives and neighbors of Hartman, yet there was no trace of him. His family was growing gravely concerned. His friends said they last saw him at a saloon on Sunday evening, the day after the murder. They said Hartman looked pale, nervous, and exhausted. Hartman manufactured a story that he had just left the hospital after a ten-day stay. Joe's friends insisted he was not a murderer and that something must have happened to him.

On March 4, Judge Hine read the complaint to Gottschalk and told him that he could have a hearing or waive it. "I want a hearing," Gottschalk told the judge. The assistant county attorney, Hugo O. Hanft, then asked for a ten-day continuance, but Stan J. Donnelly, Gottschalk's lawyer, asked the court to refuse it. He told the court his client has been in jail almost ten days and the state was stalling because they could not find Hartman. The defense attorney said the prosecutors were waiting for the grand jury to convene next week. I was pleased that the judge did the right thing and didn't accept the defense motions. He continued the hearing until March 14, and Gottschalk remained locked up. If the judge had ruled the wrong way, I would have come up with something to keep him in jail.

The citizens were still a little unsettled, and some people were critical of our treatment of the suspect, like the writer of this March 9 letter to the editor of the *St. Paul Pioneer Press*:

> *There seems to be a distinct change in sentiment coming over the community regarding the case of Gottschalk, the suspected murderer of Schindeldecker. The public is becoming sick and tired of the daily report of conjectures, opinions, the theories and suspicions of the police department paraded before them in place of facts. They have heard all the evil reports his neighbors were able to bring against him. And the American sense of fair play begins to proclaim loudly that it is time Gottschalk was given an opportunity to be heard in his own behalf. This conviction strengthened by the fact that what little has leaked out seems to be strongly in his favor. For instance, the public was told that he had an evil countenance and the wickedest eye the chief of police had ever seen. About when his photograph appeared it revealed a face at least as good looking as some members of the police force. When brought before a judge, he pleaded for an immediate hearing. But was ordered back to prison for ten days longer, to give time to find better evidence against him. But can a man be imprisoned on account of his looks? Can a man be put in chains because he has a little money hidden in a teacup under his bed? Can a man be imprisoned because he pays his landlord and grocer after a murder has been committed in the community? Can he be thrown into a dungeon because there are dark stains on his overalls? If so, why can a citizen be held in solitary confinement like a condemned felon until some chemist expresses an opinion whether the stains are human or animal bloodstains? If it were human blood, would it prove, in this case, that it was Schindeldecker's blood and not the prisoner's? Can a man*

be held in duress, without evidence sufficient to convict him, until the real murderer is found? If such things are possible, what is the difference between the United States and Russia, between St. Paul and St. Petersburg?

—W. F. Markoe, St. Paul, March 9, 1905[73]

I would have been more irritated by this apparent lack of trust in and regard for my police department, but the writer admitted later in the letter that he was "a friend and admirer" of mine and didn't share the belief some had that Gottschalk was a scapegoat used by the police to put off "recent outrages committed in our city whose perpetrators are still at large." Still, it was irksome that we hadn't built enough of a case yet to get the public off our backs.

Normally I try to keep the public thinking I have more information about criminal cases but am not revealing it. In this case, however, we needed the public's assistance, so we were very generous in sharing information via the newspapers. Specifically, we needed Hartman—preferably alive.

On March 14, the preliminary hearing was held in the courtroom of Judge Finehout. Mrs. Nelson testified that on the day of the murder she observed Gottschalk and another man, about twenty years old, leave the rooming house a little after 11:00 a.m. and return about two hours later. Adam Aydt testified that Gottschalk had asked him for an extension to pay his February rent, which was due on the fifteenth of February. On the twenty-fifth, a week after the murder, Gottschalk paid Aydt his room rent with a five-dollar bill. The meat market driver, Walter Gerenz, testified that he saw Gottschalk—the person he knew as Ed—talking to another man on the day of the murder. My officers testified to the blood-stained clothes they found in Gottschalk's room. Once all the witnesses'

73 This letter to the editor appeared in the *St. Paul Pioneer Press* on March 10, 1905. The writer, W. F. Markoe, lived in White Bear Lake, Minnesota, and was a salesman for Wm. J. Dyer and Brother, 21–23 West Fifth Street, St. Paul. The company sold pianos and musical merchandise.

testimony was completed, Judge John W. Finehout issued his ruling: "I think the evidence at hand is sufficient to prove that Gottschalk had knowledge of facts which he did not tell the police when first arrested."[74] The case was then turned over to the sitting grand jury for them to hear testimony and for their deliberation.

Joe Hartman's home, 606 James St., St. Paul. Source: *St. Paul Dispatch*, February 28, 1905.

A newspaper reporter who attended the hearing wrote that, in his opinion, Gottschalk talked like an innocent man. Gottschalk told reporters at the jail that whoever did this to Schindeldecker ought to be chopped to pieces—a suspicious comment to my ears.

On March 17, at 1:00 p.m., the body of a young man was found floating in the Mississippi River near Mendota. Stephen McLain and Patrolman George W. Guion found the body in ten to twelve feet of water.[75] The men had been dragging the Mississippi, near Mendota in the vicinity of Pike Island, for five days. The body was pulled toward the island because of the strong current. When they finally got the body out of the water, the men were astounded to see that two flatirons had been tied to the feet. The men notified the coroner, who promptly joined them. Detectives, police officers, and the attorney for Gottschalk, Stan Donnelly, viewed the body. Their first guess was that the victim was Hartman. At that point there was no obvious evidence to implicate Gottschalk in his murder.[76]

---

74 *St. Paul Pioneer Press*, March 18, 1905.

75 The area was located 150 feet below the government dam and about 100 feet from shore below the bluffs.

76 *St. Paul Pioneer Press*, March 18, 1905.

Joseph Hartman's photo from the city morgue. Source: *St. Paul Dispatch*, March 18, 1905.

That evening, Charles Hartman identified the body to be that of his son Joseph. He left the morgue weeping: "It is my boy Joe, my poor misguided son. There is no doubt. I would know him by the boots if his face was covered up."[77] The victim's brother Charles stayed and identified the boots and some articles from the pockets of the dead man. Two firemen also identified Hartman because he used to spend a large amount of time at Station #10, located on Randolph between Bay and View. Albert Gottschalk, Edward's brother, said, "This makes it look gloomy for my brother, but I still believe him innocent of such a charge."[78]

Coroner Miller performed the autopsy. Dr. Joseph M. Finnell and Dr. H. T. Nippert assisted him. The results proved conclusively that Hartman was murdered. Miller reported that there were three fractures of the skull, which was "crushed like an eggshell."[79] The autopsy revealed Hartman was approached from behind and hit just above the right ear. He was then struck on the back of the head and at the base of the skull. The deepest wound was the one at the base of the skull. The temple above the right eye was crushed. The murder instrument had to have been a blunt object, but the doctors could only guess what it might have been. Miller said the victim died of a fractured skull from wounds at the back of his head. My theory was that the gashing wound on the

---

77 *St. Paul Dispatch*, March 18, 1905.

78 *St. Paul Pioneer Press*, March 18, 1905.

79 *St. Paul Pioneer Press*, March 19, 1905.

back of Hartman's head was from a chisel or maybe an iron bar used by fishermen to cut holes in the ice. I was sure that Hartman was killed to silence him about the Schindeldecker murder.

After viewing Hartman's body, Gottschalk's attorney and brother went to the jail and told Gottschalk about the discovery of the body. Attorney Donnelly later told the press, "Not even an eyelash of the accused man moved as his brother confronted him with the terrible circumstances. Though he is accused of a crime that for brutality and ferocity exceeds anything in the criminal annals of St. Paul, he has maintained a calm self-possession that astounded the police, accustomed as they are to dealing with all kinds of people. Marvelous self-control or absolutely callused heart, which?"[80] Jail employees described Gottschalk as having no feelings about anything.

The press and the citizens of St. Paul were now happy Gottschalk was incarcerated and Hartman's body found. My early instincts on this case were once again proven correct, and in the following days, the *Pioneer Press* rewarded me with complimentary coverage. I explained to the reporters that it was my theory all along that Gottschalk killed Hartman to keep him silent. The *Press* praised me, stating that my investigation "from the horrible crime scene, to a witness that saw a man known as 'Ed' near the meat market, then determined the Ed to be Gottschalk, and then associating Hartman as an accomplice was a work of genius." The *Pioneer Press* wrote that the people of St. Paul were nervous until an arrest was made, and described the case as one "to test the shrewdest of detectives." "Chief O'Connor had all his men follow every clue, then it was easy for the genius of the department to accumulate fact after fact until an arrest was justified."[81] They acknowledged that I had worked "systematically and persistently" on the case and that Hartman's body was found "where the police determined it was." It's always gratifying to see the papers acknowledge the great work done by my police department.

---

80 Ibid.

81 *St. Paul Pioneer Press*, March 19, 1905.

On Sunday, March 19, the body of Joseph Hartman was removed from the county morgue and taken to the Hartman residence at 606 James. A brief service took place at the home before the casket was transported to St. Francis de Sales Church. A large crowd attended the funeral service—so many that some had to stand outside the church. Most of the people attending were friends or relatives, but some were curious onlookers. The body was taken to Calvary Cemetery for interment.

On Monday, March 20, chemist Nicholas Lehnen issued a statement. He reported that although the examination was not quite complete, he felt certain the stains on Gottschalk's clothes were from human blood. Two weeks later the Ramsey County grand jury met and heard testimony on the Schindeldecker and Hartman murders. On April 4, they issued an indictment against Gottschalk for the murders of Christian Schindeldecker and Joseph Hartman. The trial date was set for May 8.

Gottschalk's background showed he worked in Kansas City as a tinsmith (or welder), a fisherman, and sometimes a mechanic, as he did in St. Paul. He was originally from Ottawa, Kansas, and lived in Omaha and Kansas City before he moved to Minnesota. We wrote and telegraphed all major police departments in the Midwest asking them to give us any information they had on our defendant. We received very little for our efforts.

On Monday, May 8, the trial of Edward Gottschalk, for the murder of Christian Schindeldecker and Joseph Hartman, began. Ramsey County District Court Judge Olin B. Lewis presided. Ramsey County Attorney Thomas Kane represented the State of Minnesota, and Stan J. Donnelly was the attorney for the defense. The courtroom quickly filled, for this was going to be one of the most sensational trials in the history of Ramsey County. Deputy Picha and six other deputies escorted the prisoner into the crowded courtroom. Judge Lewis entered at 10:00 a.m. The first thing spoken by Gottschalk's attorney was a request to withdraw the plea of not guilty and enter another plea.

The clerk of the court, Mr. Lamb, read the indictment to Gottschalk and asked the defendant what he had to say. Gottschalk whispered, "Guilty." This was totally unexpected. The courtroom buzzed with speculation.

The defendant was sworn in, and Judge Lewis initiated the questioning. Gottschalk said he was from Ottawa, Kansas, and he was thirty-three years old. He was self-employed as a tinner, cleaned gasoline stoves, and sold fish for an income. He was married twice. His present wife lived in California with their infant child and was suing him for divorce. He had a sister who committed suicide by jumping into a well and a brother who killed himself with a revolver.

Gottschalk said he was approached by Hartman to rob the Schindeldecker butcher shop. Schindeldecker was thought to carry a large amount of money on his person and also in his shop. The two agreed to the robbery, but Gottschalk warned Hartman that Schindeldecker knew him. They agreed Hartman would do the hold up by himself and Gottschalk would be the lookout. Gottschalk testified he was across the street on Banfil during the crime. The front door of the butcher shop is on Seventh; the back door faces Banfil. Hartman was going to ask for some eggs, so when Schindeldecker went into the refrigerator, Hartman was going to push him in and lock it. But when Hartman went into the shop, there were eggs on the back counter in a bag. Hartman tried to rob him anyway. A fight followed, and Schindeldecker was killed. Hartman came out of the back and told Gottschalk he had murdered the butcher, so they went to Gottschalk's room and divided the money.

Gottschalk testified that the two met the next day, Sunday, and went fishing at Pickerel Lake. They met again the following day by the dam and did more fishing. Later that afternoon, Gottschalk sensed Hartman was nervous. Once the sun had gone down, Hartman made a fire. It was then that Gottschalk noticed the razor in Hartman's hand. Hartman came from behind Gottschalk in an attempt to stab him. Gottschalk said he jumped back and grabbed a log. He hit Hartman with it, and Hartman went down. He hit him again when he was on the ground. He soon realized he had killed him. Gottschalk said he was so scared that he grabbed some irons that were used for setlines, tied them to Hartman's feet, and threw the body in the river.

Once returned to the jail, Gottschalk told a reporter, "I had to kill him or be killed myself. When I went out to the dam that day I had no more thought of killing Hartman than you did."[82] I thought Gottschalk was lying to save his neck.

The May 9, 1905, *Pioneer Press* read:

> *The law of this state formerly provided that where a person indicted for murder in the first degree pleads guilty, the maximum penalty was life imprisonment, but this law was repealed after the Younger brothers had been sent to Stillwater for life. By taking advantage of this provision of the law, the Younger saved their necks, but this very fact led to the repeal of the law. As the law now stands the crime of murder in the first degree is punishable by death unless the trial court intervenes. The only thing that stands between Gottschalk and death by hanging, therefore, is clemency on the part of Judge Lewis, or, in case he imposes the death sentence, the pardon board.*

On the following Thursday, May 11, the self-confessed murderer of Joseph Hartman was scheduled to be sentenced at ten o'clock by Ramsey County District Court Judge Lewis. I got there a little after ten and found out that people of all ages started to fill the courtroom when the courthouse opened at eight o'clock. At nine o'clock, the courtroom was completely full. At ten o'clock the entire courthouse was crammed with spectators, especially in the stairwells. I had to go in the back way through the judge's chambers. Anger was prevalent throughout the crowd, causing the sheriff to fear that the prisoner would be

82 *St. Paul Pioneer Press*, May 9, 1905.

lynched. Every available deputy was assigned to the courthouse and jail to protect Gottschalk and prevent spectators from being injured. The overcrowding and security problem caused the hearing to be delayed until eleven o'clock.

The deputies escorted Gottschalk from the county jail[83] across the street to the courthouse. The deputies split the crowd to form a path for Gottschalk. He was guided up the back stairs and entered the courtroom by a side door. A hush spread across the courtroom. People who could not see from where they were seated quietly stood. All eyes were upon the pale Gottschalk, who walked over to his appointed chair, sat erect, and looked straight ahead. The door from the judge's chambers opened and broke the silence. Judge Lewis appeared serious and did not look at anyone when he entered. He said in a firm tone, "Edward Gottschalk, stand forward."

"You Edward Gottschalk, having been accused by the grand jury of Ramsey county, by indictment, dated April 14, 1905, of the crime of murder in the first degree, and having been arraigned and pleaded not guilty before this court, and this case having been duly continued till the May term of court, and you, Edward Gottschalk, having appeared before this court May 8, and then and there at your request, having withdrawn your former plea of not guilty, and having then and there pleaded guilty to the crime of murder in the first degree, it is considered and adjudged that you, Edward Gottschalk, are convicted of the crime of murder in the first degree, and it is considered and adjudged, and the sentenced is that as a punishment for this crime, you, the said Edward Gottschalk, be taken hence to the county jail, and therein confined, and thereafter, after the lapse of two calendar months, at a time to be fixed by the governor of this state, you be taken thence to the place of execution chosen by the sheriff, and there hanged by the neck until you are dead."[84]

Governor John Johnson set the date for Gottschalk's hanging to be on August 8. Ramsey County Sheriff Miesen immediately ordered a

---

83 The county jail was located on the southeast block of St. Peter and Fourth.

84 *St. Paul Dispatch*, May 11, 1905.

twenty-four-hour-a-day deathwatch on Gottschalk. No sheriff, including Miesen, wanted an inmate to commit suicide at their jail for it would indicate poor supervision, and it could hurt the chances of the sheriff being reelected.

In addition, every sheriff ordered to hang a convicted murderer receives five hundred dollars from the state. This is reimbursement of expenses, including construction of the scaffold, rope, additional deputies, gravesite, and other things of that nature. Any remaining money belongs to the sheriff. If the condemned inmate dies prior to his execution, the entire five hundred dollars has to be returned. Personally, I would do the job for a lot less and still make money.

One of the jailers told me that Gottschalk felt that the sheriff was mistreating him just because the sheriff did not want to be cheated out of the execution money. Deputies Phillip Martin and George Sherman were assigned to a suicide watch on Gottschalk to ensure the sheriff of his money and his reelection. Martin worked the twelve-hour day shift, and Sherman worked the night shift.

At 11:00 a.m. on July 20, Martin told jailer John Feltz that he was going home for dinner. He planned to return at 1:00. Gottschalk, who was generally despondent about his incarceration, ate his dinner at noon. He then asked for something to drink, and Deputy Hilger brought him a glass of lemonade. At approximately ten after one, a deputy walked by Gottschalk's cell and saw the prisoner hanging from a rope tied to the top of the cell. At first the deputy thought that Gottschalk was playing a trick on him, but he soon realized that the body wasn't moving. The deputy called out for help. Jailer Feltz and Deputy William Mullane ran to his assistance. They entered the cell and cut Gottschalk down. Then they rubbed his limbs in an attempt to bring him back to life, but to no avail.

A number of angle irons extended up and down the walls of Gottschalk's cell, all about an inch and a half in width. They ran from the floor to within two inches of the ceiling. The top of each one was flat and protruded like a peg from the wall. The theory is that Gottschalk

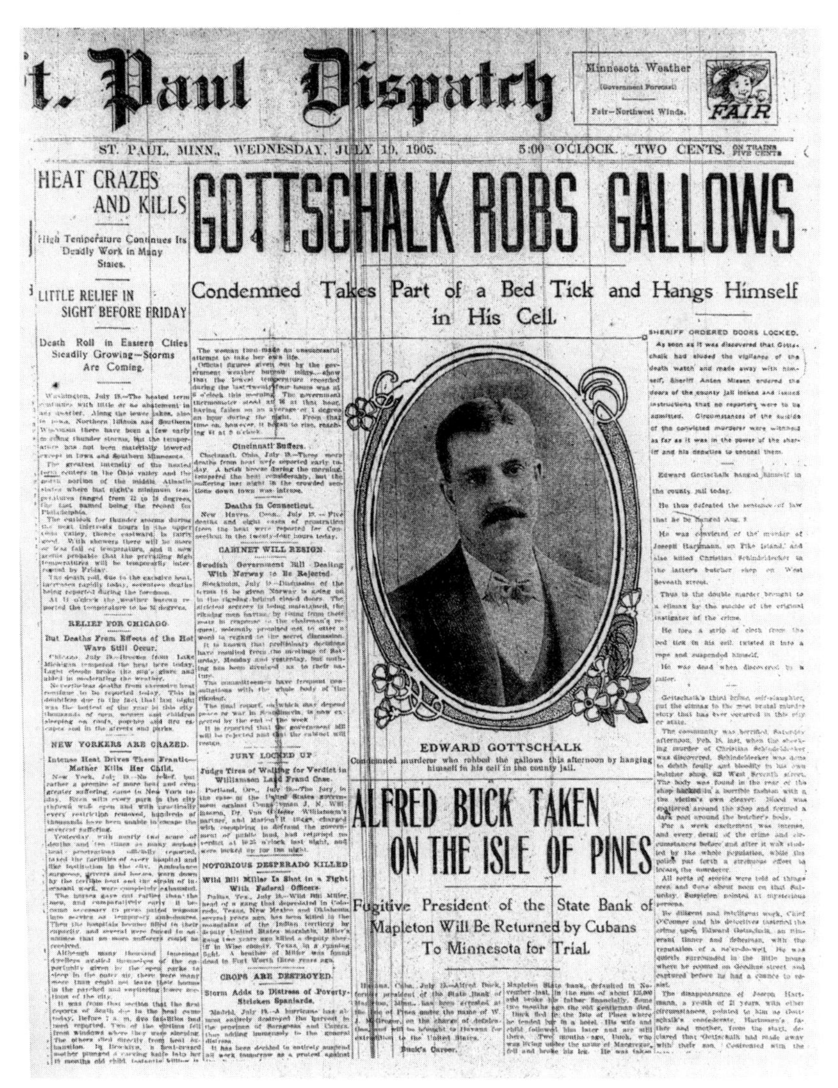

St. Paul Dispatch

Minnesota Weather (Government Forecast) Fair—Northwest Winds. FAIR

ST. PAUL, MINN., WEDNESDAY, JULY 19, 1905. 5:00 O'CLOCK. TWO CENTS.

GOTTSCHALK ROBS GALLOWS

Condemned Takes Part of a Bed Tick and Hangs Himself in His Cell.

HEAT CRAZES AND KILLS

High Temperature Continues Its Deadly Work in Many States.

LITTLE RELIEF IN SIGHT BEFORE FRIDAY

Death Roll in Eastern Cities Steadily Growing—Storms Are Coming.

RELIEF FOR CHICAGO.

But Deaths From Effects of the Hot Wave Still Occur.

NEW YORKERS ARE CRAZED.

Intense Heat Drives Them Frantic—Mother Kills Her Child.

Cincinnati Suffers.

Deaths in Connecticut.

CABINET WILL RESIGN.

Swedish Government Bill Dealing With Norway to Be Rejected.

JURY LOCKED UP

Judge Tires of Waiting for Verdict in Williamson Land Fraud Case.

NOTORIOUS DESPERADO KILLED

Wild Bill Miller Is Shot in a Fight With Federal Officers.

CROPS ARE DESTROYED.

Storm Adds to Distress of Poverty-Stricken Spaniards.

SHERIFF ORDERED DOORS LOCKED.

As soon as it was discovered that Gottschalk had eluded the vigilance of the death watch and made away with himself, Sheriff Anton Miesen ordered the doors of the county jail locked and issued instructions that no reporters were to be admitted. Circumstances of the suicide of the convicted murderer were withheld as far as it was in the power of the sheriff and his deputies to conceal them.

Edward Gottschalk hanged himself in the county jail today.

He thus defeated the sentence of law that he be hanged Aug. 3.

He was convicted of the murder of Joseph Hartmann, on Pike Island, and also killed Christian Schindeldecker in the latter's butcher shop on West Seventh street.

Thus is the double murder brought to a climax by the suicide of the original instigator of the crime.

He tore a strip of cloth from the bed tick in his cell, twisted it into a rope and suspended himself.

He was dead when discovered by a jailer.

Gottschalk's third crime, self-slaughter, put the climax to the most brutal murder story that has ever occurred in this city or state.

The community was horrified, Saturday afternoon, Feb. 18, last, when the shocking murder of Christian Schindeldecker was discovered. Schindeldecker was done to death foully and bloodily in his own butcher shop, 823 West Seventh street. The body was found in the rear of the shop hacked in a horrible fashion with a the victim's own cleaver. Blood was spattered around the shop and formed a dark pool around the butcher's body.

For a week excitement was intense, and every detail of the crime and circumstances before and after it was studied by the whole population, while the police put forth a strenuous effort to locate the murderer.

All sorts of stories were told of things seen and done about noon on that Saturday. Suspicion pointed at mysterious persons.

By diligent and intelligent work, Chief O'Connor and his detectives fastened the crime upon Edward Gottschalk, an itinerant tinner and fisherman, with the reputation of a ne'er-do-well. He was quietly surrounded in the little house where he roomed on Goodhue street and captured before he had a chance to resist.

The disappearance of Joseph Hartmann, a youth of 21 years, with other circumstances, pointed to him as Gottschalk's confederate. Hartmann's father and mother, from the start, declared that Gottschalk had made away with their son. Confronted with the

EDWARD GOTTSCHALK

Condemned murderer who robbed the gallows this afternoon by hanging himself in his cell in the county jail.

ALFRED BUCK TAKEN ON THE ISLE OF PINES

Fugitive President of the State Bank of Mapleton Will Be Returned by Cubans To Minnesota for Trial.

Buck's Career.

"Gottschalk Robs Gallows" in the *St. Paul Dispatch*, July 19, 1905.

ripped a strip from his mattress, formed it into a six-foot rope, tied both ends together, and stood on the toilet basin to hang the looped rope over the flat iron. He put the knot under his chin so it would press against his windpipe and then stepped off the basin. He had removed his shoes—probably so that if he went into convulsions, no one would hear his feet hitting the basin.

GOTTSCHALK HIS OWN EXECUTIONER

Sheriff Anton Miesen and Deputy Phillip Martin. Source: *St. Paul Pioneer Press*, July 20, 1905.

The sheriff's son, John Miesen,[85] walked through the jail corridors, saying, "My God it is awful to have a bunch of ninnies in charge of the jail. If we had one man with a grain of common sense, this would never have happened."[86] I never place any blame on my men. I am in charge and thus accountable for their actions.

At the inquest, Deputy Martin gave a statement saying that he had notified the other jailers before he left on his break. He presumed Gottschalk would be monitored in his absence. He put no blame on the sheriff and explained that it was poor communication on the jailers' part. I'm sure Martin was trying to keep his boss out of trouble because he thought it would help him keep his job. It didn't work. Martin was fired.

On Wednesday evening, July 19, and on the following morning, Coroner Miller allowed the public to walk through the morgue and

---

85 An actor.

86 *St. Paul Dispatch*, July 20, 1905.

Jail cartoon published in the *St. Paul Dispatch*, July 20, 1905.

view Gottschalk's body. There was no age restriction on the visitors, so both children and adults viewed the body. They all shared a morbid curiosity. An estimated two thousand people went through the morgue. Once Miller asked the police to stop the viewing, it took two of my police officers forty-five minutes to get everyone out of the morgue.

After the autopsy that afternoon, Coroner Miller made some interesting statements, as quoted in the following day's *Pioneer Press*:

- Gottschalk's skull was abnormally thick in the front, indicating that there could be no normal development of the brain in that region, and as a consequence the man would have had peculiar, if not criminal, traits.

- The head, to outward appearance, was indicative of a high intelligence. The forehead was not low at all, as is often found in the heads of hardened criminals.
- Gottschalk had a marvelous physique that would do credit to an athlete.
- Gottschalk's brain weighed fifty-one ounces. The average brain weighs forty-nine ounces.
- Dr. Miller stated in his report that the portion of Gottschalk's brain in the crown of the head was in excess of the normal development. This indicated that the man had an extraordinary shrewdness along certain lines.

After the suicide, it was revealed to the public what I already knew from the jailers: Gottschalk had developed a hatred for Sheriff Miesen. When he heard that Miesen would receive five hundred dollars for the hanging, he was amazed. He replied that he would bet the jailer that the sheriff would never get his money. He was right.

On Saturday, July 22, A. A. Devore of Hopkins took responsibility for the body from the J. J. Hurley Undertaking Rooms at 378 South Wabasha. This was at the request of Gottschalk's father and brother. I heard that Devore had a difficult time finding a cemetery that would bury this notorious murderer. Finally, Superintendent Horton of Roselawn Cemetery allowed Gottschalk to be buried in his cemetery. He said, "If we were to inquire into the morals of everyone brought here for burial we would have fewer graves."[87]

At 3:00 p.m., the body was placed in a plain black wood coffin and carried to a wagon. It took exactly one hour for Devore and Hurley to transport the body to the cemetery located on Larpenteur Avenue. The men, upon arrival, found the superintendent, six cemetery employees, and a hastily dug grave in a remote part of the cemetery. Devore and Hurley were the only nonemployees present. There was no ceremony. The men took the coffin from the wagon and lowered it into the grave

87 *St. Paul Pioneer Press*, July 23, 1905.

and immediately started to fill in the site. Within minutes everyone had departed.

I am proud of solving this case because it took an animal off the streets. Of course I took most of the credit for solving it—why wouldn't I? If it hadn't been solved, you know whom they would be trying to get rid of, don't you?

Oh yes, one last thing. I admit that I let a few crooks roam our city, because they give the police valuable information on criminal activity. All I ask is that if they're to pull some shenanigans, they have to go somewhere else, *not* St. Paul. I run a safe city.

Whatever happened to . . . ?

The Schindeldecker Meat Market, located at 523 West Seventh in 1905, today would be located at the north end of Mancini's restaurant, 531 West Seventh, where the parking lot is now.

Edward Gottschalk is buried in Roselawn Cemetery in plot number 91. There is no marker on his grave.

Joseph Hartman is buried in Calvary Cemetery in section 39, block 19, lot 34. There is no grave marker.

Christian Schindeldecker was born in Germany on October 7, 1870. His funeral was on Tuesday, February 21, 1905, at the German Lutheran Church located on Goff and Dearborn, St. Paul. He is buried at the old German Cemetery, which today is called the Riverside Cemetery, located at 333 Annapolis Street East in St. Paul.

John J. O'Connor was born in 1855 in Louisville, Kentucky. The O'Connor family moved to St. Paul the next year. He went to the St. Paul schools and began his working career at age fifteen in the employment of P. H. Kelley & Company, a wholesale grocery company. He worked there ten years before joining the police force in 1881. He became the chief of detectives in 1885 and obtained national attention for his special ability in ferreting out criminals. He married Miss Annie Murphy in 1890. A change in administration put him out on the streets from 1892 to 1894 and again from 1896 to 1900. He ran his own private detective agency during that time and was a state representative from the thirty-sixth district in 1899. In 1900, he was appointed chief of police of the St. Paul Police Department. His office was at 97 West Third Avenue, and his residence was located at 144 West Fourth Street, St. Paul. He moved to Glendale, California, in 1921 and died there in July 1924 at the age of sixty-eight. He is buried in Calvary Cemetery in St. Paul.

The O'Connor System started out as a crime-prevention process in the 1920s and 1930s. Every criminal, famous or not, was supposed to check in with the St. Paul Police Department when they arrived in the city. They would then be worry free because the police would not touch them as long as they behaved themselves in St. Paul. As a result, gangsters of the era were everywhere in St. Paul, which had a national reputation as a haven for murderers, bank robbers, and kidnappers. And history blames O'Connor. But the fact is that he was no longer chief of police by the time the system named after him was officially in place.

CHAPTER 4

Not in Traverse County

1905

"A wronged child led by honey words and promises to her ruin, her childish confidence and love changed to the blackness of a despair which dethroned reason."

—Defense Attorney F. W. Murphy, Traverse County, July 3, 1905

TRAVERSE COUNTY, FOUNDED IN 1882, had a population of 7,573[88] in 1905. It was located in west central Minnesota with its western borders neighboring both North and South Dakota. Wheaton was the county seat of this 574-square-mile fertile farming community, which produced, of course, wheat as its major product.

Crime was not a grave problem in Traverse County, so it had only a part-time county attorney, Edward Rustad. The Rustad family settled in Wheaton in 1889 and had been active in county politics ever since.

88 1900 census.

Traverse County Attorney Edward Rustad. Source: *Wheaton Gazette-Reporter*, June 30, 1905.

Edward received his degree in law in 1900 from the University of Minnesota and was elected county attorney later that year. Rustad would prosecute his first murder case in 1905 at age thirty-eight. Here he recalls the trial of that case.

"He asked me to marry him and I said that I would, but he would have to be true to me and promise not to pay any attention to other girls. He said that I should not think anything about that Miss Martin, as he did not care for her. I said I would marry him. He said to me that, if I should break my promise, he had the right to kill me and I had a perfect right to kill him if he should break his promise, and I believed him at that time."[89]

So testified Antonette Seidensticker in answer to her attorney's question about a conversation she had with Herman Shipp. A year after the engagement she would kill Shipp and attempt to kill herself. It was my job to prosecute Miss Seidensticker, who had confessed to the murder. I thought that with the evidence, the facts, and the confession, it would be an easy case to win, even for my very first murder case as county attorney. I made an oath when I became a public prosecutor that I would do my best, using all my God-given talents, in all the cases I prosecute. She would be no exception. I intended to convict her of murder. When, or if, convicted, she would be hanged. I didn't find it a simple matter, hanging a woman, especially this one. Antonette was only thirteen years old.

89 Trial transcript.

Two days after the murder, May 27, E. H. Boley, Traverse County coroner, conducted the inquest at Burton's Bank building in Wheaton. I questioned all the witnesses.

Antonette Siedensticker. Source: *St. Paul Dispatch*, June 26, 1905.

My first witness was a clerk at the Erickson and Hellekson hardware store in Wheaton named Otto Dokken, and he testified that he was working at the hardware store on May 25. He said that young Antonette entered the store and told him that she wanted to borrow a gun. She said she wanted a revolver, not a shotgun, because she had been attacked by a wolf at the farm and that the wolf had also attacked the stock. He asked if she wanted a box of cartridges. She replied that if he would just load a gun, that would be enough. Dokken then loaded and gave her a secondhand, five-shot .32 hammerless revolver. He said she then walked over to the buggy and laid it in the seat and that was the last he saw of her.

Dr. J. A. Healy was summoned. He stated that he has been a practicing physician in Wheaton since 1901. He had gone with the sheriff to the crime scene on May 25. There they found a young man dead, whom Mrs. L. P. Deal identified as farmhand Herman Shipp, age twenty-one, of Cokato. They found Mr. Shipp lying face up between the front left wheel and the side of the buggy. "There was a frothy blood oozing from the mouth. I noticed a black stain, which proved afterwards to be a burn on the chin to the left of the median line." He added that the left chest and shoulder area of the deceased's clothing were charred from burns. He found the young girl at the house who had two gunshot wounds in her side. He arranged for her to go to the hospital in Wheaton.

Herman Shipp. Source: *Wheaton Gazette-Reporter*, June 3, 1905.

Later that day Healy conducted a postmortem examination of Mr. Shipp at Boley's undertaking room. He found that the aorta was perforated about two inches from the heart, causing death by internal hemorrhage.

Mrs. Deal testified next. She said that she knew Antonette and the farmhand Herman Shipp. She was home in the early afternoon of May 25, when Antonette came to her farm and asked for Herman, who was working in the field. As they were talking Antonette said, "I see a team of four white horses and a covered buggy coming. Is that him?" Mrs. Deal confirmed that it was, and suggested that she get out of the buggy and tie her horse, but she answered no, that she had to go to Graceville. She said that she had a message from Mrs. Vern Smith for Mr. Shipp, which she wished to deliver personally, and she would wait in the buggy until he got there. Shipp drove into the yard, unhooked the horses, put them into the barn and then came over to the house. He stopped at the buggy where Antonette sat, placed his hand on the iron of the seat and his foot on the wheel, and stood there just a moment. Mrs. Deal said she did not hear a word they were saying, but I bet she was trying. The greetings seemed familiar and very pleasant. Then he raised himself up into the buggy alongside her and they immediately drove away. They drove across the railroad tracks east and traveled around the farm for some time, finally stopping north of the tracks by the gate, about five rods[90] from the farmhouse.

Mrs. Deal continued testifying:

> *I heard what I know now must have been a pistol shot. I heard two reports. I went to the window and could see*

90 A rod is 5.5 yards or 16.5 feet.

Mrs. Ida Deal, the only eyewitness to the murder of Herman Shipp, near Wheaton, Minnesota. Source: *St. Paul Dispatch*, June 28, 1905.

only one in the buggy—that was Antonette. I went out to the corner of the house and looked down the track to see what had become of Herman. Just as I stepped inside the door, I heard two more shots fired, and looking out the window, I saw Antonette lying across the seat. I saw what was supposed to be the lap robe hanging down from the buggy.

I watched her and the horse for a few minutes to see if Herman would not come up from somewhere. The horse continued to come right along. She was not handling the lines at all. She raised up in the buggy seat, looked over the corner to where Herman proved to be and then sat down and laid right in the buggy seat. The horse continued to come until he got a wheel caught on the gatepost.

I looked down the track to see if I could see anything of Herman. Then I looked at the clock and saw that it was just

> *one o'clock, by my time. I watched Antonette and waited for ten minutes for someone to turn up, for most young people don't want an old woman sticking her nose into their affairs. I then could not stand it any longer, I went to the buggy.*
>
> *Antonette had not moved that I remember, from the time the buggy had stopped at the gatepost. When I got to the buggy, I think Herman was entirely dead. I did not think there was any life. His clothes were on fire from the gunshot[91] on his chest and I got a pail of water and put out the fire, opening up his heavy overcoat to make sure I had all the fire out. Then I shook Antonette to find out what her condition was and tried to get a response from her. I saw her hands covered with blood, and there was blood oozing from her chest, and also some of her clothes appeared to be on fire. I put out the fire and decided that she was dead also.*
>
> *I unhooked her horse and hooked it onto my own buggy and drove across the field to a neighbor, living to the south of me. I asked the gentleman to go to Dumont and telephone for Sheriff Hopkins and tell him there's a dead lady and gentleman at the gate of Charley Teare's farm. Then I got their hired man to go back with me to the house. I never went near the buggy again.*

Sheriff P. J. Hopkins was summoned. He stated that he had been sheriff in Traverse County for three and a half years. He testified that he received a telephone call from Dumont, a neighboring town, stating there were two people dead along the roadside at the old Teare farm. Upon arriving, the sheriff found the body of a young man held between the buggy box and the front wheel. It appeared to the sheriff that the man had been shot and then slumped over and fell into the wheel while the buggy was still moving. The sheriff said it looked like the man died

91 Close range gunshots can ignite clothing because of the exploding gunpowder.

immediately after being shot. He continued testifying that he found a hammerless .32-caliber handgun on the seat of the buggy. He took the revolver into his possession at that time.

The sheriff went to the house and asked Antonette who did the shooting, and she answered, "I did."

"Was it because you wanted to get married and he wouldn't?" he asked.

"No," she said.

The sheriff asked again, "Why did you shoot him?"

Sheriff P. J. Hopkins. Source: *Wheaton Gazette-Reporter*, June 30, 1905.

She answered, "We agreed to die together, and kissed, and I shot him through the heart, I think, and I shot myself." She said she did not remember anything else.

The coroner's inquest concluded that Mr. Shipp's death was caused by a gunshot fired by Antonette Seidensticker. A grand jury was quickly impaneled on June 20, and the following day the jury issued an indictment against Antonette for first-degree murder. The murder trial date was scheduled for five days later. The penalty for first-degree murder in Minnesota is death by hanging.

I determined that after shooting Shipp, Antonette turned the gun on herself. She held the pistol in her right hand as she shot herself twice in the left side. Each bullet glanced off her ribs, circled around under her skin, and lodged in her back. The doctor at the scene easily removed the bullets and determined that the wounds were not life threatening. She remained in the hospital because of the possibility of blood poisoning.

I was told by the hospital staff that Miss Seidensticker was despondent and depressed during her nine-day stay, causing the medical staff to treat her as a suicide candidate. She was released to the care of Sheriff Hopkins's wife, whose home is attached to the jail, where special accommodations were made for the young inmate. I think Mrs. Hopkins established a maternal relationship with Antonette, showing her some compassion and support. Antonette, by the start of the trial, appeared to have regained her mental and physical health.

The most publicized trial in the history of Traverse County caused a stir in the community. Members of the Twin Cities press arrived at the Wheaton train depot to report on the trial. The hotel quickly filled up, and the residents of Wheaton rented out rooms to accommodate the travelers.

On Monday, June 26, the trial of Antonette Seidensticker commenced at the Traverse County Courthouse District Courtroom, just a month and a day after the murder. The Honorable S. A. Flaherty of Morris was the trial judge. Charles Houston, former Judge F. J. Steidl, and I made up the prosecuting team for the state. F. W. Murphy represented the defense. It took three days to select the jury, with more than fifty men interviewed. Most potential jurors were asked questions about whether they believed everything they read in the newspapers, whether the age of the defendant would influence their decision, and whether they had already formed an opinion about the guilt of the defendant.

The trial started with Mr. Dokken explaining how Antonette received the gun and Mrs. Deal explaining how the murder happened. The sheriff and doctors explained what Antonette said after the murder of how she was implicated. The coroner testified to the condition of the deceased body and the cause of death.

Mrs. Ada Smith testified that her husband, Vern, previously hired Herman Shipp to assist them on their farm. The Smiths were neighbors of the Seidenstickers, and Antonette stopped over to visit them on May 23, two days before the shooting. Mrs. Smith testified that she noticed "Tony" was interested in Herman and decided to have a private conversation with her. She told Antonette not to keep company with Shipp, as he was not a respectable man for her to go out with, because he was intimate with other girls and was the father of an illegitimate child.

Mrs. Smith explained to the court that Antonette's mother was confined to her bed for about ten months before she died. Antonette came over to their farm on errands during that time and sometimes stayed a couple of hours. She testified that at that time, Antonette became the acting mother of the family.

August Shipp of Cokato, father of the deceased, then testified. Mr. Shipp stated that his son was twenty-one years old when he died. He was told about the death of his son by telephone. He had picked up a letter at the Cokato post office on May 26; the letter was from the defendant to his daughter Hulda. He had given it to the county attorney before the trial.

Antonette's cousin, Lizzie Kruse, testified that she had known Antonette since she was a baby. Miss Kruse attended school with her and had seen her handwriting frequently. The county attorney gave her the letter from Cokato and asked her if she recognized the handwriting. Miss Kruse replied that the handwriting was Antonette's. The letter was entered as evidence. The defense objected, but was overruled. The letter was read to the jury:

> *Wheaton, Minnesota, May 25th 1905.*
> *Miss Hulda Shipp, Cokato, Minnesota.*
>
> *Dear friend:*
>
> *It is with reluctance that I write of a subject which has given me great pain, and of which silence is impossible. It is a very dangerous subject to talk about. I've been going with him for a whole year and always considered him a very honest and industrious man. He is a father of a little child, the mother of the little daughter lives in our neighborhood, and if I get hold of him, I shall kill him. The audacity of such a man!*
>
> *From your departed friend.*

Miss Kruse testified that she also knew Shipp, saying that Antonette came to her workplace—a home in town she was cleaning—between ten and eleven on the morning of the shooting. She testified that her sister was there when Antonette arrived. They thought Antonette was acting queer that morning. "We talked with her concerning Herman. She asked where he was and where Addie Deal lived. We told her, and she went to Deal's and then returned to where we were. She asked if we had seen Addie out with Herman. We said yes. She said she heard the same thing." Antonette then related to the girls that she had told Addie "to wait until I see him and I'll kill him," and also told them, "Need not mind because I'm going to do that."[92]

Dennis Merry was the next witness. Merry was the man for whom Shipp was working the day he was killed. He identified a letter from Antonette to Herman as the one he picked up at the Wheaton post office and gave to the sheriff. The letter was admitted as evidence and read to the court:

> *Dear Herman:*
>
> *It is with great reluctance that I enter upon a subject which has given me great pain, and upon which silence has become impossible if I would preserve my self-respect. You cannot but be aware that I have just reason for saying that you have much displeased me. You have apparently forgotten what is due to me, circumstance as we are, thus far at least. You cannot suppose that I can tamely see you disregard my feelings by conduct toward other girls, from which I should naturally have the right to expect you to abstain. I am not so vulgar a person as to be jealous. You will not live to see my heart crushed. When there's a cause to infer changed feelings or unfaithfulness to promise of consistency, jealousy is not the remedy. What the remedy is*

92 *Wheaton Gazette-Reporter*, June 30, 1905.

I need not say—we both of us have it in our hands. I am sure you will agree with me that we must come to some understanding by which the future shall be governed. All you are good for is breaking a girl's heart, but my heart you shall never break. You are the first man I ever loved, and I always said you would be the last. I always considered the girl lucky who would get you, but I pity her now. How can you look an innocent girl in the face and commit such a crime? Why, you ought to be hung. If you want Miss Deal so bad you can have her, for she ain't any better than you are, but I tell you one thing, if I don't come to the point of speaking to you pretty soon, I shall write your sister, and I know of five different girls that you have been going with. I shall let them know also of your terrible disgrace. I shall get revenge. I am three years older than Miss Deal, I think I nearly realize what I am doing. Haven't you the least bit of respect for yourself? I also loved you with extreme passion of a woman's heart. I always thought you a very honest man and always took pity on you, but I think different now. Believe me, I write more in anger than in sorrow. You have made me very unhappy, and you'll never regret it either. But it will take much to reassure me of your own unaltered regard.

Yours truly,

Antonette G. S.

P.S. You can show this letter to Miss Deal if you want to, but you better beware, for your life hangs by a thread.

That concluded my case. The weapon, an eyewitness statement, incriminating statements from reliable witnesses, and an admission of the crime by the defendant were all presented to the jury.[93] This was an open and shut case. I tried to be kind in reference to the young defendant. I did not want the jury to feel I was too harsh on her.

I did notice the strain of the trial wearing on Antonette who sat between her father and her attorney. The young girl nearly fainted a few times during the testimony. The severity of the charge was starting to set in with her.

On Thursday afternoon, June 29, in the overcrowded second-floor courtroom of the Traverse County Courthouse, the defense commenced with their case. F. W. Murphy, in his opening address to the jury, said that the defense would be temporary insanity. He added that he had strong evidence to support his theory and that the defendant was not responsible for the death of Herman Shipp.

Fred Seidensticker, the father of the defendant, was the first witness for the defense. He testified that his wife had died a year earlier, and Antonette became the mother to her little sisters and brother. He explained that the mother had some of the mental problems that he had started to observe in his daughter. Antonette became distant and isolated the last few weeks prior to the shooting. She acted queer, as if in a dream, and grew worse each day. She did not sleep nights and wanted to be alone, brooding, and he had called a doctor to treat her. On May 25, her head and eyes hurt her. Fred Seidensticker instructed her to go into town and see a doctor about her eyes. That is where he thought she was when he was called about the shooting. He went to the Teare farm and met his daughter there. She would not talk to him; she only moaned and said she wanted to die. Her face was flushed, and her eyes glazed. He transported her to the hospital in town. He said he was sure she was insane because she was in the hospital three days before she recognized him.

93 The jurors were Burt Higgins, Herman Hassler, G. A. Palmquist, F. H. Grotemeyer, Julius Juel, Carl Riewe, John Durner, Richard Mittlestep, foreman A. J. Ramsey, Edwin Ball, John A. Good, and M. D. Foster. All were farmers, and all, except one, were married and had families.

Deputy Jim Cunningham testified that he was in charge of her for nine days when she was in the hospital. He said her flushed face, glassy eyes, and strange actions convinced him that she was insane. He said that she did not sleep well, wanted to be left alone, and begged to die. She would not answer questions, and it did not seem to him as if she knew what was transpiring around her. I got the sense that the deputy was feeling paternal about young Antonette.

Antonette Seidensticker. Source: *Wheaton Gazette-Reporter*, June 30, 1905.

The defendant's uncle, William Kruse, testified that their family had a history of mental illness and that Antonette's mother was a victim of this illness prior to her death. Several other witnesses, who were relatives, neighbors, friends of the family, testified as to why they believed Antonette was insane on May 25, 1905. The defense called two of her younger sisters, Rosy and Lena Seidensticker. They testified individually and told the court how upset their big sister became when they told her that Herman had a new girlfriend. Lena said that Antonette began spitting up blood and became very withdrawn.

Antonette Seidensticker was the next to testify. Every inch of the small courtroom was filled with spectators. Those who arrived early were seated and so were the elderly, and all the others stood on the sides and in the back. Youngsters sat in the aisles. The doors were left open so people outside could hear, as they stood on the stairs leading up to the second floor. The entire room went remarkably silent as the girl approached the witness chair. All eyes in the crowded courtroom were on her. She looked pretty in a new dress, with her hair in a bonnet, a flower attached to her blouse and white scarf around her neck. Her legs kicked nervously back and forth in the witness chair, with her toes barely touching the floor.

There were preliminary questions, to which Antonette answered that she was thirteen years old and had three younger sisters and one younger brother. She entered school at age seven but stopped at age eleven, when her mother became ill. She did the housework and took care of her siblings and a bedridden mother. Antonette said she enjoyed reading Shakespeare and playing the piano. She testified about having desponding fits and spitting blood since last December, and was worried that she was suffering from consumption, from which her mother and an uncle had died.

Murphy: When did you meet Shipp?

Antonette: I met him down at the farm about two years ago this spring. May Martin was with him. I knew May Martin; she is the girl that has been spoken about here. I was then eleven years old.

Murphy: Did he say anything when you first met?

Antonette: He wanted me to come over to Smith's and have ice cream. I told him I could not go because I was left in charge of the children, and Papa and Mama were gone. He said the children would be all right at home and that I had better come. I next met him coming home from town. He was alone, and so was I. I had some talk with him, and he said that the first time he saw me he fell in love with me. He asked me to call on him. I told him that I did not want to call on him, as I was not acquainted with him, having just seen him once. He said I could call on him; he loved me and wanted to call on me. I told him that Papa would not allow anyone to call on account of me being so young, that I didn't want to run around with anyone. I said I did not think it was right to call on him when I didn't know him. He appeared to talk honest to me when he told me

> he loved me the first time he saw me. He praised me and said I was good-looking and an honest girl as he had heard.
>
> The next time I saw him he was coming to cut some hay, but I didn't have much talk with him at that time. Saw him next when over at Smith's visiting. He seemed to be glad to see me, talked love, and asked me if I could love him in return. I told him that I didn't know him well enough. I next saw him at Smith's house, and we were left alone for a little while. He said he was so glad we got together alone. He took me in his arms and kissed me, said he loved me, and I said I could not love him, but would like him like any other friend. He said no, he wanted me to love him. I said that I loved him, but didn't want him to tell anyone.

F. W. Murphy, defense attorney. Source: *Wheaton Gazette-Reporter*, June 30, 1905.

Antonette told the court that Shipp would always give her hugs when he saw her after that. She told Shipp that she was only eleven years old and wasn't old enough to be going with a man as old as he was. He said he would call her seventeen, because he loved her and that he would make believe she was seventeen. She added that she was wearing short dresses then, a good deal shorter than she had on, which did not make her look older. She said she didn't believe much of what he said at first. As time went on she believed him when he told her he loved her. She was beginning to have confidence and began to think about him. He gave her candy, fruit, and nuts, and said he would do anything for her. Shipp said he would stop swearing, drinking, or anything she wanted him to do, and if she wanted to go to dances, just to let him know.

Murphy: Did he say anything about other girls?

Antonette: Yes, he said that this Miss Martin got mad at him because I was going out with him and that she was watching us pretty close. He said that I was the only girl that he ever loved and was going to be the last one. I believed him and put confidence in him from the way he spoke. I saw him frequently after that, and he always said the same things about loving me. Once in Mr. Smith's parlor he hugged and kissed me and then asked me to marry him. I said I had not known him very long and did not love him well enough to marry him. I saw him often, and he always wanted to be alone with me so he could talk about love.

Murphy: Do you remember last Christmas Day?

Antonette: Yes, sir. He was over to our place. Mrs. Smith sent over a cake, and he said she wanted us girls to come over there. Afterwards he winked at me and said she didn't tell him anything, that he only wanted me to come over. He frequently did that to get me over. I was alone with him again in Smith's parlor that day, and he again kissed me and said he loved me, and by this time I had commenced to think a great deal of him. I saw him after that when I was helping Mrs. Smith, when her husband was in the woods. He made love to me and asked to keep it a secret, and he would do the same. He didn't want anyone to know what was between us.

Murphy: Were you happy then, Tony?

Antonette: Yes, very happy. I thought he was an honest fellow and was very happy in his love.

Murphy: Did you see him after that?

ANTONETTE: Yes, we were in the granary. He asked me to marry him and I said that I would, but he would have to be true to me and promise not to pay any attention to other girls. He said that I should not think anything about that Miss Martin as he did not care for her. I said I would marry him. He said to me, if I should break my promise, he had the right to kill me and I had a perfect right to kill him if he should break his promise and I believed him at that time.

MURPHY: The promise was made there at the granary?

ANTONETTE: Yes.

MURPHY: What else was done there at the granary?

[At this time she broke down in tears. The judge suggested that the defense attorney could ask leading questions.]

MURPHY: Did he abuse you, Tony?

ANTONETTE: Yes, sir.

MURPHY: Did he make you promise not to tell it?

ANTONETTE: Yes, sir.

MURPHY: In order to make it binding did he tell you that you might kill him if he didn't keep his promise?

ANTONETTE: Yes, sir.

MURPHY: Did you believe him?

ANTONETTE: Yes, sir.

MURPHY: Did he exercise an influence over you?

ANTONETTE: Yes.

MURPHY: You believed what he said at that time, did you?

ANTONETTE: Yes.

MURPHY: Did you think lots of him?

ANTONETTE: Yes, sir.

MURPHY: You thought he would be true to you?

Antonette: Yes, sir.

Murphy: At that time, did you believe he had any other ladies on the string, any love affairs?

Antonette: No, sir.

She explained that after some time Shipp stopped corresponding with her. Mrs. Smith's daughter told Antonette that Shipp was writing letters to other girls. Another girl told her that he was writing to Emma Stevenson in Cokato and that he did not want to do anything with her any more. Her little sisters came home from school and said they heard that Shipp called her "Dutch bitch." She told the court that the next time she saw him he was riding past her place with Miss Addie Deal.

Antonette: The next time I saw him, he was driving by again. I was not certain who was with him. He had a new buggy and waved to me as he passed. He was watching me from the buggy as long as he could see me. I sent Lena to the Tesches' place to ask the Tesch girls if it was him and who was with him. She came from school that afternoon and told me.

Murphy: That was worrying you, was it?

Antonette: Yes, sir.

Murphy: What next did you hear?

Antonette: The boys brought a report from school that he was over to the Lubys' place and had invited them all down to the dance. The Luby boy asked if he was going to invite me, and he said he had three other girls and would not take me to the dance. He [the boy] asked him again if he would take me if I could go, and he [Herman] said no, he didn't care anything for me.

Antonette next heard from her cousin that Shipp was at the dance with Addie Deal and that they made love in public, drank from the same cup, ate from the same piece of bread, and danced together all evening.

Wheaton, where Antonette was tried for murder. Source: *St. Paul Dispatch*, June 30, 1905.

Antonette said it made her very worried and during that time she hadn't had her menstruation.

She explained that not having her menstrual period for three months led her to believe that she would soon be living in "a disgraceful exposure." Shipp had put her in such a state, causing her much worry and stress, and then abandoned her. She had no one to go to, no one she could talk to, causing her to brood over the situation "until her brain was on fire." For the four nights prior to the murder she could not sleep because of the continuous reports she was receiving about Herman "making merry with other girls."

As the *Wheaton Gazette-Reporter* wrote, "There were many tear-bedimmed eyes in the courtroom when the defendant finished her pitiful story."[94]

The trial concluded with Judge Flaherty giving his instructions to the jury. He told them their choices were "guilty as charged in the indictment, not guilty, or not guilty because of insanity." At 6:00 p.m. on July 3, the jury went into deliberation. People shuffled out of the courtroom, many patting Antonette's father on the back as they left.

94 *Wheaton Gazette-Reporter*, June 30, 1905.

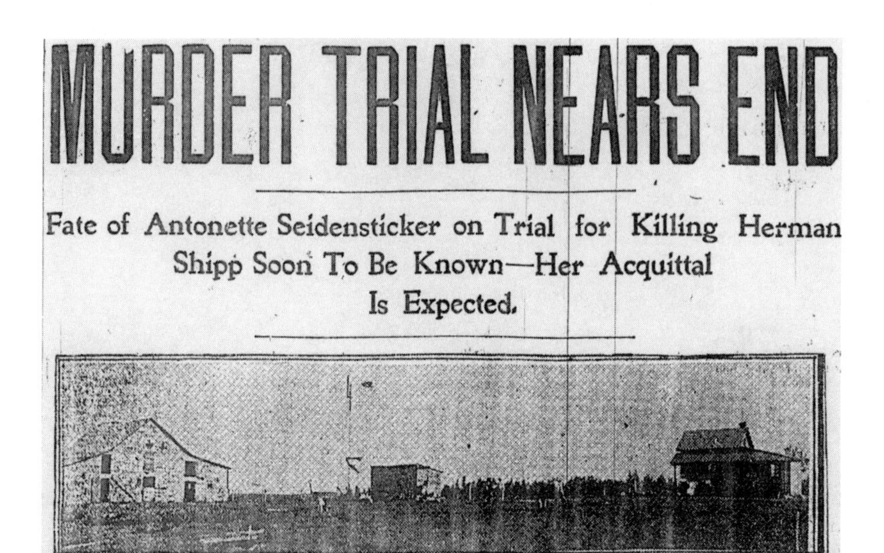
MURDER TRIAL NEARS END

Fate of Antonette Seidensticker on Trial for Killing Herman Shipp Soon To Be Known—Her Acquittal Is Expected.

THE HOME OF "TONY" SEIDENSTICKER, WHOSE FATE IS TO BE DECIDED SOON.

Source: *St. Paul Dispatch*, July 1, 1905.

Chores had to be done and many had a long distance to travel and wanted to do so when there was sunlight. The general consensus was that the jury would not make a decision that night.

The first-degree murder trial of a thirteen-year-old female defendant, tried as an adult, was the first in the state's history. Her fate was with a group of adult men, not what I would call her peers. From my point of view, the jury had to choose between one of two verdicts: guilty or not guilty because of insanity.

Foreman A. J. Ramsey later told me that inside the jury room, he immediately took a ballot without any discussion. It only took one ballot to render a verdict. The foreman notified the judge, who in turn ordered the deputies to call all the court officers to come back to court; that process took well over an hour because most had reached their rural residences. At 8:00 p.m. the jury was back in the courtroom.

Judge Flaherty asked, "Gentlemen of the jury, have you reached a verdict?"

Mr. Ramsey responded, "We have." Antonette buried her head into her father's chest, sobbing; otherwise the courtroom was silent.

Judge Flaherty read the verdict and gave it to the clerk of the court, who read it to the hushed courtroom: "We the jury find the defendant not guilty." Cheers and clapping rang through the courtroom. Antonette immediately jumped up and hugged Murphy around his neck, with her feet off the ground, thanking him in her sobbing, girlish voice. Judge Flaherty restored order while Antonette cried in her father's arms. The judge thanked the jury and told all of us attorneys that it was a pleasure working with men who were professional in their conduct toward each other and to the court. He did not have to intervene in any personal argument between the two sides. He dismissed the jury and informed Antonette that she could go home.

Antonette and her father went over and thanked each juror individually. The jury members all smiled as they shook hands with the girl and her father. Sympathetic tears were in everyone's eyes. People waited in a small line to congratulate the Seidenstickers. No one was hurrying to go home, even though it was getting dark. Small groups of people conversed outside the courthouse. They seemed pleased.

I made my civil and obligatory handshakes and quietly left. I was shocked by the verdict, and yet I didn't feel bad about losing the case. I felt regret for Herman and his family, of course. At home, I sat alone in my parlor wondering if I could have conducted the prosecution differently. Then it came to me. The jury of twelve men did not want to convict, but rather send a strong message to all neighboring young men that evening: not in Traverse County.

Whatever happened to . . . ?

Traverse County Courthouse is still there, 702 Second Avenue North in Wheaton. It was built in 1892. The courtroom has been remodeled, and it is definitely worth a visit.

Antonette Seidensticker was not pregnant at the time of the murder. After the trial her father sent her to a convent in Minneapolis to live and continue her education. She studied nursing, and in July 1912, she married Harold E. Newcomb. They moved to Ryder, North Dakota, where they worked on a ranch. They then moved to Minot for seven years, where she bore four of her six children, four daughters and two sons. In the winter of 1919–20, they moved to Ward County, where Harold farmed in the summer and worked the coal mines in the winter. From there they went to Velva, where Harold worked in a strip mine, until he broke his leg attempting to stop a runaway team of horses. Antonette had to do any work she could find to support the family, such as working as a seamstress or a cook.

Harold Newcomb died in 1930 of pneumonia. His family, after hearing of his death, did not think his wife had sent for a doctor quickly enough and thus held resentments against her. Many years later the in-laws told some of Antonette's children that their mother and a man were in a wagon and got into a scuffle. The man slipped under the wheel of the wagon and was run over and killed. Years later, one of her daughters asked her mother about the incident. Antonette replied that it was a closed book and would remain closed. She never mentioned the incident to any of her children.

Helen, Antonette's eldest child, was living and her only surviving child when this narrative was first written. She has since passed on. Helen learned of the murder and the trial only when the author contacted her and mailed her newspaper articles from the time. Helen was a widow and retired from the federal government as an administrative assistant. She lived in Virginia.

Helen wrote of her mother: "My mother was a good and caring woman. She was talented because she could sing, play the piano and the organ, but poverty stifled her. I remember her driving twenty-five miles in a buggy to hear Schumann-Heinke sing in a concert. She wrote prose and poetry. She suffered from a weak heart the last two years of her life, dying of heart failure in 1956. She is buried in Velva, North Dakota."

Edward Rustad was born in Portage, Wisconsin, in 1867. His family settled in Wheaton in about 1889. His father was county auditor, and Edward was his deputy. When his father died, in October 1892, the Traverse County commissioners made Edward the county auditor. He held that position for six years. He was elected mayor of Wheaton in 1897 for two years and then moved to Minneapolis to study law at the University of Minnesota. In November 1900, having received his law degree, he was elected Traverse County attorney. He held that position for ten years. This was not a full-time job at the time, so he also practiced law with Judge F. J. Steidl. In 1908, he became president of the Wheaton National Bank. In 1910 he sold his interests in the bank to his brother and was elected to the state senate. He served two terms until 1918.

Mr. Rustad was appointed U.S. Marshall in 1920 and subsequently moved his family to 6106 Lyndale in south Minneapolis. He served in that capacity until 1932. He married Miss Bernhadin Lundberg in September 1893. They had four children. On November 27, 1936, at age sixty-nine, he died at the home of his daughter in Painesville, Ohio. Services and burial were at Lakewood Cemetery in Minneapolis.

CHAPTER 5

Last of the Rope Dancers

1905

"Premeditation means meditation beforehand, a thinking over or a consideration in advance. To infer the existence of premeditation does not require the lapse of any precise or definite time. It may not be necessary for a day, an hour, or a minute; all that it requires is that there should be sufficient time for the operation of the mental processes in which the judgment is to be exercised and a purpose definitely formed. This period in some cases may be very brief depending upon the individual. If there is time for the mind to consider or to mediate upon the act the time is sufficient though the period is brief."

—Ramsey County District Court Judge
Olin B. Lewis, May 20, 1905

JAMES CORMICAN WAS A DEFENSE ATTORNEY who immigrated to St. Paul from Belfast, Ireland, in 1876. He went to law school later in life and at the age of forty-seven obtained his degree. His law office was located at 412 Court Building in downtown St. Paul. In 1905 he was assigned to represent a double murderer in a case in which he became personally involved—maybe too involved.

A defense attorney must ensure that his client receives the very best possible representation. This is what I tried to do for my client William Williams in 1905. Nevertheless, I cannot help thinking I failed.

It all started for me on the morning of Thursday, April 13, 1905. I had just arrived at my office when I received a telephone call from the Ramsey County clerk of the court. He asked me if I had read that morning's paper, and I said I had not. He asked me if I was available to go to the county jail and talk to a William Williams, whom the county court wanted me to represent. I needed the business, so I told him I would do it. I asked what Mr. Williams had allegedly done, and he replied, "Just a couple of murders."

I arrived at the jail about 9:30 that morning. I was directed to a small, damp cell in the drab third floor of the courthouse. There I met Billy Williams, a tall, skinny, shabbily dressed man standing by his bunk. His eyes were reddened, his face was unshaven, and he smelled as if he had been throwing up drink all night. He was in a very nervous condition.

We both sat on his bunk as I introduced myself and asked him to tell me his background. He said he was twenty-seven years old and an immigrant from St. Ives, Cornwall, in England. He had been in the United States for seven years. He was incarcerated in 1898 for several months at Camp Thomas in Augusta, Georgia, for leading a military mutiny while serving in the Minnesota Volunteers. The next year, he was arrested and convicted of killing an Italian laborer in a bar fight. He had served two years in the St. Cloud Reformatory.

I told him that he had been accused of killing two people and I wanted to know who they were and how he had met them. He proceeded to tell me the following story.

In June 1903 Billy was a patient at St. Paul Hospital. There he met fourteen-year-old Johnny Keller. They became friends, and in 1904 Billy took Johnny to Manitoba, where Billy worked as a steamfitter. Johnny had previously quit school and been a bellboy at the Windsor Hotel in St. Paul. When he took young Johnny with him, Billy promised the boy's parents that he would send him to school. The parents, or at least Johnny's mother, apparently gave their approval. But after several months, Johnny returned to St. James, Minnesota, to live with his father, who worked there as a temporary cook.

William Williams. Source: *St. Paul Pioneer Press*, April 14, 1905.

Billy found life without Johnny unbearable. He quit his job and proceeded to St. James in an effort to win Johnny back. The result was a violent argument between the boy's dad and Billy. However, Johnny decided to return to Winnipeg with his pursuer.

It was not long before the relationship soured, and Johnny's mother sent him a railroad ticket home to St. Paul. Johnny returned, and once more Billy returned for Johnny, but the young man refused to join him again. After a short time, Billy took a job in St. Louis, believing that once he saved enough money, Johnny would move there with him. They wrote letters to each other, with some being affectionate, but soon it was clear that Johnny was no longer interested in maintaining the connection. For one thing, both of Johnny's parents strongly disapproved of the relationship and told him he shouldn't leave again. Johnny agreed not to go to St. Louis. Billy then began to send threatening letters to

Johnny—something he regrets—demanding that Johnny join him or else there would be consequences.

In the spring of 1905, Billy hopped a ride on a freight car back to St. Paul. On the afternoon of April 12, he proceeded to the Kellers' second-floor apartment at Reid's Court.[95] Mrs. Keller answered the door and told Billy he was not welcome. She told him that her husband was going to shoot him if he ever bothered their son again. Billy left frustrated, went to a downtown pub, and drank until "[his] brain was on fire."

Billy returned to the Kellers' home later in the evening in a dazed state of mind. Mrs. Keller called him a son of a bitch and wanted him to leave; Johnny wanted him to stay. He told me it was as if he were in a trance—he could not clearly remember all the details about what happened after that. He saw and heard strange things that only added to his bewilderment. Abruptly he found himself talking to the neighbor downstairs from the Kellers and telling her to get a doctor. He then ran to the police for help. He felt a frenzied energy directing his actions. And he did not seem to recall shooting the two people he was accused of killing: Johnny Keller and Johnny's mother, Mary.

Finishing his story, Billy Williams fell against the wall in exhaustion. I looked at him and thought, *I don't want to help this man. If it were just that he's queer, maybe, but an Englishman? Never.*

Billy had told his story as if he were a victim of the Irish curse, viz. whiskey. Whiskey is the gateway for the devil to enter one's mind. It makes a man fight, even kill. The devil himself is the owner of the drinker's body and mind.

I stood and looked at William Williams and realized that he had no one. *I am the only one standing between him and the gallows*, I thought. I recalled my oath and duty as a barrister. I knew the good Lord introduced us for a reason. I said a quick prayer to the blessed Virgin for strength and then told Williams that I would do the best job for him that I could.

---

95 About a block west of the cathedral. The building is gone. The address today would be 262 Selby.

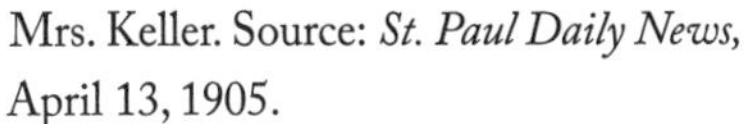

Mrs. Keller. Source: *St. Paul Daily News*, April 13, 1905.

Johnny Keller. Source: *St. Paul Daily News*, April 14, 1905.

The morning's newspaper reported the details that Billy hadn't told me. About 12:45 a.m. on April 13, a confused man knocked on the door of the Klines, the family who lived below the Kellers. Mrs. Kline answered the door. Her husband and sons were asleep. The man told her to go upstairs, that Mrs. Keller and Johnny had been shot. He then ran off. Mrs. Kline entered the apartment and saw Mrs. Keller sitting in a chair bleeding from a wound in her side. The wounded mother told Kline, "Bill shot my boy and me too. Take the lamp and see if my boy is dead."

The scared woman then entered Johnny's bedroom to find him in bed, unclothed and with two bullet holes close to his right ear. She ran downstairs and awoke her husband. She sent him to get a doctor and to notify the police. She then returned to sit with Mrs. Keller until help arrived.

Billy Williams, in the meantime, had run straight to the St. Paul Central Station. There he met with Lieutenant Hanft. Billy told the police officer to get an ambulance to Reid's Court for Johnny and his mother, who had been shot. He told the officer about an argument with Johnny's mother. Billy rambled on; he said he didn't know why he had shot two people. He was asked about his gun, a revolver, and said he had left it in the apartment. Hanft placed him under arrest while other officers went to Reid's Court. Upon arrival at the Kellers' apartment, the police found the two wounded people and the gun on the floor. Sixteen-year-old Johnny died the following afternoon, and his mother, Mary, in her early fifties, died eight days later.

The trial began on May 16, a month after the murders. The trial was in the courtroom of Ramsey County District Judge Olin B. Lewis. Ramsey County Attorney Thomas Kane represented the state. Francis Clarke and I were Billy's defense lawyers.

After Mrs. Kline and Lieutenant Hanft testified, the physicians answered questions about the autopsy results, which showed that Johnny was shot twice from close range, once in the neck and once behind his right ear. The county attorney then read to the jury some of Billy's letters to Johnny, many of which threatened Johnny if they did not reconcile. Mr. Keller testified about the obsession Billy had had with his son. He described the numerous attempts he and his wife had made to prevent Billy from contacting Johnny.

Billy testified in his own defense on May 18. I wanted the jury to see this young man in a sober light, to show them that he was obviously insane while under the direction of the devil.

In his testimony Billy described being at the Keller home on the afternoon of April 12 and said that Mrs. Keller was very angry with him, wanting him to leave her son alone. Billy said he left and started drinking heavily, returning to the flat at about eight that evening. He told the court that Mrs. Keller was cursing at him as she walked around their flat. He claimed she had said "she would see both of us dead before she would let us leave again together."

Billy felt dizzy from drinking and wanted to lie down. Johnny let him stay because he did not like the way his mother was behaving. Billy had left a trunk with his belongings at the Kellers' home. He went to

Ramsey County District Courtroom, 1905. Can you find the spittoon? Source: Minnesota Historical Society.

the trunk and took out a change of underwear, shaving brush, razor, and revolver. He testified that Mrs. Keller emptied the revolver and kept the cartridges.

Billy described how he and Johnny were "laying in bed for a while, and Mrs. Keller come in a couple of times, and she kept on walking around in the other room, moving things around, and she kept on talking, you know; and I told John, 'I guess I had better get up and go.' He says, 'No, you better stay here.' And she kept on getting worse. So I said, 'John, I can't stay here anyway. I'm darned near crazy for want of sleep now.' And everything seemed to be going around. I says, 'I don't think you will get any sleep at all if I stay here; I better go.' And he says, 'She might cool down.'"

But Billy got up and got dressed, preparing to leave. That's when he says Mrs. Keller rushed in and shouted, "You shan't go now, you son of a bitch." He grabbed her while still feeling dizzy. The next thing he realized, he was in middle of the room with a gun in his hand.

Billy showed the court how he was holding the gun when he came out of his trance. He showed the court that he was pointing it at himself. He said he could not remember anything that happened between the time that Mrs. Keller rushed at him and when he was looking at the gun in his hand. The next thing he remembered was standing in Mrs. Keller's bedroom. She was standing about a foot from her bed. She told him to go get her neighbor Mrs. Kline, and he asked her what for. She said she was hurt. He said, "If you are hurt, I better send the doctor too."

The county attorney read a letter that Billy wrote while in St. Louis on March 3, 1905:

> *Dear John,*
>
> *Say why don't you write me. I wrote you two letters and received no answer. What is the matter if don't hear from you soon shall be St. Paul and see you. Am not working yet and am not looking for any, as I guess I shall have to go back to St. Paul to see you. Had to borrow money to send this letter as I am flat broke. Have not felt well lately besides not hearing from you bothers me. Now Johnny why have you not answered my letters either you think that now I am gone you can make a fool of me as you have before or else you wish me back. You can't fool me again as you have because I won't stand for it so you better cut it out. You have been playing with me long enough. Now Johnny so it is time you tryed something else for a change. Keep your promises to me this time old boy as it is your last chance. You understand what I mean and should have sense enough to keep your promises.*
>
> *Well old boy I should like to think that it is not your fault as I used to but it looks as if it was you now.*
>
> *Well Johnny old boy you know how I love you and what I have tried to do for you. I have spoiled my own*

> *chances for your sake and what reward have I got. Well we will try once more and make a success of it or ____.*[96]
>
> *Well John I might get a letter from you yet in answer to one of mine but what makes you take so long before writing. tell me all about yourself when you write. Hoping to hear from you soon, I remain your loving friend Bill*[97]

My partner Francis Clarke and I asked Billy some personal questions about the purpose of his association with Johnny Keller. Billy said that Johnny had helped him out at the hospital, and that he wanted to help him out, to make it "square" with him. He said that he wanted to do the best he could for Johnny. I asked Billy whether he ever had immoral relations with Johnny, whether he treated the boy in an unnatural way, or whether he had any improper physical contact with him, and to all these questions Billy answered no.

In my final argument to the jury I stated that Billy Williams was obviously insane at the time of the shooting. He and Johnny had been the best of friends, and Johnny was in fact Billy's only friend. How could you kill your only friend unless you were insane? His brain was contorted because of rejection and whiskey. He was in a stupor, not capable of making a rational decision. He needed help, not a conviction.

The jury was out for five hours and came back with the verdict: guilty of murder in the first degree. Judge Lewis sentenced Billy Williams to death by hanging. The Minnesota Supreme Court turned down my appeal for a new trial in December. Governor Johnson set the execution date for February 13, 1906.

I was beside myself with guilt. I asked myself what I could have done differently. I decided to introduce Billy to my friend Father Cushen for some spiritual assistance. I needed some spiritual guidance myself.

---

96 Billy didn't complete this sentence probably because he wanted Johnny to figure what the consequences would be.

97 File in transcripts at Minnesota Historical Society.

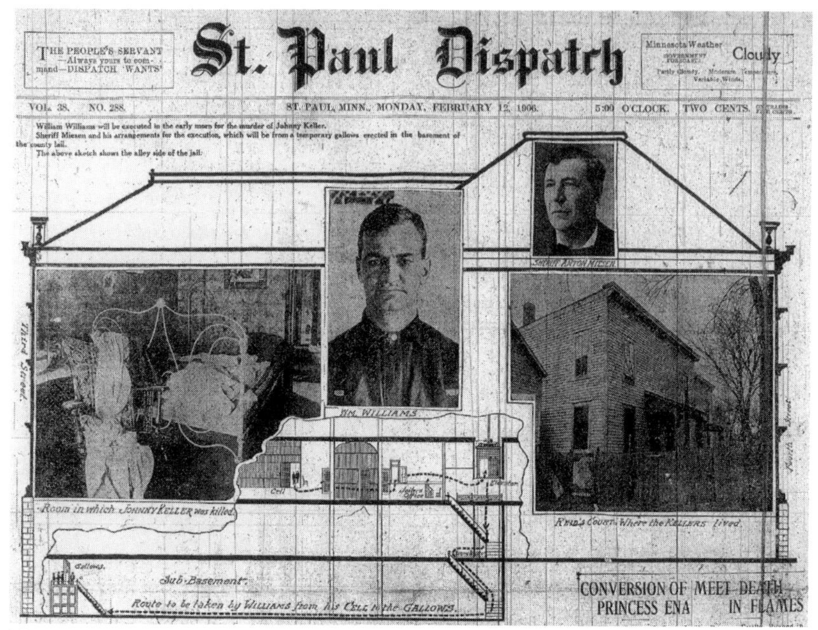

THE PEOPLE'S SERVANT —Always yours to command—DISPATCH 'WANTS'

St. Paul Dispatch

Minnesota Weather Cloudy

VOL. 38. NO. 288. ST. PAUL, MINN., MONDAY, FEBRUARY 12, 1906. 5:00 O'CLOCK. TWO CENTS.

William Williams will be executed in the early morn for the murder of Johnny Keller.
Sheriff Miesen and his arrangements for the execution, which will be from a temporary gallows erected in the basement of the county jail.
The above sketch shows the alley side of the jail:

CONVERSION OF PRINCESS ENA

MEET DEATH IN FLAMES

This illustration, published in the *St. Paul Dispatch,* shows the path from William Williams's jail cell to the gallows. Source: *St. Paul Dispatch*, February 12, 1906.

While all this was going on, the basement of the Ramsey County jail was busy. The deputies were testing the trapdoors of the gallows, which were originally constructed in July 1905 for Ed Gottschalk. They were now being reassembled for my client.

Sheriff Anton Miesen allowed no visitors at the jail that day, except for attorneys meeting with their clients. Ramsey County Attorney Kane reviewed the Supreme Court rulings pertaining to Billy's case. He told the press, "I feel certain that no substantial error was committed in the trial, and that justice has been done the condemned man."[98]

At three in the afternoon on the day of the scheduled execution, I went to the home[99] of Judge Lochren applying for a habeas corpus.[100] I

98 *St. Paul Dispatch*, February 12, 1906.

99 The Honorable William Lochren, U.S. District Court Judge, lived at 422 10th Ave. SE, Minneapolis.

100 A writ that may be issued to bring a party before a court or judge, having as its function the release of a party from unlawful restraints. *Habeas corpus* (Latin)

was beside myself with apprehension. I pleaded for a little more time because I wanted to go over everything one more time to see if there was anything that had been overlooked. I believed errors had been made by questioning Williams with no attorney present, that the letters should not have been admitted, and that he was obviously insane. The judge's wife joined me in my plea. I was probably annoying the judge, but now with his wife on my side, he was beginning to get upset. The judge denied the request on the grounds that the proceedings were not in error. He said he had gone by the book and would not overrule the State Pardon Board or grant a postponement.

It was a long trolley ride back to the courthouse, where I would once again search the law, trying to find a way to save my client. I was full of anxiety. I was the only one who could save Billy. I prayed to the Virgin Mary, Mother of God, for guidance. Faith was leaving me, and desperation was soaking into my thoughts.

The same day, February 12, the Ramsey County sheriff received the warrant for the execution from Governor Johnson. The time of execution was established at 12:30 a.m. on February 13, only a few hours away.

When I had seen Billy earlier that day, he was wearing a new black suit and a white shirt, with a stiff collar, purchased by the sheriff. Billy commented that this was one of the few times in his life that he wore a stiff collar. After lunch, he sat in his cell in silence and then called to the guards who were in the cell hallway. Several deputies were on death-watch. (The sheriff did not want another Gottschalk incident.) Billy asked the deputies to play a game of pitch with him. For several hours Williams and the guards played cards, until Sheriff Miesen showed up. He sent the men back to their stations.

At nine that evening, I appeared at the Ramsey County jail, where I met my friend Chief Deputy Frank Robert. I asked Frank to go tell Billy that all appeals had been denied. "I can't bear to do it," I told him.

Frank replied, "Come with me and do it yourself."

---

means "you should have the body."

As we entered the cell, Billy looked to me for some good news. He said, "Hello, Cormican. How are things going on the outside?"

I broke down crying, saying, "Billy, there is nothing I can do for you."

"Won't the governor do anything?" he asked.

"No, the governor won't interfere."

Williams asked me about the British consul. I had to tell him that the consul felt the matter was not in their jurisdiction.

Sitting in the small cell, I told Billy about going to Federal Judge Lochren's home in an attempt to obtain a stay of execution and failing to get it.

Billy said, "Well then, I suppose there is no help for it. You have done your best."

"Bear up like a man," I told him.

"Of course I will," he said calmly. "I am not afraid of death. Why, I had eighteen of my teeth pulled at one time. I guess the pain of that was worse than anything I can get now." I told him I would not attend the execution, we shook hands, and I left.

Deputy Pica told me the next day that Billy, the sheriff, three deputies, and Father Cushen departed the cellblock for the subbasement. The sheriff did not want Billy on the inside rail of the stairwell, in case he decided to take a dive. Miesen, the miser, did not want to take a $500 loss. The priest walked down the rail side of the stairs with his arm around Billy. When Billy finally saw the gallows, Pica said he did not stop or hesitate but walked directly to the stairs. He climbed up the thirteen steps to the platform with a steady gait.

The deputy told me that Sheriff Miesen showed Billy where to stand on the trapdoor. Pica then grabbed the three straps that were hanging over the rail on the platform. He applied one to Williams's ankles, used another strap to attach his hands to his thighs, and bound his arms between the shoulders and the elbows with the last strap.

Billy told Pica, "You certainly can work those straps."

"William Williams, have you anything to say why the sentence of the court should not now be executed upon you?" asked Chief Deputy Robert.

Billy cleared his throat and replied: "Gentlemen, you are about to execute an innocent man. I am not guilty of killing Johnny Keller. I had no quarrel with him. He was the best friend I had, and I certainly expect to meet him in the world to come. I forgive everyone who has had anything to do with this business, and I wish to thank those friends of mine who have interested themselves in my welfare."

The gallows where Williams was executed. Note how low the rope is. Source: *St. Paul Dispatch*, July 18, 1905.

Meanwhile, the police, under the command of Lieutenant Henry Meyerding, had established a line around the jail. The citizens apparently caused no problem for the police as they gathered and spoke among themselves.

Deputy Robert later told me that he put the rope around Billy's neck. The rope was new, not stretched beforehand, as was the custom in previous hangings. The deputy placed the black hood over Billy's head. The straps around his hands and legs were checked. Once the lever was pulled, the trapdoor would swing open, Billy would drop straight down, and the knot would break several bones in his vertebrae, causing instant death.

At 12:32 a.m. Deputy Frank Robert motioned to the sheriff that the rope was secure. Sheriff Miesen pulled the lever, and the trapdoor fell open. The *St. Paul Dispatch* reported, "Williams's body shot through and pulled up with a jerk."[101]

"He is on the floor!" spectators yelled.

The newspaper said that three deputies then grabbed the rope and pulled Billy up. The rope and his neck stretched. The body swayed as deputies Robert, Pica, and Hanson took turns holding the rope.

---

101 *St. Paul Dispatch*, February 13, 1906.

Sheriff Miesen gave a statement to the *St. Paul Daily News* stating that the execution went as he had planned and there were no mistakes. "There was not a slip anywhere in the procedures. I pulled the trap myself, and I helped pull on the rope. The official witnesses preserved good order, and many of them were deeply impressed."

But that morning the *St. Paul Daily News* reported:

> *William Williams has been hanged. The drop fell at 12:32 and he was cut down at 12:48, two minutes after the physicians pronounced him dead. Williams strangled to death. His neck was not broken by the fall.*
>
> *His feet touched the ground by reason of the fact that his neck stretched four and a half inches and rope nearly eight inches.*
>
> *Deputies then pulled the rope so that Williams's head was kept up and strangulation could slowly go on. His feet touched ground all the time that the death agonies were playing in his mind.*
>
> *Slowly, but surely, life was squeezed from the body until 12:46, just 14 minutes after the trapdoor was sprung and 21 ½ minutes after Williams left his cell, death relieved the murderer of his suffering.*[102]

The *St. Paul Dispatch* described Billy's last moments in its daily edition on February 13:

> *Slowly the minutes dragged. The surgeon, with his watch in his hand, held his fingers on Williams's pulse. Five minutes passed. There was a slight rustle, low murmurs among the spectators and then silence. Another five minutes dragged. Would the man never die? Fainter and fainter grew the pulsations of the doomed heart as it labored to maintain its function. The dead man's suspended body moved with*

102 *St. Paul Daily News*, February 13, 1906.

> *a gentle swaying. The deputies wiped their perspiring brows with their handkerchiefs. Members of the crowd shifted from one foot to another. There were murmurs from the uncomfortable audience. Eleven, twelve, thirteen minutes slowly passed. Williams's heart was beating now with spasmodic movement, fainter and fainter. Fourteen minutes—only surgeon's fingers could detect a flow of blood now. Fourteen and a half minutes. 'He is dead' Surgeon Moore announced.*[103]

Deputy Robert told me that he cut the body loose from the rope. Undertaker Schroeder's assistants put the body in a cragged[104] coffin and carried it out the St. Peter Street exit. The body was then transferred to the city morgue, at 164 South Washington.

The autopsy report came out the morning of the thirteenth. Billy had signed a release that his body be given over to me for burial. He did not want his body dissected by medical students, but he did give permission to have his brain analyzed. The concluding report stated that Billy's brain was developed more on the animal type than on the human type. The brain proper was comparatively small, especially the frontal portion. The autopsy report said the neck was neither broken nor dislocated. The report concluded that death was from strangulation and painless.

Dr. Justice Ohage,[105] surgeon, was a little more opinionated in his evaluation:

> *Williams was a miserable brute, a human dog. He had a head like Gottschalk, the back part of his brain a great deal more developed than the front part. This typifies the dog or brute. He was born and bred with lack of intellect, a human brute. We examined his brain and the lobes showed*

---

103 *St. Paul Dispatch*, February 13, 1906.

104 Rugged, not smooth.

105 Dr. Ohage was the commissioner of health for St. Paul. He resided at 589 Irving.

The Ramsey County Courthouse, where William Williams's trial was held. Source: Minnesota Historical Society.

> *about the same kind of brain as Gottschalk. It was the brain of one of cunning, deceit, and vicious tendencies. He was of animal intellect, a low state of human instinct, a natural born man of brutish nature. We determined that his neck and spine were not broken by the fall, but we did not open the body further than this.*[106]

I admit I was shocked by these statements, but they did not know him the way I did.

The following Thursday morning, two days following Billy's death, his body was placed in an oak casket. It left Schroeder's Undertaking Parlor by wagon and slowly made its way to Calvary Cemetery, 753 Front Street, St. Paul. The casket was placed in a pine box and quickly lowered into the ground. Aside from Father Tom Cushen, I was the only mourner.

106 *St. Paul Daily News*, February 13, 1906.

Billy Williams was to be the last of the rope dancers—his was the last lawful execution in the state of Minnesota. Because of his prolonged, painful manner of death, all capital punishments were set aside until the repeal of the Minnesota death sentence six years later.

Before I defended Billy Williams, I had no opinion on capital punishment. Now I wonder if capital punishment turns all of us into murderers.

Whatever happened to . . . ?

William Williams was buried in Section 39 of Calvary Cemetery. His grave site is unmarked.

Sheriff Anton Miesen was defeated on November 11, 1906, after only one two-year term in office. He then purchased and operated the Café Neumann, 36-38 East Sixth Street, St. Paul. On Sunday, May 30, 1909, two men, Dr. C. W. Young and Prof. John A. Nye of the Law Enforcement League, went to Miesen's café and ordered two beers. They were served and the following week filed a complaint with Ramsey County Attorney O'Brien's office. A warrant was issued for the former sheriff, stating he sold liquor on a Sunday, a violation of the Sunday alcohol law.

John Aubler, brewmaster for the Schmidt Brewing Company, was the primary witness for the defense. He testified that he had prepared a special brew for the café's Sunday trade. The special brew he made for Miesen was less than 2 percent alcohol. The special brew was delivered to Miesen the Friday before he was busted. There was not a test on the beer the two men ordered. The jury was out eighteen minutes before returning a not-guilty verdict. Miesen sold his business in 1911.

He was appointed to the Ramsey County Board in 1915 to fill a vacancy caused by a resignation. He held this position until his death in March 1918. He died at the city hospital following a stroke. He was seventy-five. He resided at 630 Ashland, St. Paul, at the time of his death. He left a wife and four adult sons. He is buried at Roselawn Cemetery, St. Paul.

James Cormican died of natural causes at his home, 349 North Snelling, on May 28, 1931. He was seventy-six. His funeral was at St. Mark's Church in St. Paul; he was buried at Calvary Cemetery. He practiced law up to the time he died. He was considered a compassionate, hard-working, and successful attorney. He was survived by his wife and four grown children.

CHAPTER 6

Northern Hardships

1907

"If I were sure that you were guilty, there would be no hesitation on my part in imposing the death sentence."

—Beltrami County District Court Judge
Marshall A. Spooner, April 13, 1907

CHARLES W. SCRUTCHIN WAS THE defense attorney in two of the most notable murder trials in Beltrami County history. In late 1899 he moved to Bemidji and set up a law practice. He had worked as a porter for the Great Northern Railway to pay his way through law school at the University of Michigan. He chose Bemidji because the area was beautiful and growing rapidly as a result of the expanding lumber industry. Bemidji was an unsettled town when he arrived, with no schools nor churches, but forty-three saloons. According to the 1900 federal census, there were only nine "colored" Americans in Bemidji. He was one of them.

Charles W. Scrutchin, attorney at law.
Source: Author's collection.

I would like to start this dissertation by describing the residents and the environment of Beltrami County. The county is principally known for its virgin timber. Lumber, being the major commerce in the area, means the building of camps, logging roads, rail lines, and waterways, and the establishment of communities. Sawmills, such as Shevlin-Carpenter in Bemidji, have an output of thirty-five to forty-five million board feet annually.[107] All this industry makes it an exciting place to live.

Lumberjacks are recruited to the area to fill the many winter jobs available. Most lumberjacks work on farms in the summer and lumber camps in the winter. They work six-day weeks to saw and transport logs throughout the cold, windy winters. Their long day begins before sunrise, when they dress and have a breakfast of flapjacks, hash, beans, and fried cakes. During the day they are subject to serious injuries, such as being hacked by an axe, being crushed by timber, falling, getting cuts, having their hands and feet smashed, and developing frostbite.

They return to the campsite at sunset to have a large supper, which usually consists of meat, potatoes, flapjacks, bread, and pie with coffee. After supper, they hang up their wet clothing, light their pipes, play cards, and tell stories. The wood stoves push out smothering dry heat.

107 Harold T. Hagg, *Mississippi Headwaters Region* (Bemidji, Minn.: Beltrami Historical Society, 1986).

Mealtime in a Nixon Lumber Camp near Akeley, Minnesota. Source: Minnesota Historical Society.

The oily-smelling kerosene lamps are extinguished at nine o'clock in the bunkroom. Bedbugs are a constant plight.

Besides the lumbermen, most of my clients are settlers who come to Beltrami County to seek land and develop the property. They face many hardships, like extreme weather, insects, diseases, and loneliness. The amended Homestead Law of 1862 allows any U.S. citizen over twenty-one, male or female, to claim 160 acres of public land by living on it for at least fourteen months and improving it. When the fourteen months are up, the settler can sell the lumber and keep the profit.[108] Once the land is cleared, the government hopes that improved wheat farms will result.

One settler, Mr. N. O. Dahl, was a sixty-year-old lumberyard worker from the Red River Valley near Crookston, Minnesota. A widower, he moved to northern Beltrami County[109] in 1901 and claimed a site located

108 Homestead Law of 1862, Amended. The original law stated that to acquire property one had to reside on and improve the property for five years tax-free, or reside on the property for a fourteen-month period, at which time a settler could secure a deed by a cash payment of $1.25 per acre.

109 The county was founded in 1866, and settlers arrived in the 1880s. The county was

one and a half miles east of Quiring on section 33, about fifteen miles northwest of the village of Blackduck.[110] He knew about the vast timber in the county and thought he could profit from timber and some potato farming. There are very few settlers in that part of the county because of the thick underbrush and wetland that surrounded the timber.

Mr. Dahl had three daughters, two of whom are married to Crookston businessmen. His third daughter, Miss Aagot, was a schoolteacher who had various health problems. He talked her into making a claim next to his plot, telling her that the fresh pine air and outdoor work would restore her to good health. In 1903, the twenty-two-year-old made a claim next to her father's. Her shack stood near her father's. The Dahls visited and welcomed their neighbors often. They were friendly and had no quarrel with anyone.

In the fall of 1903, Mr. Dahl sold eighteen hundred dollars' worth of his timber, a large and quick profit for the new settler. He traveled to Crookston to visit family and friends the following January. He deposited most of his money in a Crookston bank and returned to Quiring with seventy-eight dollars in his pocket. He told his neighbors of his sale; he was happy that his dream was coming true. Hard work did pay off.

The Dahls were often seen at the Quiring township[111] post office, which was the gathering spot for all the settlers to check on each other's health and to visit. In April 1904, mail was accumulating for the Dahls, and no one had seen them for some time. Neighbors found no one present when they went to their shacks. Residents of the area thought that the Dahls must have gone to Crookston for a visit but wondered why they had not told someone, especially the postmaster, Mr. Carter. The postmaster wrote Mr. Dahl's other two daughters and asked if they knew the whereabouts of their father and sister.

---

named after Giacomo C. Beltrami, an Italian adventurer who explored the area in 1823.

110 Blackduck, Minnesota, is about twenty-four miles northeast of Bemidji, which is 217 miles north of Minneapolis.

111 Quiring Township is thirty-five miles north of Bemidji.

Mr. Dahl's sons-in-law from Crookston visited Quiring in early June 1904. They went to the Dahls' shacks and found that Mr. Dahl had moved in with his daughter. There were two beds in Aagot's shack and also some food and other provisions. They noticed that Miss Aagot's bed slats were broken and the looking glass was turned against the wall. They found the shacks to be in somewhat good order, yet suspected that someone might have been rummaging through them. The two men took their in-laws' belongings and returned to Crookston.

Bemidji County Attorney H. J. Loud and Sheriff Tom Bailey were notified of the mystery in Quiring. It was generally accepted that the Dahls were dead, but no one knew in what manner they had met their demise. People were nervous because of the possibility of a killer or killers in the area. The county board offered a reward of fifteen hundred dollars for the location of the Dahls. Search parties were formed. Spring was arriving, and the vegetation was growing fast. The warm weather made the ground muddy, making the search difficult. Private detectives and bounty hunters from the midwestern portion of the country were gradually joining in the search.

There was continuous gossip and rumors in the northern part of the county about who could have killed the Dahls. The names of Eugene Caldwell, Paul "Little Paul" Fournier, and James "Shorty" Wesley were bandied about. Mr. Caldwell lived on his property with his wife and family near the Dahls' shacks. Mr. Fournier and Mr. Wesley were bachelor lumbermen who traveled to the various lumber sites nearby. They had been in the area for the last couple of years. Before the Dahls' disappearance, rumors had it that these men had made statements about desiring N. O. Dahl's money. All three were considered disreputable by law-abiding citizens.

According to a later account from Eugene Caldwell, on July 26, he and his brother-in-law, Jean French, also a neighbor of the Dahls, went looking for a stray cow on French's property. They drifted over to Mr. Dahl's claim and found the cow by the old man's shack. They chased the cow, which tripped over a balsam stump as it tried to avoid capture. A strong putrid smell arose from the stump, and their dog started digging next to it. Bits of clothing were churned up as the men probed with sticks, and then they came across a skull.

They notified authorities in Bemidji, and Dr. Marcum (the deputy coroner), the sheriff, and the county attorney hurried to the scene. The badly decomposed body, later identified as N. O. Dahl, was taken to Bemidji for an autopsy, which determined that he had been shot in the head by a rifle. His remains were then transported to Crookston for burial.

It looked too convenient to the sheriff that once the reward was established, Mr. Caldwell found the body. Mr. Caldwell and Mr. Fournier were arrested. Mr. Fournier was a suspect because he had served time in prison for robbery, had talked about robbing the Dahls, and was an associate of Mr. Caldwell's. Loud convened a grand jury in Bemidji, which issued an indictment for murder for both of the suspects.

Mr. Caldwell, I believe, was quite fearful after being indicted. He told the sheriff and the county attorney that he, Mr. Wesley, and Mr. Fournier were gathering timber for a man named Martindale in the winter of 1903. The three would often eat together, and it was during one of those times that Mr. Caldwell heard Mr. Wesley talk about the Dahls. Mr. Caldwell recalled Mr. Wesley saying, "Dahl has a plant[112] and I would like to make him dig it up and show the old man how to spend it." Mr. Caldwell also said that Mr. Fournier use to "josh" Mr. Wesley about Miss Dahl.

Mr. Caldwell told the authorities that on the evening of April 7, 1904, he heard dogs barking outside his cabin. He said he remembered that date because he was hauling hay that day when he and his wife heard a scream, which his wife thought was an owl hooting. Later, about 9:15, Mr. Caldwell heard a rifle shot. Mr. Caldwell mentioned to his wife that someone might have shot a neighbor.

The next day some of his cattle were loose, and he tracked them to the area of Miss Dahl's cabin. She was not home. He noticed tracks

112 People at that time often buried their money and valuables in the ground for security, and what was buried was referred to as a "plant."

that ran from the cabin door southwest to a beaver dam, where the tracks stopped. Next he went to Mr. Dahl's cabin but found it empty. He noticed many tracks from the night before and saw that Dahl's sled was gone. From there he traveled to Mr. Fournier's place, where William Krueger, a neighbor, and Mr. Wesley were also staying. Mr. Caldwell recalled that Shorty (Mr. Wesley) didn't seem to be himself. He looked pale and kept his eyes on the floor. When Mr. Krueger was leaving, Mr. Fournier told him to take his rifle.

The authorities bought Mr. Caldwell's story. The sheriff and county attorney wanted this solved, so I believe they jumped at the opportunity to find convenient culprits. Mr. Caldwell wiggled himself out of the indictment by blaming his associates for the murders. Fournier was arrested and held in the county jail. A warrant was issued for Mr. Wesley's arrest; he was no longer in the territory. Mr. Caldwell was released.

Less than a month later, on August 17, Tom Dooher, whose farm was about a mile and a half from Miss Dahl's claim shack, discovered a human foot underneath a pile of brush while raking hay. He looked further and found a skeleton. Again, the coroner was called. From the pieces of clothing near the remains of the body he identified Aagot Dahl. During the autopsy in Bemidji, the coroner found that her skull had been crushed and her shoulder had sustained a bullet wound. He was unable to determine which invasion had caused her death. The remains of Miss Dahl were sent to Crookston for interment.

I believe the killing of Miss Aagot Dahl was one of the most ghastly crimes in the history of Minnesota. The men in this area often punch it out with each other to let off steam, but the residents of Beltrami County found the killing of a defenseless young woman inconceivable and horrendous. There are not many women in this harsh environment of the country, and the ones we do have are usually respected and protected. This was a very cruel method of killing an unarmed person. The public sentiment was that the man, or men, had to be caught and hanged immediately.

It wasn't to be. On October 11, County Attorney Loud had the indictment against Mr. Fournier and Mr. Wesley annulled. He felt that the evidence against them was not enough to gain a conviction. I agreed with him. There were an abundance of rumors but not sufficient evidence.

Gradually the investigation ran out of steam as months and then years passed. The county attorney position changed hands, police and deputies had other crimes and duties to work on, yet everyone had fixed in their minds that there was a murderer or murderers here in the midst of our beautiful timberland. The gossip did not let up among the residents. Various suspects were named by the tavern patrons, lumberjacks, residents sitting by the potbelly stove in the post office, and those attending town meetings.

The area's population continued to grow. More people were moving in, more claims were made, more real estate changed ownership, and defendants needed representation; as a result, I was busy. I did not experience the difficulties one might expect as a colored man. I am the highest educated, with a master's in law, of the eleven attorneys in the area, and am very well known and respected in the community. Even though Bemidji's fraternal organizations have banned me and my brethren from membership, I represent many of their members in court. I accept the situation for the time being. While the discrimination pains me, I am proud of my ability to help others with my law practice.

In early 1907, the new county attorney, Henry Funkley, sat down with Eugene Caldwell and squeezed out of him every fact he could recall about the Dahls' deaths. Mr. Funkley interviewed other lumberjacks and obtained a few damaging statements. This evidence prompted Mr. Funkley to convene a grand jury in January of 1907, almost three years after the murders. Mr. Fournier and Mr. Wesley were again indicted for the murder of the Dahls. There were rumors that Mr. Wesley was dead, but on February 9, he was located and arrested while working in a logging camp north of Deer River, Minnesota. He was taken to Bemidji, where both he and Fournier pled not guilty to the charge of double murder. A trial date was set for March 28.

Trial Wesley Is On Today; Charged Murder N. O. Dahl

Entire Jury Selected and Trial of Case Commenced This Afternoon by County Attorney Henry Funkley, Who States What He Intends to Prove.-- Claims Two Confessions Were Made by Wesley.

A headline printed in the *Bemidji Daily Pioneer* about the Wesley trial. Source: *Bemidji Daily Pioneer*, March 28, 1907.

Rumors and hearsay spread within the early morning crowd that waited outside for the courthouse to open. The suspects were going to be tried separately, with Wesley going first. His trial was held in the courtroom of the Honorable Judge Marshall A. Spooner of the Fifteenth Judicial District Court, Bemidji, Minnesota. Along with Mr. John M. Martin of Virginia, I represented the defense; Mr. Henry Funkley represented the state.

One of the first witnesses was Mr. Charles Laroque, who testified that he saw the Dahls at the young woman's cabin in February when he skidded logs there. Then, in late February, he purchased some potatoes and other articles from Miss Dahl and her father for forty-seven dollars. They arranged for him to pick up some of Miss Dahl's household articles in June, when she planned to return to Crookston. The county attorney concluded that no one except the murderers saw the Dahls alive after that.

Mr. Eugene Caldwell was then called. He testified that he had known Mr. Wesley for eight or nine years and that Wesley had worked for him, at different times, during the winter of 1903–04. He reiterated his stories of hearing the defendants talk of robbing the Dahls. He thought they would "do up"[113] most anyone for a plant. He claimed that a day or two after the murders he went by the Dahls' residences and recognized Mr. Wesley's footprints in the area. He said a woodsman knows the tracks of other people.

William Krueger testified next. He was a German settler and spoke in very broken English. He stated that on April 3, 1904, he had

113 *Bemidji Daily Pioneer*, March 30, 1907.

loaned his rifle to Mr. Wesley. Shortly after the murders he said that he went to Mr. Fournier's to retrieve his rifle. Mr. Wesley was living with Mr. Fournier at that time. The rifle was a .38-.40 caliber, and he used soft-nose bullets in it. His rifle was entered into evidence. He testified that he had found a strand of long blonde hair on his rifle when Mr. Fournier and Mr. Wesley returned it to him. He showed the hair to Mr. Fournier and Mr. Wesley, who laughed at him and jokingly told him that he must have been "sparking the girl." Mr. Krueger was asked if it was a woman's hair, and he answered yes. We objected, stating that a woman's hair could not connect the defendant with the killing of Miss Dahl. How would Mr. Krueger know if it was a woman's hair? He was a bachelor with no women in his life, and now the court was accepting his word on it. We felt that the hair should be brought to court for expert analysis, but the judge overruled us; I am not sure why.

A Charles Martindale was the next witness who was to collaborate Mr. Caldwell's testimony, but he was intoxicated. He was belligerent and his language was racy. In the end, the judge prohibited him from testifying. A deputy escorted him from the courtroom. A disturbing event.

Dr. Marcum was called next.[114] He was the deputy coroner in 1904 and was the one called to Quiring Township on July 27, 1904, to view the remains of Mr. Dahl. He introduced eleven parts of Dahl's skull. He testified that he had found two bullet holes in the skull made from either a rifle or a revolver. One bullet had entered from the left side, and the other at the back of the skull. Either of the wounds would have been fatal. Marcum then introduced other exhibits, which included a pair of trousers, a cap, a piece of suspenders, and a ring.

Dr. Marcum testified to the location and condition of Miss Dahl's body when it was discovered. Her skeleton had been found two miles north of her homestead, under brush, in a swamp near a creek. He said he found a woman's long black coat, a white tam-o'-shanter, a cap, mittens in the coat pocket, a ring on her finger, a hatpin, and a pair of pins. Her skull was fractured, with a blow over the left eye. There were

114 Dr. Marcum received six dollars a day for his expert testimony.

bloodstains on her underclothing and on her shoes. He found a hole in the coat just inside the shoulder where the seam was. The bloodstains indicated that Miss Aagot was in an upright position when the wounds were made. He concluded that the wound, under the shoulder, would not necessarily have caused death, but the blow to the skull would have.

On the fourth day of the trial, Grace Caldwell, Eugene's wife, was called to testify. She stated that she had heard Wesley on two occasions tell about how he wanted to dig up Mr. Dahl's plant. She described a time when "Paul told of holding up a camp on the Big Fork, and that he had turned the looking glass to the wall throwing reflections toward the bunk."[115]

Charles Martindale showed up again to testify, this time somewhat sober. The judge was not taking any chances and instructed the women to leave the courtroom while he testified. This upset most of the women: they feared they would lose their seat because of, as one woman put it, "an insufferable drunk." Once things settled down, Mr. Martindale said that Mr. Wesley and Mr. Fournier worked for him in January of 1904. He was with them when Mr. Wesley said, "I am going to quit my damn job, do up Krueger and get his money and then go dig up Dahl's wealth." He said at that time Wesley also said he was going "to ------ that round head blond." Mr. Fournier responded, "No, you want all the girls in the county. I want her. She would be good on the farm." The witness's language was obscene. He added that Wesley said he would "get rid of the old man Dahl, cut a hole in Red Lake, and dump him in or bury him in moose wallow. The Dahls should not come here and take claims. The poor people want this country."

Allan McGraw, age fifty, of Clarksville, Iowa, testified that he was in the Beltrami County jail in the summer of 1905, at the same time as Mr. Wesley. He was cutting Mr. Wesley's hair one day when he told him that Mr. Fournier had shot both of the Dahls. We asked Mr. McGraw why he didn't tell the county attorney about Mr. Wesley's story at the time. He replied that he did not like the county attorney because he was trying to put him in the penitentiary. He denied any interest in

115 *Bemidji Daily Pioneer*, March 30, 1907.

District Court Judge Marshall A. Spooner.
Source: *Bemidji Daily Pioneer*, March 30, 1907.

the reward and added that he was just answering a subpoena.

The state called witnesses to show that Mr. Fournier was broke at the beginning of April 1904 but had money after the murders. Some of the testimony was not allowed because witnesses were not sure of the exact dates that Mr. Fournier did or did not have money.[116] My question was, what did Mr. Fournier having money have to do with Mr. Wesley committing murder?

On April 2, 1907, Mr. Martin and I initiated Mr. Wesley's defense case. In my opening remarks, I told the jury that I was going to show that the Caldwells were liars and that Mr. McGraw (Wesley's cellmate) was a proven criminal. Could you really believe these men? I reminded the court that Mr. Caldwell at one time was a suspect in the murders. I concluded by telling the jury that I would prove that Mr. Dahl was killed by a 303 Savage, like the one Mr. Caldwell owns, and not by Mr. Krueger's .38-40 caliber rifle.

Mr. Fred Wilson, a volunteer searcher, was one of our first witnesses. In August of 1904, he and a detective found a rifle shell on a trail leading to Mr. Dahl's cabin. He took it, went to Mr. Caldwell's home, and placed it in Mr. Caldwell's rifle. The shell was then introduced into evidence.

The following day, before the court convened, the deputies locked the doors of the courtroom to keep the excess crowd from entering. The courtroom was starting to smell a little ripe. You see, our winters

116 Mrs. Caldwell was recalled and stated that in June 1904 she knew that Fournier had purchased a horse for twenty-five dollars, a dog for five dollars, a gun for two dollars, and fifteen dollars' worth of provisions.

here are very bitter and long; the lumbermen dress warmly and keep the same clothing on for at least a week at a time, often longer. That odor plus poor ventilation, combined with the smell of burning tobacco, manufactured a repugnant scent.

The former county attorney H. J. Loud was called to the stand. I wanted to use him as an expert in ballistics, to show that it was Mr. Caldwell's rifle that shot the Dahls. The judge would not permit it.

James "Shorty" Wesley was called to testify and took the oath in a firm voice. The seemingly confident, clean-shaven, and well-groomed defendant looked directly at us, anticipating our questions. We had prepared him for the questions we were going to ask and some we thought the county attorney would ask. He was not used to wearing a suit, but it fit him reasonably well. Mr. Martin started the line of questioning in a very quiet courtroom. Shorty testified that he came to Beltrami County in 1898 and had worked since as a general woodsman.[117]

He was at Mr. Fournier's home when a neighbor, Mr. Krueger, came to pick up his rifle. Mr. Krueger never mentioned anything about a hair on his rifle, nothing about the girl's hair, and nothing was said about "sparking the girl." Mr. Wesley said he never told anyone that he was interested in Dahl's plant. He said Mr. Caldwell was a liar. Mr. Wesley testified that he had absolutely nothing to do with the death of either of the Dahls.

After eight hours of testimony, we rested our case. A decision was made to continue court into the evening for the final arguments. No one left the courtroom. The overflow crowd remained seated. County Attorney Funkley addressed the jury about five o'clock in the afternoon, explaining his theory that robbery was the motive in this case: "In the course of bringing the perpetrators to justice, it was necessary to look about for men who would entertain motive, and among residents at the scene of the tragedy there were none he could think of depraved enough

117 Wesley explained that a woodsman does such things as swamping, sawing, teaming, landing, top loading, and following the drive.

to commit the crime except Fournier and Wesley."[118] He described the two defendants as vicious.

My colleague on the defense team, Mr. Martin, told the jury that the defendant was a wayward boy who had gotten a wrong start in life. "But gentlemen, he has the bulwark of the constitution around him—he is presumed to be innocent until proven guilty."[119] He said that he believed the defendant was innocent and that he would have his tongue cleaved to his mouth or his right arm cut off if he weren't telling the truth. He spent some time attacking the credibility of Mr. and Mrs. Caldwell and said it was Eugene Caldwell everyone was afraid of. He argued that it could have been Mr. Caldwell's rifle and not Mr. Krueger's that killed the Dahls. "Suspicion has been cast upon a strong witness for the state who helped weave the chain of circumstantial evidence around Mr. Wesley."[120] He concluded at 10:45 p.m.

Judge Spooner read the indictment and his instructions to the jury. The jury departed the courtroom, for deliberation, about eight minutes after 11:00. I could not believe it when a quick twenty-seven minutes later, the jury foreman told the deputy they had reached a decision. Such a short jury discussion, for a first-degree murder trial, meant they had not reviewed the evidence. The judge and attorneys had not gone far away from the courtroom and were able to be notified. Only about thirty people remained in the courtroom; no one had expected such a quick deliberation.[121] Mr. Wesley looked pale and nervous as he was brought into the courtroom handcuffed to the deputy.

Judge Spooner asked the Clerk of Court to read the verdict: "We, the jury impaneled and sworn to try the guilt or innocence of the above named defendant, find the said defendant, James Wesley, guilty as charged in the indictment. T. J. Miller, foreman."

---

118 *Bemidji Daily Pioneer*, April 4, 1907.

119 Ibid.

120 Ibid.

121 The courtroom had been filled to capacity all day and evening, with people in the hallways and stairwells.

James Wesley (second to right) and Paul Fournier (right) with their counsel, C. W. Scrutchin (left) and J. M. Martin (second to left). Source: *Bemidji Daily Pioneer*, April 13, 1907.

Mr. Wesley was stunned, as I was. The judge dismissed the jurors and all in attendance rushed to the street to discuss the verdict. Mr. Wesley was escorted back to his cell to await sentencing, which was postponed until the completion of the Fournier trial.

Two days after the Wesley trial concluded, the trial of forty-one-year-old Paul Fournier, aka Little Paul, commenced. There was a change in our defense strategy this time. I became the lead attorney, and Mr. Martin assisted me. The Honorable Marshall A. Spooner would preside; Beltrami County Attorney Funkley was representing the state.

The same witnesses from the Wesley case testified again to their findings. The courtroom was always completely filled.[122] One of Mr. Dahl's sons-in-law testified to the condition of the cabins when he inspected them. During the questioning, one of the jurors asked him if the doors were locked. (Yes, a juror was allowed to ask a question.) The witness answered that both cabin doors were padlocked, but nails were so loose that he was able to pull them out with his fingers. There were no provisions in the cabin, and it did not look like a "tussle" had taken place in Miss Dahl's cabin. He also stated that the bedding did not look as if a woman had left it.

Charles Martindale, the former employer of Mr. Wesley and Mr. Fournier, was called to testify. Again Mr. Martindale's language became somewhat racy, so much so that the judge instructed the women to leave the courtroom. The women were not happy about losing their seats because of an old, foul-mouth drunk, but they did what they were told. His language was repulsive, and judge told him to watch it or he would be in jail. Mr. Martindale said that the two defendants often talked about going after the old man's money and having their way with the girl. He recalled that Mr. Fournier said, "That old son of a bitch had no business to come from Crookston up there and take up a homestead where some poor man needed it worse than him. He had wealth enough to keep him in Crookston and keep him without working, if he saw fit."

Mr. Martindale said that he was afraid of the two men, not because he feared they would turn him in for cutting timber on government property, but rather because he was afraid that they would kill him because of what he knew.

William Krueger testified again to loaning his rifle to Mr. Fournier and Mr. Wesley and finding hair on it when he picked it up. He said he then returned to his cabin, which had been broken into. He noticed

122 A few attorneys were among the crowd. One was A. M. Crowell, from Turtle Lake, who represented Robert Kinney in the first murder trial in Beltrami County in November 1898. Kinney was convicted of killing police officer Jerry Root in the spring of 1898 and was sentenced to life at Stillwater Prison.

that four cartridges were missing. A juror asked him how he knew that, and Mr. Krueger told the juror that he had counted them before he left. The jury was having difficulty understanding the German witness, so one of the jurors was sworn in as an interpreter. He said he did not tell anyone about the hair because he was afraid no one would understand him. I tried hard to show that Mr. Krueger was hostile toward the defendant, which he denied.

People who attended the trial talked about the wide latitude Judge Spooner was giving to both attorneys and his unusual practice of allowing questioning by jurors.

Miss Florence Melquist, one of Mrs. Caldwell's sisters, was called to the stand. At the time of the trial, she was a resident of St. Cloud. She had lived with her sister and Eugene Caldwell in the winter of 1903–04, when she often saw Fournier. She stated that Mr. Fournier told her that "he went to rob a warehouse—I don't know where it was—but it was a warehouse that he went to rob, and they turned the looking glass towards the wall, and they put the light in the eyes, the fellow's eyes, the watchman, who laid in the camp—he gave his reasons for this—I don't remember—I know he told the story more than once—hold the gun on the man, while they was taking the things they wanted."[123]

On the morning of April 11, 1907, we initiated our case. Former County Attorney H. J. Loud was allowed to testify this time. He stated that he was knowledgeable about gunshot wounds because he read considerably on the subject and also had some experience in homicide cases. There were no powder marks on Mr. Dahl's cap or skull, according to previous testimony, so he was shot at an unknown distance. Mr. Loud said that it was his opinion that a man with a good aim could hit another man in the head at two hundred yards. He told the court that a .38-40 low-velocity, soft-nose bullet—like the ones in Mr. Krueger's rifle—fired at two hundred yards would leave a hole as large as its own size. He told the court that a 303 Savage high-velocity bullet—used by Mr. Caldwell's rifle—fired from the same distance would mushroom on impact. Loud

123 *Bemidji Daily Pioneer*, April 10, 1907.

showed the jury Mr. Dahl's skull and illustrated that the wound was enlarged by the bullet's exit. Mr. Loud then concluded that the rifle used in the homicides was not the one Mr. Fournier had borrowed.

Late that afternoon I called my last witness, Paul Fournier. The *Bemidji Daily Pioneer* described the silence in the courtroom room as "death-like" while Fournier was sworn in. He was short in stature, sported a long, dark, drooping mustache, and was dressed in a faded dark suit.[124]

Mr. Fournier said he was a lumberjack by trade who had moved around a lot. He lived in Big Fork; he stated that he had been arrested for robbing a camp there. He served fourteen months in Stillwater for the robbery. I asked him every possible question pertaining to the circumstantial evidence that the previous state witnesses testified to. Mr. Fournier denied every statement that was damaging to his case. He and Mr. Krueger did not get along, and the same was true of him and Mr. Caldwell.

Mr. Fournier admitted that he and Mr. Wesley were at Caldwell's place on the evening of April 7, 1904, but they never left the house. He recalled that evening very clearly because earlier Mr. Wesley had shot a rabbit, which they ate for dinner. He testified to the fact that he was never in either of the Dahls' residences, he did not kill them, and he did not know who did. He said he was completely innocent.

After a few questions to clear up Mr. Fournier's testimony for the jury, we rested our case. Mr. Funkley stepped up for the cross-examination. Mr. Funkley questioned him about having a son, who was half Indian, living at Leech Lake. I argued that this had nothing to do with the case at hand, but to no avail. Mr. Fournier said he did not know if he was the father. Mr. Funkley asked him if he had killed a man by the name of George Barclay at Pine River in 1898. I objected, and the objection was sustained. Mr. Fournier was then asked if he killed a "squaw" because she had threatened to turn him in for the murder of Mr. Barclay. Another

---

124 On April 12, 1907, many attorneys, court officials, and law enforcement officers from throughout the state were in attendance. The sheriff of Hennepin County, W. J. Dreger, was one of them.

objection was sustained. The county attorney questioned him about other dates in 1904, but Mr. Fournier could not recall what he did on those days. Mr. Funkley said he was surprised because Mr. Fournier was very detailed about his actions on the day of the murders. Mr. Fournier was dismissed after a total of four hours of questioning.

A. J. Wosterchill was called by the state as a rebuttal witness and an expert on the caliber of weapon that killed Mr. Dahl.[125] He said that he shot Mr. Krueger's .38-.40 rifle into a piece of wood to determine the mushroom effect from that type of cartridge. He also shot it into the head of a corpse. From his experiments, he conjectured that it was Mr. Krueger's rifle that shot the bullet into Mr. Dahl. Voluminous arguing followed.

Both sides rested at 3:40 p.m. Mr. Funkley addressed the jury first, in the final argument, summarizing the testimony. I followed, explaining how my client had been betrayed by a friend and neighbors. Judge Spooner then gave his instructions to the jury, telling them to weigh the evidence and credibility of the witnesses. The jury was given the case at 5:45.

At 8:10 the jury informed the court that it had reached a verdict. The jury was out for two hours and twenty-five minutes with a half-hour break for supper. The word of the decision hit the streets of Bemidji quickly. People immediately scrambled up the stairs into the musty second floor courtroom to hear the verdict and see the reaction of the defendant. The jury entered the room, and the viewers were quiet. The jury showed no sign of what the verdict was, looking straight ahead as they entered and took their seats. Judge Spooner asked the jury to listen to the reading of the verdict. The clerk read: "We the jury, sworn to try the guilt or innocence of the above named defendant, find the said defendant,

---

125 Wosterchill, age twenty-three, was a trick-shot showman who worked for Peters Cartridge Company of Cincinnati, Ohio. He did a show following the trial that included shooting coal, walnuts, and washers out of the air with his .25-caliber rifle. With a .38 Smith & Wesson he hit two beer bottles twenty feet apart with two shots. He was so fast that it looked as if he shot both bottles at the same time. He used his .22 rifle to shoot 213 shots, creating a profile he called Chief Bemidji.

Paul Fournier, guilty as charged in the indictment. Dated at Bemidji, Minnesota, this twelfth day of April 1907. H. C. Wood, foreman."

Mr. Fournier swallowed two or three times as he sat quietly absorbing the verdict. A poll of the jury was requested, and all twelve men agreed that they voted "guilty." The defense notified the court that a motion for a new trial would be presented in the morning prior to sentencing. The crowd did not leave the courtroom. They stood around talking among themselves, making it difficult for the deputies to walk Mr. Fournier back to his jail cell.

A reporter from the *Bemidji Daily Pioneer* was permitted an interview with the two convicted murderers. Mr. Wesley told him that he had nothing to say to the "damn newspapers" and that he had nothing to fear. He did not give a damn. He said some other "vile"[126] comments, none of which could be repeated in the press. Mr. Fournier was more cooperative while he smoked his pipe and showed no nervousness. "I don't know what to say, it is so sudden. I didn't expect a verdict of guilty. I am innocent of that crime, but they thought me guilty."[127] The reporter described Mr. Wesley as being "cranky and querulous and [using] the most vile language, he is the most obstreperous prisoner in the entire jail."

The following morning, we stood in the crowded courtroom and made an appeal for two new trials based on errors in the proceedings of the trials. We hinted that we would be appealing to the Minnesota Supreme Court. Judge Spooner denied our motion.

Mr. Fournier stood for the sentencing. The judge said to him:

> *I think it cannot be said that you did not have a fair trial in every respect. And the jury have seen fit, on the testimony of the various witnesses, to find you guilty of the charge. The crime of killing N. O. Dahl and the circumstances are of a most cold-blooded character. Few instances in the annals of crime have been of a more brutal character.*

---

126 *Bemidji Daily Pioneer*, April 13, 1907.

127 Ibid.

> *If I were entirely sure that you were guilty, there would be no hesitation on my part in imposing the death sentence. While I think the jury was right in bringing in the verdict of guilty under the circumstances, there may be a possibility that someone else committed this crime. I think it is my duty to give you the benefit of such doubt as may exist. Consequently I shall not impose the death sentence.*
>
> *Paul Fournier, as punishment for the crime of murder in the first degree, of which you have been duly convicted, you are hereby sentenced to be punished by confinement at hard labor in the state's prison at Stillwater, Minnesota, for and during the full term of your natural life.*

Judge Spooner gave the same sentence to Mr. Wesley, using almost the exact words he did in sentencing Mr. Fournier. A sigh of relief passed through the courtroom as the prisoners were escorted back to the jail through a small path formed by the large crowd. I couldn't believe a judge would not hang a man because he didn't know if he was guilty or not, yet still give him life in prison.

On April 15, nineteen days after Mr. Wesley's trial had begun, the sheriff escorted him to the Bemidji train depot. Shorty said he was "standing pat" about his story. The newspaper reported that since the trial Mr. Wesley "has been exceedingly cranky and exceedingly profane, using the most vile language."[128] Mr. Wesley arrived the next day at the state prison, where he was assigned inmate number 2120.

The paper said that Mr. Fournier spent time crying in his cell while proclaiming his innocence. Fournier was transported to Stillwater two days later and was issued inmate number 2123.

It was not over for Mr. Fournier. I argued before the Minnesota Supreme Court that there had been serious errors in his trial and therefore he deserved a new one. The Court ruled on July 16, 1909, that

128 *Bemidji Daily Pioneer*, April 15, 1907.

errors had been made during the trial[129] and he was thus awarded a new trial. The following is a summary of the errors the High Court found in Fournier's trial:

1. Allowing Mr. Dahl's son-in-law to testify that he found the looking glass turned against the wall at Miss Dahl's cabin, and then Florence Melquist testified to a conversation with Mr. Fournier, who told her how he had turned a looking glass toward the wall during a previous crime.

   "To permit a witness to testify to a conversation with the defendant, in which the defendant stated that he had committed a crime in no way connected with the one for which he is on trial, is reversible error."

2. Allowing the county attorney to ask Fournier at some length about his illegitimate son who was living on the reservation. It appeared the state was trying to portray Fournier as a negligent father.

   "The persistent asking by the county attorney of incompetent and improper questions with reference to matters which are of a nature to create prejudice in the minds of the jurors and prevent the defendant from having a fair trial is such improper conduct as to require the granting of a new trial."

Mr. Fournier's second trial began in Brainerd on December 9, 1909, this time with Judge W. S. McClenahan presiding. The prosecutor for the state was Beltrami County Attorney Chester McKusick, and I was once again Mr. Fournier's attorney.

On December 10, the judge ordered all witnesses to be out of the courtroom when other witnesses testified. The witnesses in the new trial were pretty much the same as in the original trial. The major difference

129 *State v. Fournier*, 108 Minn. 402, 122 N.W. 329 Criminal law.

this time was that the prosecutors could not bring up my client's former arrest and imprisonment, an alleged crime in which he turned the looking glass toward the wall, and any allegations about the defendant not related to this case. That was enough. I picked apart the witnesses with whom I had become so familiar. I attacked the truthfulness of key witnesses for the state. I accused some of deliberately lying. Finally, on the following Wednesday morning, the jury returned with a verdict of not guilty.

Mr. Fournier jumped to shake the hands of the jurors with tears in his eyes, thanking them profusely. He would not stop hugging me. Later that day he was transferred back to the Bemidji jail to face another trial for the murder for Aagot Dahl. It never happened. Given the tired witnesses and the expense of another trial, probably in another county, the state gave up. Mr. Fournier was free.

I don't know if these two men were guilty, but I do believe they each deserved a fair trial. Our tools of investigation are limited, and it usually comes down to one man's word against another's. Just like the terrain in Beltrami County, our judicial system is a little rugged. Fair as we humans can be, we go by the book. We all know that God is the only one to issue perfect justice. With that in mind, while respecting everyone, we do the best we can.

Whatever happened to . . . ?

John M. Martin passed away within two years of the trial.

Charles W. Scrutchin resided at 820 Bemidji Street, Bemidji. He was a prominent and well-respected man in northern Minnesota. He was about forty during the trials, but his exact birth date is not clear.[130] His parents moved from Richmond, Virginia, to Atlanta, Georgia, when

130 Mr. Scrutchin used September 11, 1866, as his birth date; birth records of black people in the South were often not recorded.

he was two years old. His father died when he was ten, and shortly afterward his mother moved to Spokane, Washington. There she worked as a domestic servant for General Frank Wheaton. The young Scrutchin graduated from high school in Spokane and then attended the University of Washington. When he was twenty-five, he entered law school at the University of Michigan and graduated with a law degree in 1893. He went on to get his master of law degree in the next year and the same year passed his bar exam. In 1895 he worked in Chicago for E. H. Morris, another black attorney. In 1897 the Democrats swept the elections in Chicago, so Scrutchin, a hard-line Lincoln Republican, decided that Chicago was not the place where he wanted to practice law.

Morris told him that Minnesota was a good place to work because of a friendly reception he had received when he gave a speech there. In 1898 Scrutchin moved to St. Paul; at the time there were about 1,400 black citizens in the Twin Cities area. There were five black attorneys in the Twin Cities, headed by Frederick L. McGee, the first black attorney in Minneapolis, and William R. Morris, the first black attorney in St. Paul. At that time, there was much talk of a rapidly expanding community in the Bemidji area, a newly founded lumber town. It sounded exactly like what Scrutchin desired: beautiful landscape and promising business.

He moved there in 1899, when there were only eight other black people in the township: Charles Sykes, an elderly man who was hired by Scrutchin as his cook; Andy Cannon and Moses Taylor, barbers; Charles Cruip, a baker; James Godetts, a laborer and prizefighter, and his two children; and Tom Wright, a saloon waiter. Scrutchin quickly became a prominent attorney, handling mostly lumbermen's civil and criminal matters. He won a few of his first cases and was soon one of the town's busiest attorneys. He was smart, educated, well liked, honest, and hard working.

Among the six African Americans practicing law in Minnesota in 1900, Mr. Scrutchin was the only black attorney who lived outside of the Twin Cities.[131] He was the lawyer for the laborer, the woodsman, and the poor person. He was known as their "favorite counsel because

131 In 1900 there were 2,497 lawyers in Minnesota.

of his ability" and his friendly disposition.[132] His fees were economical compared to other attorneys, yet he provided a first-class legal service to all his clients. The courts and other attorneys in the area respected him highly. When the Beltrami County Bar Association was formed in 1900, he was immediately accepted, and in 1904 he was elected vice president of the association.

On August 27, 1900, Scrutchin married Laura P. Arnold, whom he met in Chicago. She was white. (Of the eight other African Americans living in Bemidji, three were married to white women.) The couple had two babies who died shortly after birth. In 1907 Mrs. Scrutchin was seriously injured when she fell through a wooden sidewalk on Irving Avenue in Bemidji. She broke two ribs that were torn off at the vertebra with severe bruising of her head and legs. Her disabilities and health gradually declined so much that in 1918 Scrutchin had to send his wife to Hot Springs, Arkansas, for healing. She returned to Bemidji, where she died in December of 1928 of myocarditis. She was sixty-two.

After a distinguished career in representing the "little guy," Scrutchin passed away on July 14, 1930, of "apoplexy, dropsy."[133] He was about sixty-five. He had been fighting diabetes since 1925. His wife's medical bills exhausted his finances to the point that he died poor. The Bemidji Bar Association handled the funeral arrangements and expenses, since he had no living relatives. He died with a drawer filled with his client's bills that had not been paid. He is remembered as an advocate for the poor and uneducated, an excellent, dedicated attorney for whom no case was too small. He is buried next to his wife at Bemidji's Greenwood Cemetery.

Paul Fournier's fate is unknown.

---

132 Former Beltrami County Attorney Clarence Smith quoted in Steven R. Hoffbeck, "Victories Yet to Win: Charles W. Scrutchin, Bemidji's Black Activist Attorney," *Minnesota History* 55, no. 2 (summer 1996): 66.

133 Loss of muscular control, with diminution or loss of sensation and consciousness, resulting from a rupture or blocking of a blood vessel in the brain.

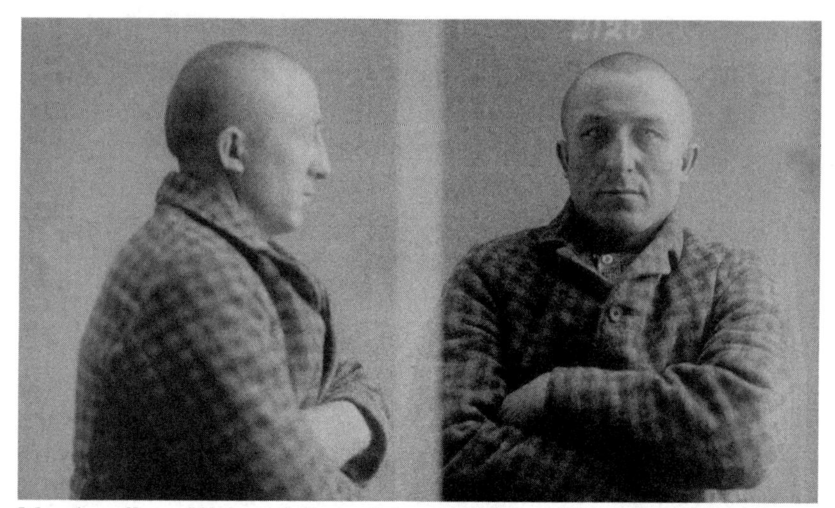

Mug shot of James Wesley in Stillwater Prison, 1907. Source: Minnesota Historical Society.

James Wesley was born on October 12, 1876, in Green Bay, according to his reception papers at Stillwater Prison. The documents describe Wesley as five foot three inches, 141 pounds, with a stout build, dark blue eyes, dark hair, and a florid complexion. The report states that his habits were liquor, chew, lewd women, and gambling. He answered "no" to drugs, cigarettes, and snuff. He had two children, Nellie and Edith, and his wife was deceased. He and his second wife, Jessie French, were no longer together. He had completed the fifth grade.

A prison agent reported that Wesley was "sullen and hard to get much from him. He was held for nearly a year in jail, released and three years later re-arrested and convicted as was his alleged accomplice Fournier [later found not guilty in a new trial], who was sentenced here for life. If innocent cannot blame him for his attitude."

He died an inmate of the new Stillwater Prison, succumbing to tubercular peritonitis, on December 18, 1921, at the age of forty-five. He was buried in an unmarked grave in St. Michael's Cemetery located south of the prison.

Eugene Caldwell remained in Quiring. He died of an accident in which his skull was crushed in April 1927. He was fifty-five. He is buried at the Quiring cemetery.

CHAPTER 7

A Double Hanging

1907

"I am not here to commute sentences; that power lies with another tribunal."

—Beltrami County District Court Judge W. S. McClenahan, October 5, 1907

The Honorable Judge William S. McClenahan of the fifteenth district court of Minnesota was born in Baltimore, Maryland, in June 1854. In 1880 he received his law degree from the University of Maryland. Two years later he moved to Brainerd, Minnesota, to enter general law practice. He chose Minnesota because George Holland, another lawyer, wrote to him about the beauty of the area and the plentiful opportunities for an attorney.

When I moved here, I found the streets were muddy, the winters brutal, and the insects unforgiving. Trees and lakes were everywhere. Everyone

District Court Judge William S. McClenahan.
Source: Minnesota Historical Society.

worked very hard and was always happy to greet one another. People concluded a transaction with a handshake and willingly offered assistance to others. I joined George Holland in his law office and slowly started to grow my practice, especially in real estate and criminal matters. I thought I would stay a short time because life on the East Coast had been a little easier. Nevertheless, I was a Brainerd city attorney for twelve years, and in 1900 I was elected district court judge. I grew to love it here. I will never leave.

In mid-September 1907, I had to leave temporarily to go by train from Brainerd to Bemidji. There I was assigned two first-degree murder trials. The defendants in these cases were Merton Munn, accused of killing his business partner's husband, and Peter Mathieson, who was accused of killing his friend. These two murder cases were conducted in a record time of just thirteen days, including one Sunday. In that short time period the juries were selected, all testimony was given, and verdicts were delivered. I like to keep things moving, for idle time is the devil's workshop.

The first trial began at 10:00 a.m. on Monday, September 23, at the Beltrami County Courthouse. County Attorney Henry Funkley[134] was the prosecutor, and E. D. Clough of Crookston represented the defendant, Merton S. Munn, a thirty-two-year old bachelor, who was accused of shooting August Franklin. Munn and the victim's wife were partners in a boarding house-restaurant in Spooner, where the Franklins and Munn resided.

---

134 J. D. Taylor of Warroad assisted Funkley.

Jury selection commenced that morning and was completed the following evening. The next day, Wednesday, September 25, County Attorney Funkley examined his witnesses. The first was T. J. Williams, who owned a hardware store in Baudette, just across the river from Spooner. August Franklin worked for Williams as a tinner.[135] Williams told the court that Franklin worked until nine the night he died.

Emil Engebretsen, who ran a saloon next to the restaurant, testified that he heard a shot at 1:00 a.m. and went over to the restaurant to find out what happened. He met Munn at the front of the restaurant, and Munn told him to take the gun because he had just shot Franklin. They went inside and waited for the marshal to arrive. Engebretsen testified that everything looked in order; that is, it did not look like a room where a fight had just taken place.

The state then introduced two men who testified that they saw Munn in bed with Mrs. Franklin. A man by the name of Quell testified that before Munn and Franklin had purchased the boarding house and started the restaurant, Mrs. Franklin was a waitress at a house where he and Munn were boarders. One night he went up to Munn's room at about nine o'clock. The door was open and the light still burning when he looked into Munn's room and saw him and Mrs. Franklin in bed together. The son of the boarding house's cleaning lady testified that he saw Mrs. Franklin and Munn in bed together many times. There were no more witnesses for the prosecution. In the early afternoon of the first day of this murder trial, the prosecution had completed their case.

The defense called the cleaning lady as a witness. She testified that her son's testimony was not the truth. She had never seen Munn and Mrs. Franklin in bed together, something she would have known. She did not know why her son would say that.

Mrs. Franklin was then called. She testified that she and Munn had purchased a building to venture into the room, board, and restaurant business in Spooner. Her husband helped secure the financing for the venture. On the early morning of June 14, 1907, she and her husband

135 A person who makes or repairs items made out of tin; tinsmith.

were arguing. Mr. Franklin thought that his wife and Munn were more than just business partners and he was going to drive Munn out of the house. During the argument, Mr. Franklin went to look for Munn, who was in another room of the house. She heard the shot and went to see what had taken place. A table separated the two men by about nine feet. Her husband, who was shot in the chest, was leaning against the east end of the table, while Munn was standing at the west end.

My crowded courtroom was motionless when the defendant was called to testify. Munn testified that he had purchased the gun to protect himself and Mrs. Franklin from her husband. He said that he was in the next room reading, while Franklin and his wife were in the kitchen arguing. He heard Mrs. Franklin tell her husband that she was leaving with the children and going to her father's. August Franklin told her that she could not do that and that he was going to "get" her and Munn. Munn testified that Franklin entered the room, they exchanged words, and Franklin struck him. He responded by grabbing his revolver and shooting Franklin once. He then went outside to seek assistance. He said he met Engebretsen, gave him his gun, and told him that he just shot a man. They then waited for help. He said he was just protecting himself.

All witnesses concluded their testimony by Thursday afternoon. At nine o'clock Friday morning, the county attorney made his presentation to the jury. He summarized the evidence of the case as premeditated murder because Munn had purchased the gun to shoot Franklin. Next Mr. Clough, of the defense, told the jury that his client might not have made the best choice in shooting Franklin, but it was clearly a case of self-defense. He added that Munn did not flee the scene but rather gave himself up and sought assistance for Franklin.

I gave my final instructions to the jury, and off they went for deliberation. Once the jury left the courtroom, I insisted that the jury selection begin on the Mathieson trial. There was no time to waste. By three in the afternoon no jurors had been picked, but the sheriff had scheduled twenty-five men to be interviewed the next day. I thought it should have been completed before this time. As I said, *tempus fugit*, gentlemen. (Time flies.)

That same evening, at 8:12, the Munn jury notified me that they had reached a decision. Spectators rushed to the courtroom to hear the verdict. As Munn was led in, he seemed relaxed and even joked with Sheriff Tom Bailey. The clerk read the verdict: "guilty as charged in the indictment" of murder in the first degree. Munn let out a huge sigh and looked somewhat stunned. The deputies led him back to his cell to await sentencing. I was disappointed that the jury had not found Munn guilty of some type of manslaughter, which is taking another person's life without premeditation. I do not believe the jury seriously considered the *animus nocendi* (state of mind) of the defendant.

At the conclusion of Munn's five-day trial, the *Bemidji Pioneer* reported, "The trial has been somewhat drawn out, but considering that many witnesses were examined, the proceedings were very expeditious. The work of securing the jury for the trial of Peter Mathieson, indicted for the murder of Johan Johanson, has been commenced and will be taken up and vigorously pushed."[136]

On the evening of Tuesday, October 1, twelve jurors were picked for the trial of Peter Mathieson for the shooting death of Johan Johanson. The state opened their case the following morning. County Attorney Funkley represented the prosecution, and John Gibbons and Graham M. Torrance represented Mathieson. The opening witnesses for the state testified to finding the body floating in Gull Lake in the spring of 1907. The corpse had been thrown through a hole in the ice some time in the previous February. Mathieson notified no one that his shack mate, Johanson, was missing or dead. They had lived on Gull Lake, near Tenstrike.

Witnesses testified that Mathieson spent the victim's money and cashed his checks. There was also testimony describing how Mathieson, who moved to Portland, Oregon, wrote from there to the local bank asking for Johanson's money. The bank notified the Bemidji sheriff's

136 *Bemidji Daily Pioneer*, September 28, 1907.

Gull Lake murder site near Tenstrike. The cabin on the left is where Mathieson and Johanson lived. Johanson's body was found near the shore, to the right and back of the neighboring shack. Notice the stumps of trees in photo. Source: *Bemidji Daily Pioneer*, June 17, 1907.

office that someone was retrieving money from Johanson's account and having it sent to Portland. The sheriff, suspecting it was Mathieson, sent a deputy, John Bailey, to Portland. Bailey arrested him when he picked up his mail.

I noticed that there was no testimony about how the two men, who had lived together in a shack on Gull Lake, got along.

At 7:30 p.m. on Wednesday, the prosecutor rested his case. Defense attorney Graham M. Torrance immediately stood to address the jury. He told them that the defendant Mathieson was a "stranger in a strange land."[137] He said that Mathieson had only been in the United States for a year and did not understand English or the American law. The attorney explained that Mathieson had been by himself and after the accident had not known what to do. He admitted that the defendant had done some "wrong things," yet that did not make him a premeditated murderer. Torrance concluded his opening statement and paused briefly in the silent courtroom. He then asked the defendant to go to the witness box to give testimony.

Peter Mathieson was a pale young man of twenty-eight, calm, and not the type one would expect to be on trial for first-degree murder. He answered questions in a low voice. I often had to remind him to talk

137 *Bemidji Daily Pioneer*, October 3, 1907.

louder. He said that he was from Denmark, where his parents farmed. He and some friends had left Denmark for the United States more than a year before, arriving in New York by boat in September 1906. He had traveled to Stillwater, then up to Blackduck. He had walked fourteen miles to Oakwood, where he found his friend Bigelow Peterson. The trip from Denmark to Oakwood had taken him a month and a half.

Mathieson described how he and Johanson were partners on the cross saw in cutting cordwood. On a February morning, they both awoke early. Mathieson made a fire and then told Johanson he was going to shoot some rabbits for breakfast. They had jointly purchased the revolver a few days earlier, and Johanson had taught Mathieson how to use it. Mathieson laid the gun down on the table and proceeded to put wood into the stove. Suddenly the gun went off by itself, and the bullet hit Johanson in the eye. Johanson, who was sitting on his bed, fell onto it and did not move.

Mathieson testified that he then went outside for a short time. He returned to find that Johanson had not moved. Not knowing what to do, he walked to the town of Tenstrike and drank. He returned to find Johanson dead on his bed. Mathieson stripped him of his clothes, chipped a hole in the ice of Gull Lake, and put the body in the water. He took Johanson's clothes and hid them in the woods, miles from their residence. I interrupted the testimony, stating that it was after eight o'clock and getting too late for further testimony. The court was then adjourned until the next morning at nine o'clock.

On Thursday morning, Peter Mathieson completed his testimony. He said that, shortly after the shooting, he moved from Tenstrike to Bemidji. There he cashed the checks belonging to Johanson and "blew in"[138] the proceeds. He then traveled to Portland, where he was arrested. The county attorney questioned Mathieson about how he had cashed Johanson's checks, how he had learned to write Johanson's signature so well, and how he had communicated so successfully to get certificates of deposits from a dead man's account. Mathieson explained the

---

138 Ibid.

procedures he used. The county attorney then attempted to introduce evidence that he had men examine the revolver that shot Johanson and that they were unable to make it fire on its own. I denied the state's request because I knew the defense would come up with some men who would say the revolver could go off by itself. That would just lengthen the time of the trial, something I seldom approve of.

The following day, Friday, October 4, the state made its presentation to the jury. The county attorney went after Mathieson rather aggressively, telling the jury that the death of Johan Johanson was not accidental. He said the gun could not have gone off by itself, and explained how the defendant hid the body and clothes and then spent the victim's money. The defendant was not an ignorant immigrant, the county attorney argued, but a "shrewd criminal."

At 1:20 in the afternoon Torrance made the defense presentation to the jury. He explained how his client was ignorant of the ways people live in the United States and doubted that Mathieson would intentionally kill his closest and maybe only friend. He said that his client had made poor choices, but that they did not make him a murderer. I gave the jury their instructions to determine if this factum (deed) was accidental or premeditated, which would be murder in the first degree. They left for deliberation at 3:30.

The following morning, Saturday, October 5, at 10:30, the jury reached a verdict. The clerk read their decision. "Guilty as charged!" It was another first-degree murder conviction for the Beltrami County Attorney's office. Mathieson looked shocked and on the verge of crying.

Since it was October in Beltrami County, everyone was very busy preparing for the winter. The courts were no different. The same day the jury returned a guilty verdict of murder, everyone left for lunch and returned at two o'clock for the sentencing. I had only two hours to determine their sentences.

Now here was my dilemma. There was no doubt in my mind that Mathieson killed his friend to get his money. It was premeditated, period. He hid the body and the victim's clothes, then fled the area.

I had no trouble issuing him the sentence of death by hanging. That was what he deserved according to the law. Munn, on the other hand, shot his victim but then ran to get help for him. His motivation was not for money, but rather, as he testified, to protect himself. He did cooperate in the investigation. I did not like witnesses testifying that Munn was having sexual relations with the victim's wife. True or not, it did him no good, especially in the eyes of the good Christians on the jury. I disagreed with their verdict. I wanted to show him some leniency for his immediate repentance and cooperation. However, if I showed leniency for Munn, such as life in prison, I felt I would have to do it for Mathieson too. That I could not do. Mathieson was a premeditated murderer. I prayed on it and decided to follow the rule of the law. God help me.

The sentencing for Munn was held at two o'clock in the afternoon. Mathieson's sentencing would follow immediately. Munn appeared with his attorney, E. D. Clough, and was escorted by Deputy Arne Solberg. I asked him if he had anything to say, and Munn replied, "Nothing to say, except some awful lies have been told." His attorney then pleaded to the court that his client could not be guilty of premeditated murder. I told the attorney, "The jury has passed on the facts in this case. There could be but one defense; that did not exist."[139] A newspaper reporter described the silence in the courtroom as "painful" when I read the sentence, which I did with some difficulty:

> *It is ordered and adjudged that you, Merton S. Munn, indicted under the name of Martin S. Munn, as punishment for the crime of murder in the first degree, be taken hence to the common jail of Beltrami County,[140] Minnesota, and confined there in, and thereafter for the period of three calendar months, from this date, to wit: the fifth day of*

139 *Bemidji Daily Pioneer*, October 5, 1907.

140 Judge McClenahan broke down at this point and had to leave the courtroom. He returned a short time later and completed the sentencing.

> *October, 1907, and at a time to be fixed by the governor of this state and upon his warrant, that you be taken hence to the place of execution, by the sheriff of Beltrami County, and there be hanged by the neck, until you are dead.*

Officer Andrew Johnson escorted Munn out of the courtroom. Munn broke down in tears as he left the courtroom.

Mathieson appeared a short time later, at 2:31. His attorneys, Gibbons and Torrance, accompanied him to the courtroom. I asked Mathieson if he had anything to say. Mathieson replied, "Nothing." Graham Torrance then made a plea to the court for clemency. He asked that justice be tempered with mercy. I replied, "I am firmly convinced of the guilt of this defendant. I cannot conceive of a more deliberate and merciless murder than that for which he has been convicted."[141]

I then read the same statement to Mathieson that I did to Munn: death by hanging. The defendant was pale and blank faced. Officer Julius Dahl escorted him from the courtroom. A few stayed in the courtroom after Mathieson left.

I returned to my home in Brainerd by train later that evening, but my work on these trials was not over. Both defendants presented appeals to the Minnesota Pardon Board. Mathieson also wrote a letter to the Danish newspaper in Omaha, Nebraska, explaining his dire situation, and he asked for their help. The paper made an appeal to all Danish Americans to write letters on behalf of Mathieson. Many people, including some prominent Minnesotans, sent letters of appeal for Mathieson to the Minnesota Board of Pardons.[142] Not only did Mathieson have the Danish taking up his cause, but also the anti–capital punishment advocates supported his appeal.

Mr. Torrance, Mathieson's trial attorney, appeared before the state Board of Pardons on Tuesday, January 14, 1908. He requested that the

141 *Bemidji Daily Pioneer*, October 5, 1907.

142 The board consisted of Governor John A. Johnson, Chief Justice Charles M. Start, and Attorney General Edward T. Young.

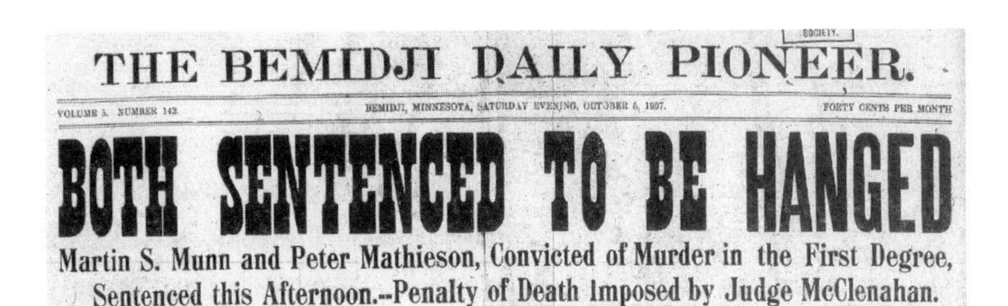
THE BEMIDJI DAILY PIONEER.

VOLUME 5. NUMBER 142. BEMIDJI, MINNESOTA, SATURDAY EVENING, OCTOBER 6, 1907. FORTY CENTS PER MONTH

BOTH SENTENCED TO BE HANGED

Martin S. Munn and Peter Mathieson, Convicted of Murder in the First Degree, Sentenced this Afternoon.--Penalty of Death Imposed by Judge McClenahan.

Source: *Bemidji Daily Pioneer*, October 6, 1907.

board grant a hearing for commutation of the sentence from hanging to life in prison. He explained to the board how the gun went off accidentally. He said that after the trial was over, his experts examined the gun and concluded that the gun would snap when it received a jar. He explained that Mathieson did not know anything about the nature of the certificate of deposit until a friend in Tenstrike, a man by the name of Jacobson, showed him one and how he could cash them. Torrance told the board that the jury asked the judge for clemency in issuing the sentencing, something I had disregarded. The board continued the case.

The Board of Pardons met on the afternoon of January 21, 1908. Both the Munn and the Mathieson cases were to be reviewed at this session.

Mr. Clough, along with Munn's relatives and friends, spoke dramatically on Munn's behalf. The case was reviewed thoroughly to show the board that the killing was self-defense. Their endeavor concluded with a plea to give Munn a new trial or commute his sentence. The board discussed the case, but denied the petition for commutation of the sentence. The hanging of Merton Munn in sixteen days was still on.

Next entered Mathieson's Danish advocates, headed by a prominent Danish-American attorney from St. Paul, Harry S. Swenson. Accompanying Swenson was former Governor John Lind, Dr. John C. Nelson, the Danish Consul, and C. C. Rasmussen, the Danish publisher. The board reviewed the case thoroughly. The distinguished assembly of Danes stressed how unfair the punishment was for a person so unfamiliar with the laws in the United States. The Danish team prevailed, as the board ordered the Mathieson sentence commuted to life imprisonment.

The next day, January 22, 1908, I heard that Mathieson's life sentence was commuted and Munn's was not. I immediately wrote a letter to Governor Johnson and the Board of Pardons stating that of the two I sentenced to death, Munn was more entitled to clemency. I wrote that there was an element of self-defense in the Munn case, an element missing in the Mathieson case. "One of the elements in the case was the question of intimacy between Munn and Mrs. Franklin, this being used by the prosecution as a motive for the murder, aside from the alleged attack on Munn. When the case was being argued before the pardon board it was admitted that there was some evidence tending to prove such relations. It was also claimed that Franklin consented to the partnership between Munn and his wife and assisted in the leasing of the building in which the restaurant was conducted."[143]

Three days later, upon receipt of the letter, the board commuted the sentence of Munn to life in prison. The board stated that it had based its reversal of the previous Tuesday's hearing "on the recommendation of Judge W. S. McClenahan of Brainerd who imposed the sentence."[144]

My quandary was settled by the Board of Pardons when they commuted both sentences to life in prison. I may not agree with both of their decisions, but they were out of my hands. I believe these men will ultimately be judged by a higher power.

Whatever happened to . . . ?

Peter Nielson Mathieson was admitted on January 29, 1908, to Stillwater Prison, where he was assigned inmate number 2321. He was described as twenty-nine years of age, five foot eight inches tall, 142 pounds, with light blue eyes and sandy hair and beard.

There was no new trial in Peter Nielson Mathieson's future. He was assigned various jobs at the prison and was not considered a

143 *Bemidji Daily Pioneer*, January 27, 1908.

144 Ibid.

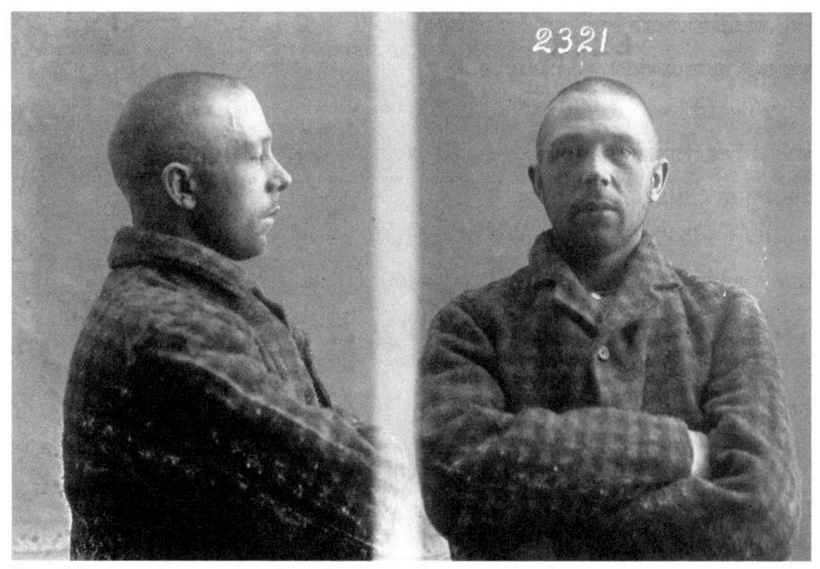

Peter Mathieson's mug shot from Stillwater Prison, 1908. Source: Minnesota Historical Society.

troublesome inmate until 1924. Mathieson did not have many visitors because he killed one of his few friends and his family was in Denmark. So he sought the attention of the daughter of another inmate, Peter Albert of Cass County, who was serving seven years. The woman, Ms. Herrick of Walker, started corresponding by mail with Mathieson and shortly after accepted his offer of marriage. She applied for permission, to the governor, to marry Mathieson in July of 1924. Governor Preus and the Board of Pardons denied her request.

Prison life was repetitive and somewhat hopeless for inmates like Peter Mathieson. "Lifers" had to spend twenty-five years in prison before they could apply for a pardon. There were not many activities outside of their work to keep their minds busy, so some of the inmates would become what was termed "stir-crazy."[145] Mathieson started to suffer from auditory and visual hallucinations, his speech was sometimes incoherent, and he was not responsive to direction from the prison staff. He was soon talking with God, who informed him that he was a brother of Christ.

145 The word *stir* is slang for prison, probably first used in the mid-nineteenth century.

On November 25, 1926, Mathieson claimed the world was going to end and tossed all of his books and personal belongs out of his cell into the gallery. He would laugh to himself and attempt to make conversation with everyone who walked by his cell. This type of conduct resulted in his being placed in the detention cell. The following day he threw his belongings out of the detention cell. When the assigned officer questioned him about his behavior, Mathieson just stared at him. A physician examined him and recommended that he stay in detention and that Mathieson was a candidate for the state hospital.

On January 22, 1927, George H. Freeman, superintendent at St. Peter State Hospital, wrote a summary of his examination of Peter Mathieson. His report stated that Mathieson talked incoherently and believed he had killed because he was supposed to. Mathieson claimed he often spoke with God and Christ and was recently informed that the Virgin Mary was his mother. The doctor concluded that Mathieson was insane and could not function at the prison, recommending that since he had committed murder, he should be sent to the Asylum for the Criminally Insane.

On January 27, 1927, nineteen years after being incarcerated at Stillwater, Peter Mathieson was transferred to the Asylum for the Criminally Insane at St. Peter's Hospital. He never left. He wrote the warden of the Stillwater Prison occasionally, telling him how Satan was running the prison. He died of pernicious anemia on October 15, 1947, at the age of sixty-nine. He is buried at the hospital cemetery, plot number 1771.

Merton S. Munn was admitted to Stillwater Prison on January 31, 1908, where he was assigned inmate number 2323. The prison admitting documents describe him as thirty-two years of age, white, single, Baptist, five foot six inches tall, 124 pounds, with a medium-dark complexion, light blue eyes, and chestnut hair and beard.

Prior to leaving for Stillwater with Sheriff Bailey and Deputy Andrew Johnson, Munn wrote a letter of thanks, which was published

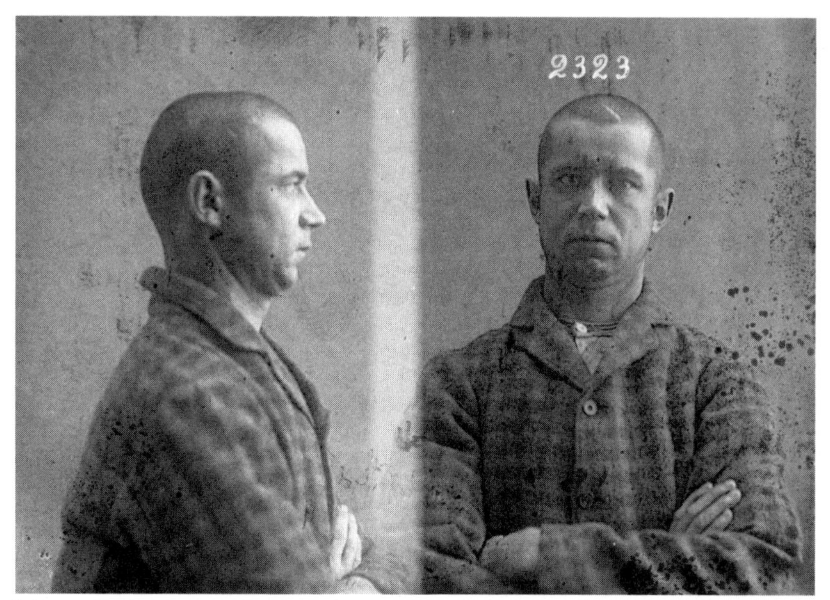

Merton S. Munn's mug shot from Stillwater Prison, 1908. Source: Minnesota Historical Society.

in the *Bemidji Daily Pioneer* on January 31, 1908. Munn thanked everyone who had supported him, including the local Presbyterian pastor S. E. P. White, the Bemidji Salvation Army, the judge, his attorneys, and his friends. He concluded his letter:

> *Trusting that at some future day the truth may be known,*
> *May God reward them all for what they have done.*

There was no new trial in Munn's future. While Mathieson had a large Danish following, Munn absorbed a large contingency of veterans from the Spanish-American War. While in prison, he corresponded with their veterans' association and subscribed to their newsletter.

As years passed Munn showed himself generally to be a model inmate. He was subject to depression, however, as shown by an incident in 1926. On Sunday, March 21, 1926, Munn attempted suicide. He cut his scrotum with a knife and sat on the toilet intending to bleed to death. He changed his mind, sewed himself up with a needle and thread, and retired to his bed. The pain was so great that he informed

Lifer Crowds 25 Lost Years Into Single Day

Much Has Changed Since 1908—Near Beer and Filling Stations.

By Paul Schmidt.

At the age of 58, Merton S. Munn walked out into a new world Wednesday.

It was a world far different from that which he had retained in his memory for a quarter of a century. It was a world that startled and amazed, but did not frighten him. Ahead lay opportunity to experience the things of which he had read and heard, but which until Wednesday had belonged to other persons, more fortunate.

Merton Munn, ex-convict, was ready and eager to take his place in that new world.

Until Monday he had been one of those beings, known only by a number, whose identities are submerged in the stern routine and uniformity of penitentiary existence.

On that day he had been granted a parole. As soon as the necessary arrangements had been made, he would be free again to take his place in the outside world. His debt to society, incurred when he killed a man at Spooner, Minn., 25 years ago, had been paid.

Wednesday all was ready for his release from Stillwater. His friends of the United Spanish War Veterans' association, who for 20 years had worked to bring about freedom for him, also had satisfied the law which requires that a parolee may be released from prison only when provision has been made for his future.

Shortly after noon Wednesday all was ready. Merton Munn walked out of the prison yard, into the friendlier atmosphere of the prison office.

That one act seemed to change everything for the small, gray-haired veteran of the Spanish war. A few minutes earlier he still had been subject to the prison regulations. Now he was free.

The scene in the clerical office of employes who had known him for years crowded around him to tell him how happy they were that at last he had been freed.

Surrounded by these friends, Munn signed cards and papers, and

(Continued on Page 13, Column 1.)

Merton S. Munn.

Merton S. Munn released from prison.
Source: *Minneapolis Tribune*, January 12, 1933.

a guard, who transferred him to the prison hospital. He recovered in a short time.

In October 1932, Munn and nine other "lifers," all of whom had served at least twenty-five years in prison, were eligible for parole. Munn contended, throughout his twenty-five year stay at the prison, that he had murdered in self-defense. The Minnesota Department of Foreign Wars and the U.S. Spanish-American War veterans petitioned for the parole of Munn. Henry Funkley, the former Beltrami County attorney, petitioned the Board of Pardons, stating that Munn should have never been convicted of first-degree murder. Documentation from Judge McClenahan showed that the judge felt that Munn should not have been convicted of any greater offense than manslaughter.

On Monday, January 9, 1933, Merton S. Munn was granted parole after twenty-five years of incarceration. However, the board would not release an inmate until the inmate had accommodations and employment. Immediately William R. Boyce, commandant at the Old Soldiers' Home,[146] wrote the board that Munn could live at the home. Munn was receiving a small pension from the military, which gave him funds to live on. His parole was approved.

On Wednesday, January 11, 1933, Munn was freed from Stillwater. He was given a new suit and his savings, his personal belongings

146 Now called the Minneapolis Veteran Home, 5101 Minnehaha Ave. S.

were placed in a small box, and off he went. His attorney, W. T. Coe of Minneapolis, met him at the prison to give him a ride to the soldiers' home. This was the first automobile ride of Munn's life. He had only been out of Stillwater Prison once in twenty-five years, and that was when they transferred prisoners from the old prison to the present facility. On the ride to the soldiers' home they stopped for a malted milk at a drugstore near the Wold-Chamberlain airfield, and then went sightseeing at some of the new housing developments along the way.

Once released, Munn worked sparingly, for his health was not the best. He wintered in Louisiana and stayed with his brother in Minneapolis during the summer. There is no death record for Munn in Minnesota.

Judge William S. McClenahan was the city attorney for twelve years before he being elected judge in the Fifteenth Judicial District Court in 1900. He was a district court judge for thirty years and very well respected in the state legal society. Many times he was offered federal positions, but he loved what he was doing in Brainerd and was not interested in moving.

Judge McClenahan was a member of the Masons, a fifty-year member of the Crow Wing County Bar, and a member of the Brainerd Elks.

He died at his home at 423 North Bluff Street in Brainerd at the age of seventy-eight, after a long and tenuous illness. His wife and their son, William E. McClenahan, survived him. His well-attended funeral was held on September 13, 1932, at St. Francis Catholic Church. He was interned at Evergreen Cemetery in Brainerd.

Spooner is a township and was named for Marshall Spooner, a state judge. Spooner was largely destroyed by the Baudette Fire of 1910. Spooner Township adjoined the Village of Spooner, which merged with Baudette in 1954.

CHAPTER 8

Family Silence

1909

"If it had been an ordinary case of murder I would have excluded nobody, but this was a case in which a lot of morbid curiosity seekers, attracted here by an unfortunate girl's distress, simply wanted to crowd in and satisfy their desires to look at another person's trouble and that person possibly demented."

—Ramsey County District Judge Hugo O. Hanft,
May 20, 1909, after clearing his courtroom

HENRY A. SPANGENBERG, THE THIRTY-YEAR-OLD owner and operator of a butcher shop at 313 West Seventh Street in St. Paul,[147] was a neighbor and friend of Louis Arbogast, the victim in this case. Henry lived above his meat market, which was across the street and a little south of the Arbogast residence.

147 Corner of Grand and West Seventh, St. Paul.

I will start from the beginning and let you experience it just as I did. It was about 4:25 a.m. on Thursday, May 13, 1909, and I was coming downstairs to prepare my shop for the day when I heard terrible screams from the front porch of 286 West Seventh Street.[148] "Won't someone help Papa?" Ida Arbogast pleaded hysterically. I raced over and saw the paperboy, Isadore Abrahamson, rushing into the house. When I arrived, Ida's sister Minnie had just joined her on the porch. I followed young Isadore into the house to determine the trouble. I ran up the stairs to the second-floor bedroom, where I found my friend Louis Arbogast on fire in his smoldering bed. His head was bashed in, and blood was spattered everywhere. I had never seen such a gruesome scene. The paperboy had grabbed a rug and begun to put out the fire, and I joined him, using another rug.

Dr. Gauger, another neighbor, arrived a short time later, followed by the ambulance and police. Louis was transported to St. Luke's Hospital, where he died as he was being rolled into the operating room. Ramsey County Coroner A. W. Miller pronounced him dead. The preliminary conclusion was a possible suicide.

When I heard about the coroner's preliminary report, I could not believe it. I knew the wound on Louis's head could not have been self-inflicted. I think the police were trying to minimize the tragedy in order not to alarm the public. But that was no suicide.

I was shaken up by what I'd seen. Louis and I had been competitors. His butcher shop was located just down the street from mine, at 201 West Seventh Street.[149] (Of course, with 157 meat markets[150] in St. Paul, some of them are bound to be near each other.) But he was also a friend of mine.

---

148 St. Croix Cleaners, 286 West Seventh, St. Paul.

149 South of Kellogg on West Seventh, St. Paul, next to the Liffey Irish Pub.

150 *Polk St. Paul Directory*, 1909.

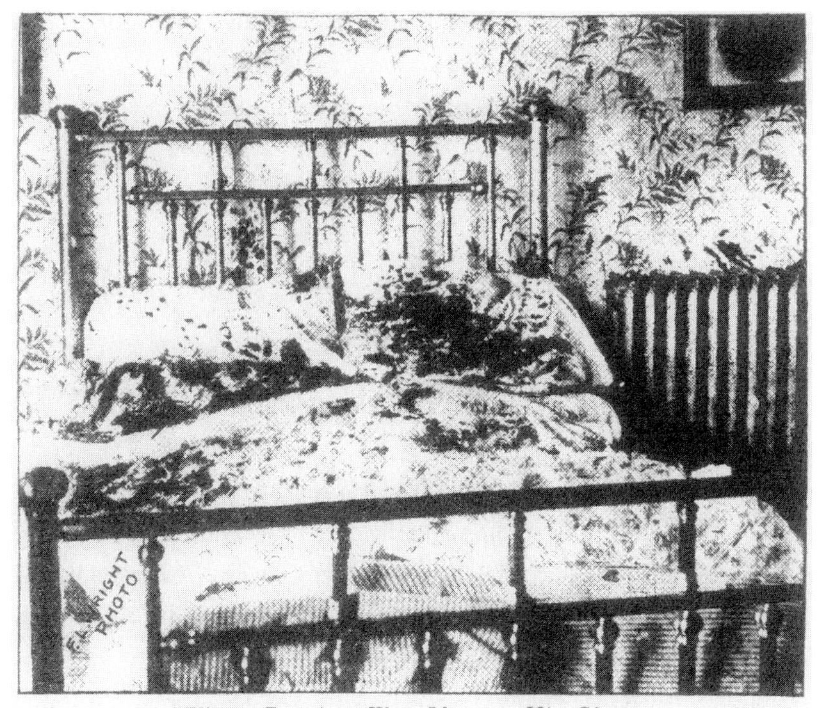

Bed in which Louis Arbogast was killed. Source: *St. Paul Dispatch*, May 15, 1909.

Louis had told me that he was born in Germany and immigrated to the United States when he was seventeen. I knew that he'd worked odd jobs in St. Louis and then moved to St. Paul in 1879 to work for the MacMillan Packing Company. After five years there, he opened his own shop. He was a stout man with a mustache. I always thought of him as a good and loving father to his five daughters. Four of those daughters lived with Louis and his wife, Minna, at their home: Louise was twenty-three, Ida twenty-two, Minnie eighteen, and Flora—nicknamed "Babe"—fourteen.

Louis and Minna's bedroom was located on the east side of the house on the second floor. Ida and Louise shared the bedroom next to theirs, and Minnie and Flora were in the bedroom across the hall.

I was still at the Arbogasts' home, offering my support to Minna and her daughters, when the police arrived. They spoke first to Minna, who was sitting in the front room. She was suffering from burns on her back. She and her daughters were nearly hysterical, and the confusion and chaos kept the police from getting much information about what had taken place.

At about 6:45 a.m., their married daughter, Emma Ulmer, arrived with her husband, Lawrence. They lived two blocks away on South Exchange Street. I left shortly afterward. I later read in the paper that around 9:30, Lawrence Ulmer and Detective Michael Daly walked down to the basement where they discovered a four-pound axe sticking out from underneath a coal pile. The axe was covered with blood.

According to the paper, the bed sheet was soaked in kerosene, except where Louis had laid, and blood was spattered on the floor, the walls, and the ceiling from the swinging of the axe. The police presumed Minna had not been in the bed when the kerosene was tossed on it. She had burns on her back and a small part of her left side, which they thought happened when she climbed onto the burning bed. Louis was seriously burned after he was attacked with the axe. The police found the bathtub on the second floor half full of reddish water. On the sides of the bathtub were patches of blood, some of which had dried. Behind the tub they found bloody nightclothes. The Arbogasts' daughters told the police the clothes were their mother's.

Minna (Wilhelmine) Arbogast was a small, stout German housewife easily capable of swinging an axe. The family could afford a servant, but Minna wanted to do her own housework. She had been opposed to Louise and Ida's cashiering in her husband's meat store, but Louis's word was law in the home. He insisted that his daughters help out in his store because he wanted his family to be the ones to handle the money. He was also devoted to his daughters and enjoyed their company during business hours. Minna was a nervous person prone to worry, so much so that she would become bedridden when one of her daughters was ill. None of us neighbors had seen her leave the house in months.

St. Paul police detectives Sweeney and Daly continued the questioning. Minna told the detectives that during the night she got up to go to the bathroom. She said her husband was sleeping soundly. She said she took a bath and went back to her room. Once she saw her husband and the burning bed, she screamed, fainted, and fell on the bed. Both Louise and her mother were difficult to interview. Louise, who has lovely black hair, brown eyes, and a dark complexion, could not account for her actions after she awoke. She was confused and very unclear as to what she had seen, said, or done. The family has been trying to help Louise with her mental problems for many years. She often hallucinates and has difficulty sleeping. She's been sent several times to St. Luke's Hospital for a rest. Three days prior to the murder, she returned from a three-week stay with the Henry Schwand family in Eau Claire, Wisconsin.

Louise Arbogast. Source: *St. Paul Daily*, May 18, 1909.

The police discovered that Louise was a firm believer in fortune-tellers. The police had recently rid St. Paul of fortune-tellers, sending most of them to relocate in Minneapolis. Louise had to take a cable car over to Minneapolis to meet with one. Louise once told me about a fortune-teller who said a man had been in the house while the family was asleep and predicted he would return to do harm to her and her sister Ida.[151] Louise developed a fear of this man, which in some instances caused hallucinations. She absolutely believed that a mysterious man was pursuing her and her sister. I never saw any evidence of it, but she continued to be anxious about it.

Ida told police she was awakened by her mother's screams. She rushed to her parents' room and saw her parents' bed in flames and her

151 *St. Paul Dispatch*, May 14, 1909.

father beaten around the head. Her mother was on her side of the bed with her back to her husband. Ida thought she was sleeping or had fainted. Ida grabbed her mother and pulled her to the corner of the room. Her mother tried desperately to free herself and go back to the bed. They struggled in the hallway. Minna screamed that she wanted to join her husband. Ida would not let her go. As a result, they both fell, rolling down the staircase together. The other girls were awakened and ran to the room. Ida told the police that after seeing their father on fire, Minnie and Babe ran to the street and yelled for help.

Minnie stated that she was awakened by screams and ran to her parents' room. She then ran downstairs, where she joined her sister in screaming for help. She didn't see anyone attacking her father.

Flora, the youngest, called "Babe" or "Baby," told authorities she was awakened by the screaming and ran to her parents' room. She saw her father and ran downstairs yelling for someone to help. She also didn't see anyone attack her father.

The St. Paul newspaper reported that the Louis Arbogast Meat Company manager, Charles J. Klabunde, had stated in an interview that morning, "I was never so shocked in my life. Mr. Arbogast had no enemies as far as I know. Mr. Arbogast's home life was without a jar. He never had any domestic trouble and he was a man devoted to business and his family. His daughter Ida had been bookkeeper for him for a time." When Louis didn't show up at work, Mr. Klabunde went to his house around 6:30 a.m. to see if he was sick. Louise told him, "Father is dead, and there is something wrong with the gas." Mr. Klabunde had returned to work assuming it was a suicide. When asked if Louise had mentioned the blood, the axe, or the fire, Mr. Klabunde replied, "Not a word. I thought afterward, that was unusual too. But she was very much upset and excited."[152]

At eleven o'clock that morning, police left with the axe wrapped in newspaper. The police also took Louis's and Minna's nightclothes. The police, probably at the family's request, put the bloody mattress and

152 *St. Paul Pioneer Press*, May 14, 1909.

Side view of Arbogast home showing the "murder room." Front view of Arbogast home at 286 West 7th Street, St. Paul. Source: *St. Paul Daily*, May 13, 1909.

pillows under a shed in the backyard. The reporters, eager to observe the gruesome sight, went to the shed for a look. The daughters asked them to leave. The family refused to make any comments to the press.

A beat cop confided in me that back at headquarters, the police were having difficulty finding a motive for the murder. The family has some internal disagreements, but never anything significant. The Arbogasts didn't have a history of domestic disturbances. The police learned that a friend of Louis's, William Manteuffel, was at the Arbogast home the night before the murder. Mr. Manteuffel told the police that he and Louis discussed an upcoming trip to the Yukon planned for June 1. It was Manteuffel's understanding that Louis had announced to his three older daughters that he, Minna, and Flora would be leaving with Manteuffel for the Klondike. The police considered the possibility that there might have been some sort of argument regarding the trip. Could this have created strife within the family?

Another police theory was murder for money. The family business was doing very well and had a prosperous future, but there was no insurance policy to cash in. In fact, Minna and their daughters would be more financially secure if Louis was alive. The police thought that Louis might have had an enemy, but everyone they talked to said he had no enemies. I certainly didn't know of any. By early afternoon on the day of the murder, the police had suspects but no motive.

The police decided Minna had to be involved because of the blood on her nightclothes and the fact that she did not hear anything when the murder happened just a few feet away from the bathroom. They also thought that Louise was involved because she gave confusing accounts about how her father died. She told Mr. Klabunde, manager of her family's meat shop, that her dad died from a damaged gas jet, but neglected to mention her father's injuries. She then told a neighbor a completely different story, saying her father was murdered. The police believed that Louise was insane and could not account for her actions. They concluded Louise and her mother were involved in the murder and the other family members were not.

At three in the afternoon of the murder, Minna was transported to the City Hospital under police supervision. Louise was taken to St. Luke's mental ward for evaluation. The police eventually wanted to take both women downtown for further interrogation.

The *St. Paul Dispatch* wrote on May 14, the day following the murder:

> *An ordinary murderer would have been satisfied with the deathblow, perhaps; but whoever killed Louis Arbogast made gruesome slaughter of the work. Then the axe was taken down to the cellar with tell tale drops of blood dripping on the steps to guide the detectives in their search. It is contended that a sane person would not have bungled so much.*

Police Chief John O'Connor announced that he and his assistant, John Clark, had joined Detectives Sweeney and Daly in the investigation. They drew some conclusions based on what they had learned so far.

Louis and Minna Arbogast. Source: *St. Paul Pioneer Press*, May 14, 1909.

Because the bed was soaked everywhere but where Louis was lying, the kerosene must have been poured on before Minna lay down on the bed, or she was in another part of the house when the crime was committed. The authorities concluded that Minna wanted them to believe she was in bed during the murder and the burning of the bed. It stood to reason she would have been burnt as badly as her husband if she had been in bed when the fire started and up until the time Ida came into the room.[153] Her burns began at the shoulder and worked their way down to below her waist and onto part of her leg. She had also changed her story, saying she was in the bathroom when the murder occurred.

On Saturday, May 15, Minna told the police she was well enough to speak to them. County Attorney Richard O'Brien, Assistant Chief of Police John Clark, and Detectives Sweeney and Daly questioned her at City Hospital. I was surprised the big fellow, Chief O'Connor, was not involved in the interviews. Dr. Arthur Ancker, superintendent of

153 Summary from *St. Paul Dispatch*, May 14, 1909.

the City Hospital, gave strict orders that Minna could not be spoken to except by the police. She was suffering from exhaustion and nervousness.

I think the police assumed they would obtain a confession from her but were surprised when Minna implicated Louise as a suspect in the murder. She said Louise should have stayed in St. Luke's Hospital, where she was undergoing treatment. Minna said on the night of the murder that Louise was walking around the house when everyone else was sleeping. (Louise does that often—she has trouble sleeping.) Minna said that at about four in the morning she did not feel well, so she went to the bathroom. When she returned to the bedroom, Louise was standing in the doorway. Minna entered the room and saw her husband lying in the bed, which was on fire. She recalled that she yelled and fell on the burning bed next to her husband.

Minna told authorities that Louise and her father were very close. For several years, Louise was his cashier at the store. Minna told the authorities that once everyone in the household realized what Louise had done, they began to clean up the blood. The family wanted to protect her. However, the younger girls panicked, ran downstairs, and screamed for help. Other people then came running up to the bedroom. Minna also told the police that the Wednesday before the murder, Louise was unusually restless during the night. As the questioning concluded, the police had a new prime suspect. A meeting was arranged for the following evening with Minna, Louise, the police, and the county attorney.

Dr. Belle Walrath, the doctor who was treating both Minna and Louise, discussed her beliefs and findings with the *St. Paul Dispatch*:

> *I am sure Ida was asleep at the time of the murder. But I am just as sure that Louise was awake. She never sleeps, except under the influence of a drug. It was evidently the work of a crazed mind. Louise did come back from her visit very much improved in health. She gained eight pounds and looked very well, she had not of course, fully recovered. When she was at St. Luke's Hospital last winter they [the*

> *family] were afraid of her, and I did not think she was well enough to go home. But her father insisted that she was. Of course the expense of keeping her there was considerable. And when I wanted them to send her to Hudson, the same objection was made. Dr. Riggs has treated her, and Dr. Sweeney helped me with the case at St. Luke's Hospital.*[154]

When the reporters asked the doctor about Louise's present mental state, Walrath responded:

> *Louise talks continually at the hospital about the crime, about what the papers are saying, what people are saying. She said this morning that they were discussing the purchase of an automobile the night before the murder. And that the father thought of buying an old automobile, but the daughters wanted a new one. But she is extremely nervous and what she says has little value. She cannot be left alone for a moment. Mrs. Arbogast wants me to go to see her at the City Hospital, which the police have given permission.*

On May 18, Dr. Arthur Sweeney, who also evaluated Louise before she left St. Luke's during her last visit, told the *St. Paul Dispatch*:

> *There are reasons why it would not be proper for me to go into details at this time, but I will say that Miss Arbogast [Louise] is now insane and has been for the past six months, as least. I warned her father not to take her home in her mental condition, and told him that if he did so she would probably injure herself or someone else.*

The *Dispatch* also wrote, "One of the St. Luke's interns said today Louis Arbogast committed suicide, because he took the chance which proved

---

154 May 15, 1909.

fatal, with his eyes opened to the truth." Dr. Walrath added, "There is no doubt whatsoever of Louise's mental condition. She was a victim of advanced melancholia, with a strong suicidal tendency, and always with the homicidal possibility. As a rule, melancholia tends to suicide, but there are cases, and this was one of them, in which the homicidal tendency is strongly developed."[155]

Now before I go any further, I have to tell you that Louise and I were engaged at this time. She is a pretty girl who suffers from severe mood swings. When we first started seeing each other, we would go for walks, and I would never know what mood she would be in. When she is happy, she is loving, caring, and a delight to be with. I know someday the doctors will make her better for good, but I think the death of her father really put her in a dark place. Sometimes she acted as if she didn't know me. During this time after the murder, our relationship diminished. Few people knew of our love for each other.

On the following Sunday afternoon, I attended Louis's funeral. Family members, relatives, and close friends, including me, were the only people allowed into the Arbogast home before the funeral. There were thousands of people in the streets, and hundreds looked on from nearby buildings as members of the family moved in and out of the house. The crowd followed the procession down Seventh and Fourth Streets to Christ Church,[156] where they stood during the ceremonies. The procession was made up of thirteen closed carriages with three or four open carriages in the rear. The blinds were pulled on the carriages carrying the family. After the funeral, Louis was buried at Oakland Cemetery.

I learned from a police customer of mine that after the funeral, about 5:00 p.m., a meeting was held in Minna's room at City Hospital. Louise, Minna, Assistant Chief of Police Clark, County Attorney O'Brien, detectives Sweeney and Dale, and an interpreter were present.

---

155 *St. Paul Dispatch*, May 18, 1909.

156 Fourth Street and the northwest corner of Franklin (The church and street are gone. The church used to be located about four blocks west of Assumption Catholic church, which is still there.)

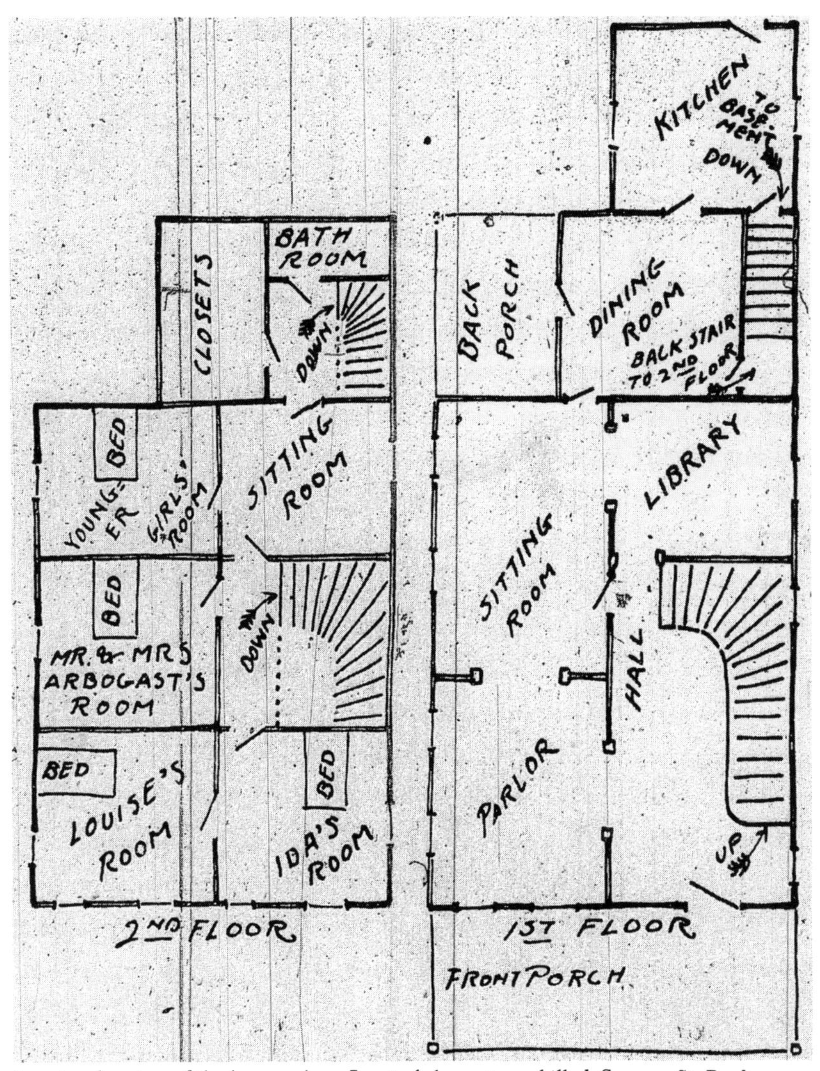

Interior drawing of the home where Louis Arbogast was killed. Source: *St. Paul Dispatch*, May 25, 1909.

(It really bothered me that Louise and Minna had no one there to support them, like a lawyer, family member, or even me.) Minna was silent until Louise came over and sat next to her on the bed. Minna said to her daughter, "Louise, it is either you or me. Tell the truth. You were outside Father's door when I came from the bathroom. You must tell the truth." Louise looked straight ahead in silence. Her mother then spoke in German and said, "You said you did not do it, but I know you did."[157] Her statement was followed by silence from everyone present. Suddenly both women broke down in tears as they hugged each other. The police officers and county attorney were not able to obtain any other statements from them that day.

The next morning, the Ramsey County Attorney Office issued a criminal complaint against Louise, based on her mother's statement. Louise was escorted from St. Luke's Hospital to Judge Hugo Hanft's courtroom for arraignment. After the clerk read the complaint that charged Louise with premeditated murder, the judge told her that she did not have to enter a plea at that time. I was there and could tell that Louise understood the severity of the situation. She responded to the judge by saying, "God will be my attorney. I did not harm my father, truly. I did not harm my father. Good sir, I don't need an attorney, Mr. Daly." She then turned to Detective Daly and said, "I don't need an attorney, do I? I did nothing. Mr. Daly knows I did nothing."[158] I wanted to get up and embrace her. She looked so vulnerable.

Louise then turned toward prosecuting attorney Michael Doran and repeated that she had done nothing wrong. Detective Daly and two nurses escorted her from the courtroom to a waiting carriage. Sheriff William Gerber returned her to the hospital ward. The Ramsey County Attorney's Office believed she killed her father in a moment of demoniacal frenzy, caused by hallucinations that she had been experiencing for months. Chief O'Connor told reporters that "she plainly is irresponsible."[159] County Attorney O'Brien stated, "According to the hospital and other facts known to us, the girl is insane and was not responsible for her actions."

On Tuesday, May 18, the Arbogasts' butcher shop was reopened by the manager, Charles Klabunde. The man appointed administrator of Louis's estate estimated it to be worth about $200,000.[160]

---

157 *St. Paul Dispatch*, May 17, 1909.

158 Ibid.

159 Ibid.

160 The administrator was Myron McMillan of J. T. McMillan Company.

County Attorney O'Brien told the press he believed Louise was insane at the time of the murder and that she was still insane. "If she does not have counsel, I shall ask the court to proceed with an examination as to her mental condition. Even if she had counsel and such a motion were not put by the side of the defense, I should myself make the motion. A woman in her condition should not be tried for murder." Chief O'Connor added, "Beyond question, Louise Arbogast is insane and was insane when she killed her father."[161]

Now with the spotlight squarely on Louise as the prime murder suspect, the police released Minna from custody. It was clear to me that she still suffered from shock and depression.

The next day, the case took a strange turn. William Manteuffel, the man who was going to the Yukon with Louis and had been a guest at the house the night prior to the murder, gave a public statement that Louise was sane and did not commit the murder. The county attorney was forced to admit the investigation contained all circumstantial evidence. The only direct evidence was Minna's statement that she thought Louise had committed the murder.[162]

Mrs. Mary Garvey, a neighbor of the Arbogasts, informed the county attorney that Louise was the only family member to tell her that her father was murdered. The rest tried to cover it up. The neighbor quoted Louise on the morning of the murder as saying, "Mrs. Garvey, Papa was murdered." Mrs. Garvey had been the first neighbor to enter the house, and she said Minna said nothing to her about being sick in the bathroom. Mrs. Garvey told the county attorney that Minna told her she was in the kitchen preparing breakfast for her husband at the time of the murder. After the interview, County Attorney O'Brien came out of his office remarking, "My God. I wish someone would tell me more about this case."

Louise finally hired a lawyer, William Mitchell of How, Butler, and Mitchell. On May 20, at her arraignment, Judge Hanft asked the

161 *St. Paul Dispatch*, May 18, 1909.

162 *St. Paul Dispatch*, May 19, 1909.

spectators in his crowded courtroom to leave. No one moved. Everyone wanted to see Louise in person. Judge Hanft told the crowd that Louise Arbogast would not be in court that day. No one believed him. After a short time, a group of deputies escorted a woman who was shielding her face down the hall toward another courtroom. Most of the courtroom spectators rushed out hoping to see Louise. Photographers snapped photos as people circled around the deputies escorting the lady. Deputies pushed into the crowd to make an opening for the woman to walk through. Suddenly, the spectators discovered that the woman being escorted was in fact an employee of the police department. Too late: the doors of the courtroom were now closed, and the deputies would not let anyone back in. Judge Hanft ordered the remaining people in the courtroom to be escorted out. Louise's sisters and I were allowed to remain. Louise then came in through the judge's chambers dressed totally in black.

Judge Hanft explained his actions: "If it had been an ordinary case of murder I would have excluded nobody, but this was a case in which a lot of morbid curiosity seekers, attracted here by an unfortunate girl's distress, simply wanted to crowd in and satisfy their desires to look on another person's trouble and that person possibly demented."

When Mr. Mitchell asked the judge if he was passing judgment on the question of the defendant's mental condition, the judge replied "Not at all."[163]

Friends, relatives, and meat-market employees were telling everyone that Louise had been her father's favorite daughter. She had been his companion. If she asked for money, he always gave her more than she asked for. I wasn't the only one who thought that Louise would be the last one on earth to hurt her father.

The county attorney was now grudgingly faced with transferring Minna from the witness list back to the suspect list. The investigators speculated that the mother hid the axe in a closet the day before the murder. She grabbed the axe at about four in the morning and attacked

163 *St. Paul Dispatch*, May 20, 1909.

her husband, then poured gasoline on him, and went downstairs carrying the bloody axe. She hid it and returned upstairs to light the fire. Minna had said she was in the bathroom, which is within hearing distance of the bedroom. She consistently told the police she never heard Louise go up and down the stairs and did not hear the attack on her husband.

On June 3, Louise and her mother were indicted for the murder of Louis Arbogast. The prosecutor believed Minna's plea would be "justifiable homicide, committed in a frenzy of fury when she discovered conditions in her household that robbed her for the moment of reason." The press was informed that a long time family skeleton would be revealed.[164]

The *Minneapolis Tribune* was extremely harsh, in opinion, when they wrote that the investigators believed there were "unlawful relations between father, pretty Louise Arbogast, followed by the inevitable discovery by Mrs. Arbogast of the wrong doing." The article continued, stating that "Mrs. Arbogast's discovery of her husband's sin is believed to have preyed on her mind until finally she plotted his death."[165] I promise you, it is not true. Louise never mentioned anything like that to me.

The investigation continued for the next few months, but the police didn't find any more evidence. The county attorney decided to try Minna first and then Louise. The trial began at the Ramsey County Courthouse on October 20, with Judge Orr presiding. Patrick McLaughlin represented Minna. She was allowed to sit behind the counsel table with her five daughters. She wore a hat with a black veil that hid her face. But then she was informed she would have to lift her veil so the court could see her face. Very slowly, as if it caused her the greatest mental agony, she lifted her veil and turned toward the jury. Her face showed the signs of suffering and sadness.

The jurors were selected the first day, and the testimony started on the following day. The crowd was unruly.[166] I am surprised no one was

---

164 *St. Paul Dispatch*, May 4, 1909.

165 *Minneapolis Tribune*, June 3, 1909.

166 The *St. Paul Dispatch* described the spectators' behavior during the trial: "The

injured as men and women pushed and shoved to get a chair. I myself stayed out of the fray by standing against the wall.

One of the first witnesses was Ida, who testified that she was the first person awakened by the screaming. She said she climbed over her sister Minnie to go to her parents' room. Ida saw her mother either on the bed or standing next to it. She forced her mother out of the room by dragging her by the nightgown down the stairs. Minnie followed behind them. Ida returned to the bedroom and attempted to pull her father from the bed but could not. She then ran to the street screaming. She stayed at a neighbor's house for the next four hours. She could not account for the actions of her mother prior to the murder.

Minnie was called to the stand. She said she was out until nine with a friend the night before the murder. When she came home, her father was talking with Mr. Manteuffel, and Louise was in their parents' bedroom talking with her mother. Minnie went directly to bed. Awakened by screaming, she was the second daughter to go into the bedroom. She testified, "I went to the room and up to my father's bed. I don't know how long I was there. I had a rug. The bed was burning, and I threw a rug on it. Abrahamson and Babe stood beside me on the side of the bed toward the door." She left the room, ran to the street, and cried for help. She said she could not remember if her father was in the bed when she was attempting to extinguish the fire, but she thought he was. She couldn't remember anything else about the morning of the murder.

---

crowd began to gather unusually early and jammed into the hallway until it was impossible to get near the door. When the doors were opened they rushed in the courtroom, with men and women engaging in a battle of equal rights for the chairs. The men got the best chairs because they were quicker and stronger, and not at all sensitive or especially considerate. After those in the first rush had been seated there were at least a hundred women standing in the main courtroom, and in fact the women occupied all the standing room while the men seemed to have the street car habit and stayed right where they were." Often during this trial, many of the young women in attendance climbed over the rows of seats instead of going down the aisles in order to get a seat as close as possible to the witness box.

Later in her testimony, Minnie changed a portion of her story. She had testified earlier that she was not sure if her father was in the burning bed, but later testified that she tried to help her father by putting the fire out. She had no idea how the murder might have happened. Her testimony, like her sister's testimony, consisted mostly of answering the questions with "I cannot remember" or "I don't know."

William Manteuffel testified he was at the house until 10:30 the evening before. He said he played cards and talked with Louis before leaving. Only family members remained in the house when he left. He said he witnessed no arguments or hard feelings by any members of the family toward Louis.

On October 22, Flora gave her testimony. She was out until 9:30 the night before the murder. When she arrived home, she went directly to bed. She was awakened by screams. She ran to her parents' room, where she saw her father in the burning bed. Unable to put out the fire, she attempted to grab her father's feet to drag him to the other side of the bed. Ida and the paperboy appeared. She did not see her mother until she went downstairs, and she knew nothing of her mother's activities before the murder. She went to her sister Emma's home and stayed there most of the day. Flora testified she "did not know" or "did not remember" in response to most of the questions. Mr. O'Brien asked her if she had a bad memory. She replied, "Yes."

Mr. McLaughlin then asked her a series of questions pertaining to how easy it would be for a person to enter their home at night undetected. He brought out the fact that one door was held only by a latch. There was testimony about possible open windows, such as the coal window, which a person could have used to gain entry into their home.

The *Daily* wrote that many people marveled at the composure the daughters showed during the trial. "The trial is a sad one, and the scene in the courtroom excites the sympathy of nearly everyone, but the Arbogast girls are apparently the least concerned persons in the room. One woman who attended the trial said all of the girls were either very fine actresses or human icebergs."[167] She does not know them like I do, for they all were very nervous and didn't like being the center of attention.

Isadore Abrahamson, the paperboy, testified next. He said he left his house at a little after four that morning. He was en route to meet another boy who was going to do his own route when he heard screaming coming from the direction of Seventh and Sherman Streets. He ran toward the screaming and met Ida, whom he knew. She asked him, "Won't someone help my poor papa?" He ran to the house, which was only two houses from the corner. He passed Minnie, who was on the front porch. The other sisters were at the door and at the foot of the stairs. They were all very excited, he told the court. He asked where their father was, but they did not answer. He ran up the stairs three at a time, and he passed Minna on the stairs. He could not recall the condition of the nightgown she was wearing.

The boy went into the smoky bedroom, where he found Louis lying naked on the bed. Young Abrahamson testified he saw Louis bleeding profusely from head wounds and that part of his body was on fire with the bed partially in flames. Mr. O'Brien asked him about the condition of the bed. Isadore said the bed looked as though it had been burning about ten minutes. He touched Louis on the arm and noticed he was still breathing and his head was covered with blood. He attempted to pull Louis from the bed, but the butcher was too heavy, so he grabbed some bedding and started to pat Louis's body to extinguish the fire. He testified that I had joined him and we had used rugs to smother the fire. Once the fire had subsided, he went downstairs. A daughter stood at the doorway and watched him put out the fire. He could not recall what daughter it was.

When it was time for me to testify, I told the jury that I lived across the street from the Arbogasts and was alerted by Ida's screams. I said that I ran to the house and up the stairs to the smoky bedroom. Once there I found Louis smoldering in his bed and Abrahamson attempting

167 *St. Paul Daily*, October 21, 1909.

to smother the fire. I helped him extinguish the fire, and then I went downstairs and called an ambulance. I recalled seeing Louis naked on the burning bed but did not recall seeing a wound on his head. (I didn't admit to seeing his head bashed in because I didn't want Louise to think I was on the side of the prosecution.) I testified that I arrived at the house about 4:30 a.m. and was not told by anyone that Arbogast was killed by a blow to the head until eight that morning.[168] Once the police secured the home I went and opened up my shop. That was all I knew.

The *St. Paul Daily* commented that "Mr. Spangenberg, like the Arbogast girls, also suffers from a bad memory."[169] Bad memory, my rear quarter. I answered the questions the best I could. If I didn't know, I said I didn't know. What was I supposed to do? Guess?

Emma, the married daughter, testified that on the morning of the murder, her sister Flora awakened her at about 6:30. She and her husband immediately went to her parents' house. Emma said she asked no questions when she got to the house and she did not remember if she spoke with her mother. She said she cleaned the lower portion of the house but not her parents' room because there was a policeman guarding it. She hired Mrs. Vincent to clean her parents' room about a week later. As with the testimony of her sisters, Emma answered almost every question with "I don't know" or "I don't remember."

In the face of those consistent answers, the county attorney gave up. The judge ordered a recess until two o'clock. As spectators left their seats, women hurried in to take the emptied seats. They settled in for a two-hour wait. Many had their lunch with them and ate in the courtroom.

Lawrence Ulmer, the son-in-law, testified that he went over to the Arbogast residence with his wife about 6:30. There he was told of the death and of the fire. The policemen were talking about a suicide, but they did not find a gun. About 9:30, Mr. Ulmer went to the cellar with Detective Daly and found an axe by the stairs, underneath some rags.

---

168 *St. Paul Dispatch*, October 23, 1909.

169 Ibid.

The county attorney asked him if the Arbogast family owned any dogs. Mr. Ulmer told the court that the family had three dogs: a bulldog, a terrier, and a spaniel. The state prosecutor would argue later that the dogs would have barked and awakened the family if some stranger was entering the residence the morning of the murder. Mr. Ulmer also found a bloody shirt in the living room closet and gave it to the police.

Flora was recalled to the stand on October 28. The county attorney asked her whom the shirt belonged to. Mr. McLaughlin objected but was overruled. Flora reluctantly said that the shirt was her mother's. Mr. McLaughlin argued the state did not show the shirt had anything to do with Minna Arbogast and the crime. The state contended the shirt had blood on it and someone tried to hide it. The judge ruled the item of evidence inadmissible.

Ernest Vincent, a young man who did errands around the house, testified that he had looked for the axe the day prior to the murder but could not find it. It had already been established that the kerosene found on the second floor was used for cleaning.

On October 29, Detective Daly testified that Minna had told him she was in the bathroom taking a bath during the time her husband was murdered. When she left the bathroom, she saw smoke and rushed into the bedroom. The detective said that Mrs. Arbogast was trying to help her husband and fell on the bed and was burned. Her daughters then entered the bedroom. The policeman told the court they picked up bloody clothes that belonged to Minna. There was blood on the tub, and the water was bloody as if someone had attempted to wash in it. Detective Daly testified no one could have entered the house through the coal window because cobwebs on it were undisturbed.

The next day, Mrs. Vincent testified she cleaned Louis and Minna's bedroom four days after the murder—not a week later, as Emma had testified. Mrs. Vincent said she found a bloody shirt in a wastebasket, and Emma informed her the bloody shirt belonged to her mother. Isadore Abrahamson was recalled to the stand. He stated there were pools of blood on the bed and on the floor and feathers were scattered all around. He was wearing worn-down tennis shoes, and he later discovered the shoes were red with blood nearly to his ankles. He said that after putting out the fire, he went downstairs for a short time. He returned to the bedroom but was not allowed in because firefighters were there. He walked down the back stairs and left through the back door to do his paper route. The defense would later claim it was Abrahamson who left blood on the back stairs, not Minna when she hid the axe. Abrahamson said he did not go all the way down to the basement.

Mrs. Garvey testified she arrived at the Arbogast home about an hour before Louis was transported to the hospital. She told the court that Minna and Louise were standing at the top of the stairs when she arrived. She could see that Minna was terribly burned on the back from the neck to the knees but able to walk without assistance. Mrs. Garvey helped dress the wounds and asked where Minna had been when the fire broke out. Minna told her she had been in the kitchen preparing breakfast, and when she heard Ida scream, she ran to her husband's room.

This was the third location for Minna at the time of the murder, according to various testimonies. Ida heard her mother's scream and found her either in bed or next to the bed, and Minna told Detective Daly she was taking a bath at the time.

Detective Michael Sweeney testified that an officer asked Minna if she had blood on her feet earlier in the morning. She responded that her feet did not have blood on them. Captain Clark said that if she had taken a bath that morning, there would be no blood on her feet. She replied she had not taken a bath that morning.

Mr. McLaughlin then took Sweeney to task for all the things the police did not do. Sweeney admitted that there was not a systematic search of the home after the axe and bloody clothing of the victim and defendant were found. He testified he did not observe a wastebasket in the murder room containing a bloody gray shirt, which was later found by the cleaning lady and belonged to Minna. Sweeney admitted they did not examine all the outside windows to see if any of them were forced open or if there were any screens missing. He said he checked them from the inside. In answer to a question from the defense, he said the police did not search the front room or the outside of the house on the west side. He testified he made a quick search of the bathroom and other rooms of the house. According to his testimony, none of the rooms were thoroughly searched.

On November 2, the defense made a motion to dismiss the defendant on the grounds that the state failed to connect Minna to the murder. Judge Orr denied the motion and also ruled that a motive was neither essential nor necessary for a conviction. Mr. McLaughlin announced the defense would rest without presenting any evidence or witnesses. "There being no preponderance of the evidence, no reasonable doubt having been raised, there is nothing for the jury to determine," he told the court.

On Wednesday, the county attorney initiated his closing arguments to the jury. Mr. O'Brien told the jury this was the most atrocious crime in the annals of Ramsey County, possibly in the United States. He insisted the murderer was someone who resided at the Arbogasts' house. He explained the motive was within the family and each member refused to talk; the motive was a quarrel, a difference of opinion, serious enough to cause a premeditated homicide. He continued by stating someone in the family committed the crime, and that person was Minna Arbogast, evidenced by the bloody clothing. It was for the jury to determine if witnesses refused or failed to tell all they knew. "I don't believe a man on this jury who does not believe that those witnesses knew what happened that morning, and refused to tell it. It would be an utter impossibility for this atrocious crime to occur within a room's distance of these four girls and not a one of them knew or had any idea of what had happened."[170]

Mr. O'Brien told the jury that Minna killed her husband with the axe, poured gasoline on him, lit the fire, and lay down next to him to

170 From the November 3, 1909 final argument of Ramsey County Attorney Richard O'Brien.

Sheriff Gerber Tricks the Curious.

Nurse, Miss N. L. Brown, dressed as Mrs. Arbogast to trick watchers. Source: *St. Paul Dispatch*, May 20, 1909.

commit suicide. She could not bear the frightful pain of burns, so when the flames began to burn her, she screamed in agony. Ida, hearing the screams, rushed into the room and found her in that condition. Ida then pulled her out of the burning bed. He referred to the paperboy as a total stranger who rushed up the stairs to try to put out the fire, something that should have been the first thing a blood relative would do, yet his own daughters did nothing. The blows to Arbogast's head came from the wife's side of the bed. If someone else had done it, they would have had to lean over the sleeping wife, which certainly would have awakened her. He described the blood trail from the upstairs landing down the back stairs to the basement from the murder weapon. He concluded that if she did not do it, she was certainly there and was guilty as a principal: "The daughters of the family know it was not an outsider, and they knew instinctively who committed the crime, but they won't tell. They have taken the stand, and it is the only stand for them, that they must stand together, so the state won't find out. And they have stood together, and refused to tell what they know." He concluded that the state had made its case a moral certainty.

The defense argument to the jury started later in the day. Mr. McLaughlin told the jury, "It is not sufficient in this case to say that Mrs. Arbogast probably killed her husband, but the circumstances must show that he could not possibly have been killed in any other way." He told the jury that Minna had no motive to kill her husband and the Arbogasts had a happy home. The inability of the girls to remember was easy to explain because of the shock and excitement of the time. Maybe someone from the outside had broken in and killed Louis. Whatever happened, the defense attorney concluded, the state failed to prove that Minna had killed her husband.

The case was placed in the jury's hands at 4:30 p.m. on November 3. They deliberated that evening, and the next morning, the jury sent a message to the judge that they had a question for him. The judge ordered the court back into session with the defendant and the attorneys present. The foreman asked the judge if the jury could find the defendant guilty in any other degree than first degree. The judge explained that there were only two possible verdicts: one for acquittal and the other for murder in the first degree.

Two and a half hours later, the jury foreman told the court that they had reached a decision. The county attorney was notified. Mr. Mitchell and Mr. Pierce Butler were seated at the defense table. Sheriff Gerber escorted Minna into the courtroom. Minna looked around for her daughters, but they were not present, even though they had been there every day during the trial. (Flora later told me that they did not want to be shoved and pushed by the crowd and the reporters, so they stayed home.) The spectators were settled when the jury walked in and sat at their assigned chairs. No sound was made. The clerk read the verdict: "Not guilty." Minna showed no emotion on hearing the verdict, but quietly asked if she could go home. I was stunned but relieved. I went up to her and said I would take her home.

The following day the papers all blamed the police department for a poor investigation. The county attorney told reporters the police had done the best they could. The reporters wanted to know the status of the case against Louise. The county attorney didn't want to respond to the question until he gave it considerable thought. I think many residents of St. Paul believe that Minna did kill her husband and the police lost the case.

Less than a month later, on December 3, Ramsey County Attorney O'Brien dismissed the indictment against Louise. The reason he gave for the dismissal was that he didn't feel he could win a case against the daughter of the victim without the conviction of the wife. The physical evidence was placed in storage. The case was filed as unsolved.

I must admit I was surprised that Chief O'Connor and his Irish snoops apparently never considered me a suspect. I was up at that early hour, reside very close to the Arbogasts, am known to the family's dogs, am strong enough to swing the axe, am engaged to the prime suspect and, being a butcher, also commonly have blood on my clothing. Moreover, some might consider my love for Louise a motive for murder.[171]

Whatever happened to . . . ?

Mrs. Minna Meile Arbogast lived in her residence at 286 West Seventh Street, St. Paul, with the exception of a few years of residence

---

171 The building across from the Arbogast residence, 269 West Seventh Street, St. Paul, is still standing. Built in 1885, it witnessed the murder that early morning of May 13, 1909. If you look up at the top of the building, it will tell you who committed the murder.

in her hometown of New Ulm, until she died of a cerebral hemorrhage on April 17, 1930, at the age of sixty-seven. She is buried next to her husband in Oakland Cemetery in St. Paul.

Emma Arbogast Ulmer and her husband moved into the Arbogast residence at 286 West Seventh after the murder.

Ida Arbogast married John H. Magnus of Jackson County, Missouri, three years after the murder. It is believed she lived her remaining years in Missouri.

Flora Dorothy (Babe) Arbogast and **Minnie Helen Arbogast** did not marry. They lived together at 286 West Seventh until the early 1930s, when the house was razed to widen West Seventh. They moved to 89 Douglas in St. Paul. Flora died of bronchial pneumonia on August 15, 1941, at the age of forty-five. She suffered from arthritis for twenty-five years prior to her death. Minnie died of heart failure on January 3, 1964, at the age of seventy-three.

Louise Arbogast worked for many years as a bookkeeper at the meat market. She married Asher Webster when she was in her early thirties. She died of a stroke at the age of thirty-eight in Avon, Michigan, on January 4, 1932.

Henry A. Spangenberg operated a meat market located at Seventh and Grand, St. Paul, for over forty years. He died in November 1945 at the age of sixty-six from heart disease. He had been residing at 565 Portland, Apt. 305, and was survived by his wife, one sister, and three brothers.

CHAPTER 9

Mr. Fridley's Sorrow

1915

"Divorced husbands get no money in this state."

—Assistant Hennepin County Attorney
George R. Armstrong, January 5, 1916

David Fridley was the son of Abraham McCormick Fridley, a pioneer in Minnesota who was involved in real estate, politics, general merchandising, railroads, and the University of Minnesota. The township of Fridley was named after him. David, like his father, developed land in and around Anoka County and the Minneapolis area. In 1915, he was considered the largest landowner in Minneapolis. He was generally conservative in his habits, not living in extravagance and known to complete transactions with a handshake. One would think a man like this could have anything he wanted, but he could not.

Photo of Mr. David Fridley. Source: *Minneapolis Journal*, January 11, 1916.

I'm a seventy-seven-year-old widower, a Minneapolis land developer, and the proud father of two daughters, Louise and Mary. It's 1926, but the events of more than a decade ago still haunt me. They've turned me into an empty shell of a person. I haven't been truly happy since the day I learned my daughter Mary was dead. I find myself going over and over those memories, as if the incidents happened only yesterday. I think back to life before the tragedy and wonder if I could've prevented it.

October 1908

I'll soon be attending Mary's wedding to Frederick Price from Neenah, Wisconsin. He's a cigar-smoking salesman for Anglo-Dial Scale Company in the Kasota Building in downtown Minneapolis. He always has a line on how he can make big money. Louise and I hardly know anything about the man, and I've got serious concerns about him. I've tried to ask Mary about him. She says he's honest, hard working—doesn't say much more than that. She thinks he'll make her happy. I love my daughter, and her happiness is the most important thing. I'll keep my worries to myself and reserve judgment on Fred Price.

July 1913

Fred seems to be traveling more and more often. Mary's left alone for long periods of time. He's tried other adventures in sales, and I admit he's quite persistent in his endeavors to make money. Still, he's something of a blowhard, always looking for an easy way to make a fast buck. I wish he didn't leave Mary alone so much. They don't have any children, so the house seems empty. At least she's got her cocker spaniel, Chum, to keep her company.

Mary and Fredrick Price shortly before her death. Source: *Minneapolis Journal*, December 14, 1915.

SEPTEMBER 1914

Fred got a job as a salesman for a printing company, and his travels leave Mary constantly alone at home. I see how lonely she is, and I can do very little for her. But I've given her and her sister each a substantial piece of land and a large diamond ring. They agree that if one of them dies, the surviving sister will get the other's ring.

NOVEMBER 1914

Late in the evening of Saturday, November 28, Louise arrives without warning at my house and gives me terrible news: Mary is dead.

Charlie Etchison, a friend of Fred's, picked up Louise and her husband earlier in the evening. He told them that Mary had been in an accident. He drove them to the St. Paul Midway General Hospital, but Mary was dead by the time they got there. Fred is in great grief, according to Louise.

When I finally see Fred and his friend Charlie, they tell me what happened. They and Mary ate lunch at Mary and Fred's apartment.[172] From there, they attended a matinee of *The Prince of Pilsen* at the Metropolitan Theatre in Minneapolis. Mary loved the operetta. Etchison said she was laughing throughout the entire performance.

---

172 1365 Spruce Place, Minneapolis.

Mr. and Mrs. Price with Chum in their 1913 Cadillac. This is the same automobile Price was driving at the time of his wife's death. Source: *Minneapolis Journal*, January 11, 1916.

After the play was over, Fred wanted to drive over to St. Paul to look at some vacant lots on Marshall Avenue he had heard were for sale. Mary agreed to go so she could window shop for material for new curtains for their apartment. En route, Fred stopped by their apartment to pick up Chum.

Fred was driving his 1913 Cadillac—a car he can't afford, but he thinks it makes him look important. They drove along Franklin Avenue, crossed the bridge into St. Paul, and turned right on East River Road. As they were approaching the Town and Country Golf Club, which overlooks the Mississippi from a steep cliff, Fred stopped the car. He told his passengers the car engine was misfiring, and he wanted to check the spark plugs. Mary asked him how long it would take, and he assured her only five to ten minutes. He asked Etchison to help him and asked Mary to exercise the dog.

The men raised the hood of the car, while Mary got out to walk the dog. Suddenly they heard Mary cry, "Oh Fred!" The two men ran around to the side of the car to see Mary and the dog at the bottom of the cliff. The two men ran down to her and found her unconscious. The dog was seriously injured. Fred told Etchison to go back up to the road, stop a car, and ask the driver to call an ambulance. He then asked him to drive to Louise's home[173] and tell her about the accident. Fred said he would go with Mary and meet everyone at the hospital.

Some pedestrians helped Fred carry Mary up the cliff to await an ambulance. The police and ambulance arrived shortly after. While Dr. Beckley was tending to Mary, Fred told the police the dog had fallen off the cliff, and he thought Mary fell attempting to save him.

I'm able to speak to Dr. Beckley at Midway General Hospital. He tells me that Fred insisted on riding with his wife in the ambulance. During the fifteen-minute ride, Fred constantly distracted Dr. Beckley with his exclamations and his repeated efforts to get his wife to speak to him. Mary didn't regain consciousness and was pronounced dead on arrival at the hospital.

Fred tells the family that Chum had to be shot because of two broken legs. He gives Louise Mary's gloves. Louise notices the third finger of the left hand glove was ripped open. Mary wore her diamond ring on that finger. There are no other tears on the gloves. Fred says that the diamond ring must have been come off her finger during the fall.

December 1914

The days following Mary's death are devastating for us—something no parent should ever have to go through. We have the funeral and bury Mary in the family plot in Lakewood Cemetery.

The county coroner determines Mary's death to be an accident. My family has doubts. We constantly talk among ourselves about the accident. One thing that bothers everyone is the missing diamond ring. Louise decides to call Fred and ask him to look for the ring. Her husband, Bill Dye, meets Fred on River Road, and the two go looking for the ring at the scene of the accident. As luck would have it, they find the ring underneath a rock at the bottom of the cliff. They give it to Louise.

Through my banking connections, I hear that Fred's going to various banks attempting to withdraw money from Mary's account. Her

173 1019 Knox Ave. South, Minneapolis.

mother and I gave her that money and her own accounts. Fred's apparently petitioning the probate court to make him the sole heir to his wife's estate, which is worth about $23,000. This includes $10,000 worth of railroad bonds we gave her the day before she died. I also discover that Fred has transferred all of Mary's land to his sister in Wisconsin.

The news about him keeps getting worse. I hear from some other reliable banking sources that he's attempting to unload the bonds. His wife just died, and this son of a bitch is out grabbing her money. Meanwhile, he's stopped communicating with our family.

My son-in-law Bill hears that Fred is seeing a Carrie Olson, a former stenographer who used to work for him. Bill tells me that the courtship started prior to Mary's death. I can't take it any longer, so I call a private detective friend, John P. Hoy, to look into Fred's background. John, a former police officer, started his own business, Hoy Detective Bureau. I should have hired him before Mary married Fred.

April 1915

It's just over three months after my daughter's death, and Price has decided to sue the City of Minneapolis for $7,000. The lawsuit states that the City was negligent for not having a guardrail on the East River Drive where Mary fell to her death. The city, in preparation for the lawsuit, has the city engineering office take surveys of the death site and hires an attorney, C. J. Rockwood.

The city's attorney sends his investigator, John Junell, along with John Hoy to Wisconsin and Illinois to look into Fred's background. The two return with information that Fred was previously married to a Rose Smith in Wheaton, Illinois, in 1896. He was never legally divorced from her, yet he went on to marry Marie Schwartz in Rockford, Illinois, in 1902. She divorced him on grounds of cruelty. They also discover that he served a prison term from December 1894 to April 1896 in the Wisconsin Reformatory for an assault in Neenah, Wisconsin. By this point, I'm not surprised by this news.

PAGE SIXTEEN Monday Evening THE MINNEAPOLIS JOURNAL January 10, 1916

PICTURES TAKEN FOR PRICE AT SCENE OF RIVER ROAD CLIFF TRAGEDY

CITY SINKING FUND WILL MEET BONDS AS THEY ARE DUE

M'INERNY OUTLINES TRACTION PLATFORM

MISSION MEETING PRAISED

RETAIL BUSINESS GAINS 21 PER CEN[T] IN MINNEAPOL[IS]

AMUSEMENTS

PLAYERS WELCOMED

ROBBERS HIDE; LOOT SAFE AT LEISURE

These are the pictures taken six days after the death of Mary Fridley Price, for use by Frederick T. Price in the $7,500 damage suit brought against the city by Price as the result of his wife's death. Source: *Minneapolis Journal*, January 10, 1916.

October 1915

The civil suit begins on October 29 before Hennepin County Judge W. E. Hale. I attend the hearing in court. Price and Etchison tell the same story as before. Then an expert from the city engineering office states that Mary's body was found twenty-seven feet from the bottom of the cliff. This fact is consistent with the body being pushed or thrown. The medical expert reports that the body didn't have any broken bones except for the compound fracture on her head. The fracture isn't consistent with a fall.

My thoughts were mostly suspicions—until now. I know the son of a bitch killed my girl. Hatred would be a weak word for my feelings toward him. In a sense, he killed me too.

They then put Price on the stand to talk about his previous marriages. He does a poor job explaining them, especially the fact that he wasn't legally divorced from his first wife. The city attorney questions him about his marriage in Kansas City to Carrie Olson in July, less than seven months after his wife's death. The attorney makes a point about how unusual it is for a person to marry so quickly after he's lost his wife.

Price is then asked to account for an assault for which he was sent to prison. The report of the incident states that he climbed in his neighbor's kitchen window while the man of the house was out. He encountered a woman in the dining room and hit her over the head. He immediately left the home, taking nothing. The attorney asks him how he could leave the scene with a woman possibly dying. Price gets red in the face, growing visibly frustrated as the questions increase in intensity. Suddenly he says, "I drop the lawsuit." The city attorney asks him if he's dropping the lawsuit because things are "getting too warm." "No sir!" Price replies. I enjoy watching that egotistical money-grabbing cur[174] rush out of the courtroom.

November 1915

I go back to probate court in an attempt to stop Price from raiding Mary's accounts. I was unsuccessful before, but now I've got proof he wasn't legally divorced from his first wife and thus couldn't be legally married to my daughter. My attorney further argues in court that Price must be disqualified as her surviving heir. The court agrees and issues a bench warrant for bigamy.

This whole procedure costs me money, but it's worth every penny to prosecute the man who killed my daughter. My life is now entirely occupied by getting this man into criminal court where he belongs. I'll not rest until he's convicted.

December 1915

I hear that Price is very upset over the recent court rulings, but those are the least of his problems. The information that Hoy discovered about him is turned over to the Hennepin County Attorney's Office.

---

174 Cowardly person or a mongrel dog.

On December 1, over a year after my daughter's death, Hoy and city detectives testify before a Hennepin County grand jury. The jurors, in addition to hearing testimony, go to the location of Mary's death. They ultimately indict Frederick Price and Charles Etchison for first-degree murder.

Price is picked up immediately, but Etchison is back in Washington, DC, where he works for the Encyclopedia Britannica. The authorities wire the DC police, who then pick up Etchison on December 2. Detectives Archie Buck and Michael Duffy take the train to DC to transfer Etchison to Minneapolis. On their return trip, they stop in Chicago late on December 4, where they're joined by Assistant County Attorney Armstrong. They take Charlie Etchison out of jail and to the Brevoot Hotel, where a long interrogation commences. At first, Etchison doesn't crack. Then suddenly, as if something new has entered his mind, he asks for a moment to pray. He kneels facing a wall. The detectives and the attorney are silent as Etchison bows his head and asks for strength. This silence is soon shattered as Etchison says, while still kneeling, "Price killed her."

The authorities are seeking permission to exhume Mary's body for further examination. Believe it or not, the damn fool Price signs off on the agreement along with his attorneys, with the stipulation that their pathologist accompany the state doctor during the autopsy. Mary's body is exhumed on December 29. The autopsy is performed at the cemetery shortly afterward.

January 1916

The trial of my former son-in-law begins on January 4. I'm told that the spectator line is the longest ever in the history of any trial in Hennepin County. The first young lady in line tells the press she waited over three hours to get into the courtroom. Mr. Armstrong, the prosecutor, saves a seat up front for me every day.

Judge Hale was scheduled to preside, but he was the judge assigned to Price's disastrous civil lawsuit against the city. So Judge Fish is assigned instead. Price seems confident and somewhat disinterested as he watches his attorney, Michael Brady, question prospective jurors.

On January 5, the deputies are sent out to issue subpoenas for two witnesses to testify. Mary Nierengarten and Rosalind Cripe lived with Carrie Olson at 1002 Hawthorn, Minneapolis, before she moved in with Price. They can explain her relationship with him before Mary's death, but they've disappeared. The deputies can't find them to serve them with the subpoenas. The temperature falls to nine below zero on that day, so the deputies don't want to stay out chasing them.

The next day, the jurors are driven to the death scene in two automobiles furnished by Sheriff Otto Langum. The jurors withstand the bitter cold as they inspect the cliff where Mary was believed to be thrown and where she landed. I hear that Price was there joking with the sheriff, smoking a cigar, and enjoying himself. The bastard.

During the trial I sit in the front row, wearing an old suit, flannel shirt, and the same old scuffed shoes. I've got tears in my eyes as Armstrong, the prosecutor, tells the jury about Mary being a plain and simple girl. She wasn't to me. Armstrong says that Price found marriage ties irksome and he was determined to sever them. He didn't want Mary Fridley anymore. He did, however, want my daughter's money. Armstrong tells the jury, "Divorced husbands get no alimony in this state." Price wanted money to support the life he was leading, so he decided to kill her and get the money given to her by "her kind, old loving father."

My health as well as my appearance have deteriorated since I lost Mary. I only care about justice for my daughter. I constantly think of all the things I should have done in order to protect her. I blame myself. I'm beyond any hope of normalcy in my life, frozen in grief. I keep my eyes fixed on Price during the trial, to see if there's any remorse in his soul. But I'll never forget or forgive what he did to my Mary.

On January 7, A. C. Godward, a city park engineer, testifies that the location of the incident was exactly 480 feet from the Ramsey County line on the Hennepin County Park property. The location is described as the first curve in the road going south a short distance past the railroad bridge. He testifies that Mary landed 27 feet 7 inches from the top of the cliff. There was crushed rock where she landed. I visit that spot many times, and it gets sadder for me every time I go.

The next witness is Dr. David E. Robertson, a pathologist from the University of Minnesota. The defense attorneys want all witnesses who plan on testifying later to leave the room, and that includes me. The judge agrees, so there I am, out in the hallway, getting pieces of information from people who are coming and going from the courtroom.

Robertson states that he conducted the postmortem examination of Mary on December 30, 1915, in the chapel at Lakewood Cemetery in Minneapolis. His examination disclosed a fracture of the skull three and one half inches by four and one half inches in size on the left side of her head. There were twelve fragments of skull. He examined the collarbone, arms, and legs and discovered no broken bones.

The doctor then reaches into his handbag and pulls out the top half of my Mary's skull and puts it on the arm of the witness box. (I'm glad I don't have to see this.) I hear that everyone positioned themselves in their seats to see the skull. Finally, Dr. Robertson concludes that the cause of death was multiple fractures of the skull and attending injury to the brain.[175] Armstrong, the prosecutor, asks him if a person with these injuries could make any noise. The doctor replies that the only noise a person with this injury could make would be from the air leaving their lungs. Now we know that Mary didn't die from the fall.

I testify briefly about all the money, land, bonds, and jewelry that I gave Mary. When I gave them to Mary, I put them in her name only. I knew her husband was always looking for money. I'm not asked many questions. I think everyone feels sorry for me. The courtroom is quiet, even though it's packed with spectators. I never look at Price while on the stand.

On Monday, January 10, over three hundred spectators are squeezed close together to get a seat to sit or a spot to stand. The fire

175 Dr. Cowles, medical expert for the defense, agreed with Dr. Robertson's conclusion.

marshals aren't strictly enforcing the room capacity ordinances at this trial. Everyone's waiting for the state's star witness, Charles Etchison, to enter through the main door of the courtroom. Several hundred people stand in the hallways in an attempt to hear the testimony or to get a glimpse of this witness. About half of the crowd is women, with many bringing their lunch with them so they don't lose their seats.

Etchison's name is called, and he surprises everyone by entering the courtroom through the judge's chamber. He's wearing his salesman's smile and an immaculate blue linen serge suit. Price watches as his old friend Charlie walks up to the desk of A. E. Frost to be sworn in. Price looks at the witness as if he's a stranger. Once Etchison sits down in the witness chair, the dramatic moment I've been waiting for occurs: Price and Etchison make eye contact. There's nothing defiant in either look. For just a moment Etchison looks at Price, and Price looks steadily at him.

Etchison explains that he came to Minneapolis from Denver to work for Anglo-Dial Scale Company, where he met Price in 1909. In 1911, he and Price opened a collection agency in Kansas City. They went broke. Price lent Etchison money along the way, but he couldn't pay all of it back.

He says he moved to Washington DC and worked for the Encyclopedia Britannica. He got a letter from Price asking him to return to Minnesota to sell fuel savings stock. Price sent him forty dollars to cover expenses. Etchison said he felt indebted to Price, so he moved to Minneapolis, staying at the Vendome Hotel. Upon arriving, Price told him he was having financial difficulties and he knew his wife's dad was "loaded." He said Mary had money but it was hers, not theirs. He said he wished he could press a button and that old man Fridley, Mary, and her sister, Louise, would disappear. Charlie asked him if he really felt that way, and Price said he did.

This is what I now believe: if I hadn't given Mary all that money, stocks, and land, she might be alive today.

Etchison seems to be cut from the same cloth as Price: a fast-talking salesmen looking for the fast buck. Etchison's nothing more than a weak-kneed lizard, but he's now on our side, even if it's just to save his own neck.

In October of 1914, Price told Etchison that he needed him to be a witness to Mary's "accidental" death. Etchison said he wanted no part of it. Price reminded him of the money he owed him and all he had to do was be a witness. Price said if she was killed, he would say that Etchison did it. In court Etchison calls Price heartless. He then describes how Price took him to areas along the East River Road to pick a spot for the accident to occur.

Charles Etchison. Source: *Minneapolis Journal,* January 11, 1916.

Etchison tells how he had lunch at the Prices' home, went to the theatre and then for a ride to St. Paul. Shortly after going past the railroad bridge, Price said the engine was misfiring. He pulled over to the side, and the two men got out. They opened the hood to pretend to check the spark plugs. Price told Mary to get out and walk the dog. When Mary was getting out of the back seat of the touring car, Price grabbed her and Etchison. He pushed Etchison away and threw Mary over the cliff. Price then grabbed the dog and threw him over the cliff too. Price and Etchison quickly went down the cliff to find Mary moaning in pain. Price told Etchison to go stop a car and tell them to call an ambulance, then to go to Mary's sister's house to tell them about the accident. They would meet at the hospital. Etchison says when they arrived at the hospital, they were told Mary was dead. Etchison gave the Dyes a ride home and returned to his room. Price told Etchison to keep his damn mouth shut and everything would be all right.

On January 11, the courtroom is crowded again, and hundreds of men and women stand in line for hours in an effort to reach the courtroom. Now it's the defense's turn. I'm sure Brady feels he's got to crack Etchison if he's ever going to get his abysmal client off.

Brady asks Etchison if he was charged with first-degree murder in this case. Etchison replies that he was and that he pled not guilty. Brady then brings up the meeting that Etchison had with the prosecuting attorney and detectives in Chicago. Brady asks him if he'll be getting a deal because he testified for the prosecution. Etchison says he was given no immunity. Brady smirks at him as if he doesn't believe him. He asks Etchison if he's a narcotic addict and if he lived with his wife before they were married. Etchison denies both accusations.

Brady then asks him if he was at Price's home the night before Mary died. Etchison says he can't remember. "Will you swear you were not there the night that Mrs. Price said she was to receive a present of $10,000 in bonds from her father?" Etchison says he doesn't know, but he believes he did hear of the present the next day from Price. Etchison testifies that Price spoke to him six or seven times in October 1914 about his intent to kill his wife. Brady asks him, "And you were shocked?"

"Yes."

"So you were shocked," Brady says sarcastically while rolling his eyes.

The questioning then moves on to the day of Mary's death. Etchison says he was at his office in downtown Minneapolis before he joined the Prices for lunch. Then they went to the theatre and afterward drove to St. Paul. Etchison pretty much stays with the same story he told the police. He says that he was afraid of Price once Price committed the murder and that he lied to the police the first time he was questioned and at the civil trial.

Brady, in his attempt to make Etchison a perjurer, produces a transcript of Etchison's testimony during the civil trial. He goes through it in detail, the same questions that Etchison gave different answers to. Etchison is embarrassed and has no real explanation other than that he lied. I can only think that this man could've saved my daughter's

When Price and Jurors Visited Death Cliff

Jurors and Price visit death cliff. Note: there is a fence now at the area where Mrs. Price fell to her death. Source: *St. Paul Daily News*, January 7, 1916.

life by telling her, the police, or anybody what Price was up to. I have no respect for this man with no guts. He's just up there trying to save himself from a long prison term. He shows no sorrow for my Mary.

The following day, Brady rises and says to the jury, "If Mary Price was murdered, the murderer is not Frederick T. Price, but the man who was on the witness stand yesterday, Charles D. Etchison." He pauses for a few seconds and then says in a loud, clear voice, "Mr. Price, take the witness stand."

Price is sworn in and sits down on the seat in the witness box. He doesn't look as confident as he did at the start of the trial. He never looks at me or anyone else but his attorney. Brady has Price explain his background in business with Etchison. Price says that on the evening prior to her death, Mary told them that her father was going to give her $10,000 in bonds. He claims Etchison lied when he said he wasn't there. Later that night Price says that Etchison tried to borrow money from him again. He turned him down. Price then tells the jury about all the loans he'd made to Etchison. He also calls Etchison a liar and a drug addict.

Price is asked about the circumstances of his wife's death. He says he drove along East River Road and heard the engine misfiring. He stopped a short distance south of the Milwaukee Short Line Bridge. He and Etchison got out of the car and opened the hood. Price asked Etchison to get him a wrench out of the back of the car. Etchison came back with a wrench, but it was too big. Price said that he never took the wrench, and he didn't see what Etchison did with it. He heard a noise and ran around the car. Both he and Etchison looked for Mary and her dog and then noticed them at the bottom of the cliff.

Mr. Armstrong, the prosecutor for the state, tears Price apart. He establishes through questioning that Price had needed money, had a girlfriend, started to spend Mary's money immediately after her death, had been in prison, and had married but had not divorced. He shows how Mary's body was tossed over the cliff. I should enjoy Price being publicly castrated on the stand, but I don't. All I can think of is why I'd given Mary all that money. And why hadn't Etchison said something? I certainly would've paid him well for information that Price was planning on killing my daughter.

Finally, the trial's nearly over. In final arguments Armstrong calls Price "a cold-blooded wife murderer who killed his wife for gold." He tells the jury that Price went to prison for assaulting a defenseless woman and he'd done it again to his wife. "Can you tell me this man loved her?" Then he tells them about him calling me "poor old David Fridley" and "stingy Dave." He tells the jury that Mary weighed less than a hundred pounds and that she was easily tossed over the cliff. He concludes by telling the jury that no deal was made with Etchison for his testimony.

I'm told that there are about a thousand people in attendance—mostly outside the courtroom—when defense attorney Brady starts to address the jury. Brady asks the jury why Price would kill his wife for money. If he let her live, she would inherit half of all her father's money. He says Etchison's a proven liar and Hoy was a hired gun for the Fridley family, and calls Etchison a drug addict and points out that he often sniffed the contents of his handkerchief when he wiped his lips while in the witness box.

The next day, some nineteen hours after the jury receives its instructions from the judge, they come back with a verdict. I'm nervous because you never know what those people talk about. But I'm relieved: Price is found guilty of murder in the first degree. He's then sentenced to life in Stillwater Prison.

People are congratulating me and patting me on the back. It doesn't help me at all. I'm glad that Price will be in prison for life and die there like the caged rat that he is. But I can't stop thinking about my daughter Mary being out of my life forever. I feel like an old playground with no children on it. I'm an empty man. I'll never be happy again.

Whatever happened to . . . ?

Charles Etchison, the man who had not been given any deal for his testimony, was never prosecuted.

David Horace Fridley was found dead in his basement on March 26, 1926, by his housekeeper. The death certificate states that his death at the age of seventy-seven was suicide by hanging. He is buried next to Mary Fridley[176] in their family plot at Lakewood Cemetery in Minneapolis. The *Minneapolis Journal*[177] referred to Mr. Fridley at the time of his death as one of the wealthiest men in Minneapolis. His daughter and son-in-law, Louise and William Dye, of Coral Gables, Florida, survived him.

---

176 Her headstone reads "Mary Fridley."

177 March 26, 1926.

Frederick Price's mug shot from Stillwater Prison, 1916. Source: Minnesota Historical Society.

The Fridley family section at the Lakewood Cemetery. Source: Author's collection.

Frederick T. Price died of liver disease at the state prison on April 8, 1930. He was fifty. He worked as a laborer and a clerk while in prison. His wife, Carrie, had him cremated at Lakewood Cemetery and his ashes spread at the lake on the cemetery property.

CHAPTER 10

Cast of Killers

1917

"Evidence must not be disregarded for the reason that it is circumstantial because criminals usually work in secret."

—Ramsey County District Court Judge
Hugo O. Hanft, June 29, 1917

George N. Hillman was a court reporter for Ramsey County courts. He was so respected around the country, that he was called the dean of court reporters. He and his family resided in St. Paul, where he operated a business in court reporting with his daughter. Over the course of his long career he witnessed hundreds of exciting and heartbreaking court cases. The cases he shares here were, according to him, "the most atrocious that I ever reported."[178]

---

178 George N. Hillman, reference P2278, MHS collections.

George Nelson Hillman. Source: Author's collection.

On August 4, 1914, twenty-six-year-old stenographer Alice M. McQuillan married forty-year-old widower[179] Frank J. Dunn, a self-employed teamster who hauled mail from the St. Paul train depot to commercial businesses and the post office.[180] The McQuillans are a prominent St. Paul family with a successful family plumbing business. The newlyweds honeymooned in Duluth and returned to reside at Dunn's rented room in St. Paul. Soon problems arose. The domineering widower was set in his ways, and young Alice had trouble adapting. She moved back to her parents' home two months after her marriage.

I first met Dunn after a hearing for spousal support after the separation. I was the court reporter at the hearing, and I saw how disconcerted he was that the court ordered him to pay Alice spousal support of seventy dollars per month. Dunn came over to my office to pick up the transcript of the hearing, and he told me he was disappointed by the court decision. He believed Alice was after his money, and he was incensed.

Now it is my understanding that in the following months, Alice attempted to reconcile their marriage several times, but Dunn would have none of it. In 1915 Dunn traveled to Montana for a short time to look at some property for investment purposes. Alice traveled to Wibaux, Montana, and worked as a stenographer from 1916 to 1917.

---

179 Dunn was first married on April 11, 1904. His wife died on April 8, 1912.

180 Dunn testified that he worked sixteen-hour days. He stated that his yearly income was $2,400.

She had hoped her absence would make her husband miss her. She became lonesome for her family and returned to her family home, at 793 Selby Avenue in St. Paul, on April 1, 1917. She contacted Frank, who surprisingly was very excited to see her. Two days later, on Easter Sunday, he took her to a neighborhood drugstore[181] for a talk about their future. While there, Frank pleaded for her return, telling her how much he missed and loved her.

Her husband was a new man. Absence does make the heart grow fonder. Alice told her family of the reconciliation. She and Frank made tentative plans to live together again. She told her family that Frank wanted her to take a stenographer position in Minneapolis as soon as she could. Alice's life was finally turning out the way she wanted it.

Now let me divert the course of my dialog for a short time. On April 24, Minneapolis police officers Charles Ziegler, George Connery, and F. X. Kort, established a speed trap at Washington and Southeast Union Streets. A car sped through the trap and was signaled to stop. The driver didn't at first, but Kort hopped onto the running board and forced him to stop. The two young men in the car pleaded with the officers, saying that they had just spent all their money on a fine from St. Paul earlier that day. I imagine the officers said, "Too bad. This is the only way you young people will learn." Kort asked Connery to escort the two men to the East Side Precinct[182] and either collect the fine or book them. Off they drove to the precinct with Officer Connery sitting in the back seat.

At 4:00 in the afternoon, Officers Kort and Ziegler arrived at the precinct at the end of their shift. Where was Connery? He hadn't called in at 3:00 for his routine check-in. No, he wasn't at the station that afternoon, they were told. No, he did not book two speeders. Where was he then? At suppertime, Connery's wife called the station and asked where her husband was. No one knew. Everyone seemed to be waiting for Connery to walk in.

---

181 Freidman's Drug Store, 429 St. Peter, St. Paul.

182 Minneapolis Police 2nd Precinct, 409 First Ave SE, Minneapolis.

GEORGE CONNERY,
Minneapolis patrolman, who vanished while riding to the east side police station with two automobile speeders whom he had arrested. Police today are scouring the twin cities and neighboring towns for trace of the mysterious car.

Minnesota patrolman George Connery.
Source: *Minneapolis Journal*, April 25, 1917.

The police talked among themselves at the precinct before going back to their beat; some started checking the local watering holes. Nothing. Finally at 10:00 that evening, the precinct notified headquarters of Connery's disappearance. Detectives Burt Weare and Frank Brunskill, along with every available officer, were called in for a search of their missing comrade.[183] It was assumed that the two men stopped for speeding were wanted for a serious crime, and that they had killed Connery and dumped his body somewhere on the east side of Minneapolis. The police searched the bluffs over the Mississippi, woods near the east side, and the east side of the river. Nothing.

The following morning I was in the Minneapolis courthouse and went to see my friend Detective Burt Weare. He told me the trail was cold with no leads coming in. But the officer's family, friends, and neighbors were not giving up. An estimated five hundred people, including guardsmen, police, civilians, and students, joined in the search for Connery. His wife was convinced he was tied up somewhere and was going to be found. Late in the afternoon, the car in which Connery and the two young men departed was found behind the Rex Theater at 501 Mississippi Street in St. Paul. Blood was found in the back seat. The police learned that

183 Minneapolis police used seven vehicles in the search.

the vehicle had been stolen in La Crosse, Wisconsin. This confirmed the police department's theory that the two men were criminals from out of town. The search continued well into the evening.

Alice McQuillan Dunn. Source: *Minneapolis Journal,* April 29, 1917.

Meanwhile, at about 1:00 a.m. on April 26, Alice McQuillan Dunn and her sister, Katherine McQuillan, were sleeping in a bed at their parents' home at 793 Selby, St. Paul. Katherine heard the stairs creaking and, thinking it was their brother Jack, called out to him. She received no answer. An unfamiliar man then entered their room, pushed Katherine away, and shot Alice three times with a revolver. The gunshots and Katherine's screams awoke their parents and brothers. They were told by two other men standing guard in the hallway to go back to their bedrooms and not to interfere. The three men then ran down the stairs and exited through a kitchen window.

Ambulances and police sirens aroused the neighborhood. But it was too late: Alice was dead. Frank Dunn was contacted shortly after the police arrived. He had just returned home from an evening at the Knights of Columbus. Dunn was shocked and wanted to know the details of the crime. He accompanied the police to the central station, where he was questioned at length. The police observed that Dunn did not appear devastated. A neighbor they questioned said that Dunn often commented that Alice's family had too much influence over her and that she was "bleeding" him for seventy dollars a month. Dunn

GROWD AT FUNERAL OF SLAIN WOMAN

The crowd for Alice's funeral. Father J. C. Byrne conducted the service. Source: *St. Paul Dispatch*, April 28, 1917.

was held for suspicion of murder. He stated he was innocent and would cooperate fully with the investigators. He asked why he would kill his wife when he was trying to reconcile with her.

At the murder scene, John O'Connor, the St. Paul chief of police, stated that they had found on the window of the McQuillans' home the fingerprint of a notorious young criminal, Joe Redenbaugh. He was last seen with other well-known young criminals Frank McCool and John Doyle, aka Tacoma Johnny. A nationwide manhunt began.[184]

The funeral for Alice McQuillan Dunn was held on Saturday,

184 Tony Miranda, *Killed in the Line of Duty* (Minneapolis Police Federation, 1998), 7. In 1917 if a major offense took place the arresting law enforcement agency would take ten to fifteen photographs of the suspect as well as their fingerprints. The agency would then send the photos and prints to other major police departments throughout the nation for their files. The photos would be entered into a photo album of suspects for witnesses to review. I, the author, believe that Chief O'Connor had an informant who told him of Redenbaugh. The chief was known to feed information about investigations while they were in progress, so I expect that a found fingerprint sounded better than someone telling him.

April 28, at St. Luke's Catholic Church[185] in St. Paul. An estimated 1,500 people attended the service, which was followed by burial at Calvary Cemetery. The press reported, "There was not a flower, a message, or a representative from the Dunn family at the funeral."[186]

Frank J. Dunn and Alice Dunn. Source: *St. Paul Daily News*, April 27, 1917.

On April 29, Chief O'Connor released a summary of the McQuillan investigation to the *St. Paul Pioneer Press*. One detail in particular stood out: an informant had called the police and stated that two years earlier, Dunn had contacted two men from Montana, Sylvester C. Ferdig and Albert F. Brown, when he was looking for someone to kill his wife.[187] O'Connor immediately sent detectives Peter Lavalle and George Dawson to Montana, where they located Ferdig and Brown within the week and returned with them to St. Paul.

Ferdig and Brown told the St. Paul Police detectives that Dunn approached them in 1915 and asked them to kill his wife. Dunn said he would pay them $10,000. He instructed the two to come to St. Paul, where he would point his wife out to them. Dunn said his wife was bleeding him of his money and because he was Catholic, he couldn't get divorced and get married again.[188] Dunn told the two men that if they

185 Old St. Luke's Catholic Church, southwest corner of Victoria and Portland, St. Paul, in 1917.

186 *Minnesota Family History Research.* "On this date in Minnesota April 28."

187 The source was Brown's former wife—his fourth former wife to be exact.

188 Dunn, a Catholic, reasoned that divorced Catholics cannot remarry if the spouse

had someone else do it for $5,000, they could keep the rest. On July 23, 1915, they met Dunn in St. Paul. At that time Dunn pointed out his wife and the house she was living in on Selby Avenue. Four days later the two men told Dunn they were blackmailers, and he had better pay up before they turned him in. Dunn paid them $4,000. They returned in October for more money, and he gave them $400. That was the last they saw or heard of Dunn.

The McQuillan investigation was taking shape, but the police could not keep Dunn in jail without connecting him to the probable suspects, Redenbaugh and McCool. They now knew Dunn had wanted his wife killed, but he didn't do it, so how could they tie him to the two suspects?

On May 5, 1917, a man who wanted to remain anonymous called the National Guard Armory in Minneapolis. He asked to speak with Captain Arthur S. Gow, the chief of the Military Police unit. He told Gow that Officer Connery's body was near Rice Creek in Fridley and gave him directions to the body.

The Minnesota National Guard sent Gow and three of his military police officers out to the site to verify the tip. Following the directions, the military police found the partially decomposed, beaten, and wounded body of patrolman George Connery. Connery had been shot in his left leg and his skull crushed. Captain Gow called the Minneapolis police.[189] Detectives Weare and Brunskill were immediately sent to the scene, where they found evidence that Connery had battled frantically with his captors. His wounds indicated that he had probably been struck by the crank of the car. His uniform was in tatters, and his coat had been unbuttoned and his pockets searched. They took his service revolver. Officers searching the woods found Connery's holster and a pocketknife, which was believed to have been used by one of his attackers. The knife had been tossed away and was bloodstained.

---

is still alive. However, if he had looked a little further in his catechism, he would find that the church does not allow murder either.

189 The police thought that the caller was probably a hunter who discovered the body but did not want to get involved.

It was believed that Connery was slain in the car.[190] A note, written in very broken writing saying good-bye to his family, was found on his body.[191]

A reward of $420 was offered by the Minneapolis mayor, Thomas Van Lear, for evidence leading to the arrest and conviction on the charge of murder of one or both of the two men last seen with Officer Connery.[192] The police officers offered another fifty dollars from their own pockets.

Once it was discovered that tire tracks at the scene matched those of the stolen car found in St. Paul and the .44-caliber bullet found in Connery matched those that killed Alice Dunn, the investigation took on new urgency. It became a joint investigation shared by the Minneapolis and St. Paul police departments.[193] The nationwide search for McCool and Redenbaugh, focusing especially on Nebraska, became even more important.[194] Police were now certain that Redenbaugh and McCool were the murderers, but the motive was unclear. Why did these men kill Officer Connery and Alice McQuillan?

A break in the case came out of Nebraska on May 3. Frank McCool was arrested in his hometown of North Platte, Nebraska. The local authorities were conducting surveillance of McCool's old haunts when he finally showed. McCool admitted his participation in the McQuillan murder to the Nebraska authorities; however, he denied

---

190 Miranda, *Killed in the Line of Duty*, 8.

191 Officer Connery's funeral was held on May 8, 1917, at St. Clement's Catholic Church in Minneapolis. He was buried in St. Anthony Cemetery. He left a wife and five children, who lived at 3009 Taylor Street Northeast in Minneapolis. The Hennepin County Grand Jury investigating his murder passed the hat and came up with eighty-six dollars for the family.

192 *Minneapolis Journal*, April 30, 1917.

193 There was some disagreement on how the investigation was to be directed by the two police chiefs. Minneapolis Chief Lewis Harthill thought another man by the name of Hamilton was a possible suspect. St. Paul Chief O'Connor targeted Redenbaugh. It turned out they were the same guy using different names.

194 McCool was from North Platte, Nebraska.

Minneapolis police detectives Frank Brunskill (left) and J. A. Weare (right) with Redenbaugh (middle) arriving at a train station. Source: Minnesota Historical Society.

any knowledge of the Connery murder.[195] McCool gave a statement, which included a reference to his partner Redenbaugh. He would not sign a waiver for the police to take him back to Minnesota, so he was secured in the Omaha County jail while awaiting extradition papers. On May 10, McCool was caught sawing bars off his jail cell. Armed with razor blades and hacksaw blades, he fought off two guards. Finally, six additional guards came to their assistance and subdued the prisoner, even as he yelled that they would never take him alive. After the assault on the guards, McCool did not feel secure within the jail and agreed to be extradited. Thus, he was transported to Minnesota that night by the Omaha and Minneapolis police.

On May 11, while McCool was on his way to Minnesota, Joe Redenbaugh and his wife, Pearl, age eighteen, were arrested in San Francisco. Joe was arrested for two murders and Pearl was arrested for aiding her husband in fleeing the state and in assisting him in planning

195 At the time of his apprehension, McCool was in possession of Connery's revolver.

Mrs. Dunn's murder. Redenbaugh confessed to the San Francisco police that he was involved in the deaths of Connery and Mrs. Dunn. The information was telegraphed to the Minneapolis police, and Weare and Brunskill left immediately to pick up the couple. When the detectives arrived in San Francisco, Redenbaugh reneged on his confession and told them that he had no knowledge of the murders. They also learned of his previous name, Edward H. Hamilton.

Meanwhile, McCool and his Minneapolis police escorts arrived in Minnesota in the early morning hours of May 12. Once he was in the central jail, McCool was considered as cold as ice. The interview started at 5:00 p.m. and lasted about an hour and a half. Questioning continued in a cell with four officers, but he revealed nothing.[196] He sat in the "sweat box"[197] for a total of three and a half more hours, and all he would tell the authorities was, "I may plead guilty, but I'll not tell about anybody else."[198]

Later that evening, the detectives told McCool that Redenbaugh had been picked up in San Francisco and had confessed to the murder of Officer Connery. His confession included the statement that he and McCool killed Officer Connery and Mrs. Dunn was set up by a bartender by the name of Mike Moore. Dunn paid Moore, who in turn paid Redenbaugh, McCool, and a third man named Doyle. (The detectives were quoting the confession that the San Francisco police telegraphed to them.) The police urged McCool to corroborate Redenbaugh's confession. Finally he confessed that he and Redenbaugh killed Officer Connery.

He claimed it was an accident. As they were driving to the police station and were about one block away, Redenbaugh slowed down, turned around, and pointed his revolver at the officer. The car hit a bump, and the revolver went off, hitting Officer Connery in the leg. In

---

196 McCool sat in the cell under twenty-four-hour surveillance to assure that he would not attempt escape or suicide. John Moshik, the last man hanged in Hennepin County, was confined to the same cell awaiting his execution.

197 Unventilated holding cell with a door and no bars.

198 *Minneapolis Journal*, May 13, 1917.

a panic, the men sped past the station to East Hennepin Avenue and drove up Central Avenue into Columbia Heights searching for a place to release Connery.

McCool said, "We never intended to kill the officer. We intended to wound him and tie him to a tree so his family could go there later, but he was a fighter to the last, and I had to beat him to the ground to make myself safe as I thought then. He was tricky and while in the automobile, he led us to believe he would submit without trouble. Even after I beat him down, I thought he would come to all right."[199]

Upon arriving in Minneapolis, Joe Redenbaugh was about to be indicted for the murder of Officer Connery and his wife for aiding him in his escape. Joe quickly accepted an agreement with the Hennepin County Attorney's Office that he would plead to first-degree murder, and all charges against his wife would be dropped. The deal was made, with the understanding that Redenbaugh would have to testify in upcoming trials of his cohorts in Ramsey County.

While traveling to Minneapolis, Redenbaugh was asked by Detective Weare if he had any regret about the murders. "I was broke and up against it and had to think of my little girlie. The Connery job was an accident. Then we needed money to make a getaway. Although I've got to pay the penalty, I sure am sorry for the little wife, but you are as game as I am ain't you kid?" he asked, hugging her.

"Sure I am Joe. Guess this is the last trip we'll be making together for a while. I'll be waiting when you come out, and I won't have a very gray hairdo either."[200]

On May 24, a month after the murder of Officer Connery, Redenbaugh entered the courtroom of Hennepin County District Court Judge W. E. Hale. I heard that he had a slight smile on his face. The indictment of first-degree murder was read to him, and his smile faded and his face reddened. The *Minneapolis Journal* described Redenbaugh as a "boy about to get whipped." He kept his head down,

---

199 *Minneapolis Journal*, May 14, 1917.

200 *St. Paul Pioneer Press*, May 21, 1917.

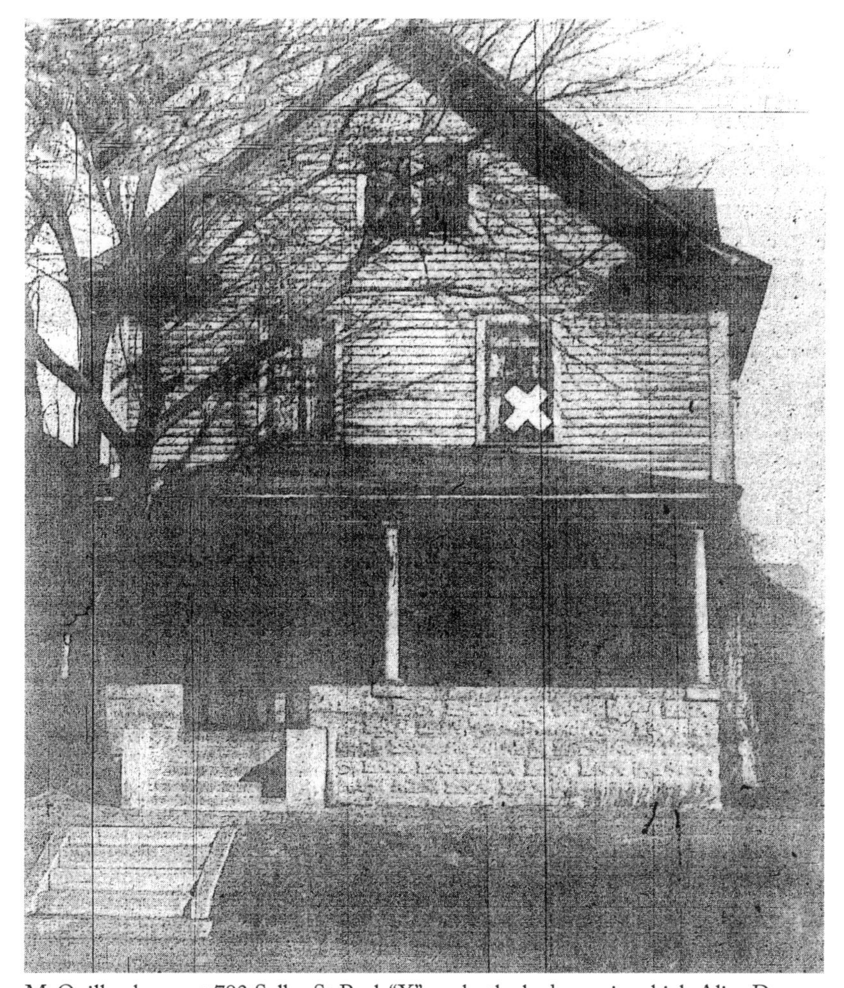

McQuillan home at 793 Selby, St.Paul. "X" marks the bedroom in which Alice Dunn was killed. An estimated 2,000 people passed through the McQuillan home for visitations prior to the funeral. Two rooms were filled with flowers and floral wreaths. Source: *St. Paul Pioneer Press.*

and when the judge asked how he pled, he softly responded, "I plead guilty." Judge Hale then asked if he had an attorney. Redenbaugh replied he did not. The judge held over sentencing until the following day, when he sentenced him to life in prison.

Redenbaugh's first reported crime was when he was nine years old. His criminal record as a teenager showed that he was arrested for a series of burglaries, car thefts, and safe robberies, and was sentenced four times to reformatories, two of which he escaped. In 1913, he cracked a safe in Ripley, Oklahoma, and was sentenced to two years in the penitentiary at Oklahoma State Prison, escaping fourteen days before his time was up. From that time until the murders, he lived, he said, by "peddling brass watches and automobiles."[201]

In a separate trial in Hennepin County, Frank McCool, twenty-three, was found guilty of third-degree murder of Officer Connery. Redenbaugh, his partner, was the chief witness for the state. Now on the other side of the river, in Ramsey County court, Redenbaugh pled guilty to Mrs. Dunn's murder and, like in Hennepin County, testified against McCool, who was convicted of third-degree murder for his participation in Alice Dunn's death.

Now came what everyone was referring to as the trial of the century: Frank Dunn was to be tried for hiring men to murder his wife. My pretrial synopsis notes stated that Dunn told Moore, a bartender, to hire someone to kill his wife. Moore got Redenbaugh to do it. Rendenbaugh brought McCool and Doyle, aka Tacoma Johnny, to assist him. This was the first trial in Minnesota history where more than one killer was hired to murder someone. These were the most despicable men that I had come across in a courtroom. I could hardly look at them.

The trial commenced on June 19, in the courtroom of Ramsey County District Court Judge Hugo O. Hanft. Representing the state was Ramsey County Attorney Richard O'Brien; representing the defendant was D. W. Lawler. I was the court reporter.

I remember that day clearly. When the deputies opened the door to the courtroom, I watched a storm of people rush in to grab a seat. Everyone wanted to see Redenbaugh testify. The scene was disgraceful. Ladies—yes, ladies—climbed over the seats in order to get as close as they could. Women's clothing was torn, hats pushed off, pocketbooks lost, and there was all sorts of shoving and pushing. The gentlemen were not gentlemen. The worst offenders were escorted out of the building.

201 *St. Paul Dispatch*, May 5, 1917.

On June 20, nineteen-year-old Katherine McQuillan testified for nearly an hour. She testified that she knew Dunn was paying her sister seventy dollars a month in court-ordered support payments. The questions then turned to the night of the murder. Miss McQuillan stated that she and her sister retired at about midnight on the evening of April 25, and that her parents and brothers, Warren and Thomas, were also home. [202]

> *I heard a noise like the stairs creaking, and I asked if it was Jack, my brother. I got no answer. I called again "Who is it?" I got no answer. My sister said, "Go to sleep Kath, you are dreaming." And she put her hand over my mouth. I saw a man step into the bedroom across the hall as I heard the noise in the hall and I cried out "Alice, Alice there is a man in the house." Then a man jumped right into the room. I clasped Alice in my arms and held her tight. The man said, "Be calm. Be calm. All I want to do is a little shooting." I took off Alice's rings and put them in my hand. The man flashed a light on us. He fired three shots. The man had on a dark suit, and his face was covered with a white handkerchief. He pushed me away from Alice. Her head bumped mine, but he pushed me away when he did the shooting.*

Joseph Redenbaugh was called to testify later in the morning. I watched as my friend Deputy Warren J. J. Sullivan took off the handcuffs once Redenbaugh was seated. Redenbaugh was nineteen, slight in build, had fair skin, and was about five feet six inches tall. He was dressed in a plain gray suit and said that he resided at Stillwater Prison. He told the jury that in June 1916 a criminal friend of his introduced him to Mike Moore, a bartender, at Chickett's. Moore told Redenbaugh that Dunn wanted his wife killed. Moore offered him the job, but Redenbaugh declined.

---

202 Testimony quoted from *St. Paul Dispatch*, June 20, 1917.

Redenbaugh returned with Frank McCool in April 1917. Redenbaugh told Moore that he would take the job. Moore told Redenbaugh to make it look like a burglary and that Dunn wanted to know when the slaying was going to be conducted so he could be someplace where he could establish an alibi. Redenbaugh was told to go to Freedmen's drugstore[203] on the following Sunday, so Moore could point out Mrs. Dunn. Redenbaugh testified that Moore pointed out Dunn's wife as they sat at a table in the drugstore. "I was there for the purpose of seeing Mrs. Dunn so that I would know her if I saw her again."[204]

Redenbaugh told the court that on April 25, he and McCool met Moore at Chickett's, 210 West Seventh Street in St. Paul, and discussed the final preparations. They decided to do the crime that night; they knew the heat would be on them after shooting a police officer. About 1:00 a.m. McCool, John Doyle, and Redenbaugh, wearing masks, entered the McQuillan residence through the kitchen window—the only one they could find open. They went upstairs and found the sisters' bedroom. Doyle and McCool covered the other bedrooms so no one would interfere.

Redenbaugh testified that he shined the light on the two women and recognized and shot Alice. The three men then ran down the stairs and escaped through the open kitchen window. They grabbed a checkbook and wallet belonging to Mr. McQuillan when they departed.[205] As they drove away, they passed an ambulance and a police car racing to the McQuillan home. They went their separate ways and they met the following morning at Redenbaugh's room.

Redenbaugh called Moore and asked when they could get their

203 429 St. Peter, St. Paul. The St. Paul insurance building now sits on the property where the drugstore was located.

204 Redenbaugh did not show because he had to pick up his wife at the St. Paul depot. Dunn thus had to return to the drugstore with his wife the following Thursday.

205 These items were found the next day by a couple of boys playing in a nearby area. Nothing was missing from the checkbook or wallet, making it unlikely that the criminals intended a burglary.

money. Moore said he would be over after he got off work. Moore arrived at Redenbaugh's room about noon. In the room were Redenbaugh, McCool, their wives, and John Doyle. Moore told them that Dunn said it didn't look like a burglary. Moore gave them sixty-five dollars, but said he would have the rest of it in the afternoon. Redenbaugh told him to tell Dunn that he had better come across with the money, and if he wasted time, something might happen to him.

Moore left around 2:00 p.m., with Doyle following him. Moore returned about twenty minutes later. Moore, Doyle, Redenbaugh, and McCool went into the bedroom, where Moore placed $2,900 on the bed. The currency was mostly in century notes and Moore told them that he held out one hundred dollars for his expenses.

Redenbaugh then testified that Doyle headed out for New York. The McCools and Redenbaughs took a train to Mankato, where they hit the saloons. They then took a train to Omaha and later to Salt Lake City, where they split up. The Redenbaughs went on to San Francisco, where they were arrested shortly after their arrival.[206]

James McQuillan, the father of the deceased, testified that he approached his son-in-law after the separation and attempted to talk to him about reconciling with his daughter. With tears flowing down his face, he told the court that Dunn wanted to have no part of it.

Mary McQuillan, Alice's mother, was the next witness. The *St. Paul Dispatch*[207] read, "The sensation came when Mrs. McQuillan told a story so dramatic, so compelling in the appeal of a mother's heart for vengeance, that it must have had a tremendous effect upon the jury." McQuillan told the jury that Dunn had urged her daughter to get a stenographic position in Minneapolis only the Saturday before the Thursday on which she was slain. Her testimony corroborated the details of the testimony of Redenbaugh. She testified on three different occasions during the trial. She said she was embarrassed

206 While in San Francisco, Redenbaugh went to Portland to case a bank. There he pawned the murder weapon for five dollars. It was retrieved for the trial.

207 June 20, 1917.

because she was not controlling her emotions, but everyone—I mean everyone—understood.

The *Dispatch* described her giving testimony:

> *Deeply shaken with emotion, her voice sobbing with the sorrow of a mother for her dead child and again ringing with denunciation of the man she believed responsible for the deed. Mrs. McQuillan carried jury and crowd with her through the most tragic tale of the undying devotion of a woman for a man that has ever been heard in a Ramsey County court room, and seldom is outlined in the most vivid of fiction.*[208]

Other witnesses for the state included the blackmailers from Montana, who described Dunn attempting to hire them to kill his wife. Ferdig shook the crowd when he testified that Dunn told him that he had tried to kill his wife himself. Dunn told Ferdig that he tried asphyxiating her but failed because he accidentally pulled down a chandelier and woke her up. Neighbors and friends testified that Dunn told them Alice was bleeding him for money.

Then it was my turn to be a witness. This was the first time in my career that I ever took the stand in a criminal trial, even though I worked in hundreds of them. My daughter did the transcribing when I was testifying. I told the court that Dunn paid me eighty-two dollars for a transcript of the court proceedings from when his wife obtained a legal separation from him. I recalled that Dunn said he "would never live with that woman again."

The prosecutors explained to the jury that Dunn's motive for his wife's murder was money. Once divorced, Dunn would have to pay her seventy dollars per month for the rest of her life. I calculated that the total came out to be around $32,000 dollars if she lived to an average age of sixty-seven.

---

208 *St. Paul Dispatch*, June 22, 1917.

On June 27, Frank Dunn took the stand. He had been scheduled to testify earlier, but got sick and ran from the room.

The *St. Paul Dispatch* described his testimony this way: "In the main, Dunn is making a good impression as a witness. He turned squarely in his chair on taking the stand, facing the jury and talks straight to the jurors, except at such times as it is necessary for him to look at counsel. He speaks clearly and distinctly; his voice carrying and distinct; his voice carrying easily to the farthermost point of the courtroom. He hammers home points in his testimony with gestures and by slapping his left palm with his right hand."[209]

Dunn testified that he was forty-four years old. He was not sure of his wife's age—either twenty-seven or twenty-eight. He was married in 1904 to a woman who died in April 1912. He married Miss McQuillan in August 1914. He and his wife lived together in his rented room at 210 Smith. They lived together there for a little over two months, and then one day he came home to find a note saying she was moving back home with her parents. She eventually moved to 202 Smith to be near him and try to reconcile their marriage.

He later traveled to Cushion and Billings, Montana, to acquire land to raise sheep. He and others in the St. Paul area were going to pool their money, form a company, and buy land. In Montana he met Brown and Ferdig, but he claimed he never spoke about killing his wife. They later approached him in St. Paul and blackmailed him. He admitted to submitting to the blackmailers.

Dunn admitted to meeting his wife at Freedman's drugstore on Sunday, April 15,[210] and again on Thursday, April 19. He said it was her idea to meet there.[211]

Dunn was stoic throughout his testimony, even as others in the courtroom were crying. Dunn did not change his demeanor during the

---

209 *St. Paul Dispatch*, June 27, 1917.

210 Redenbaugh had testified that he could not make the Sunday night appointment, so he had agreed to meet Moore at the drugstore on the following Thursday.

211 *St. Paul Dispatch*, June 28, 1917.

entire testimony. I have to admit that Dunn did a good job up until the time for cross-examination by the county attorney. Mr. O'Brien hit Dunn hard in his questions about the phone call he made to his wife asking her to apply for a job in Minneapolis, paying the blackmailers, meeting with Moore, withdrawing monies from his account the same day as the murder, and telling everyone, except his wife, that he had no intention of ever living with her again. The dagger came out when Mr. O'Brien asked Dunn to explain why Redenbaugh knew of his meeting with his wife at the drugstore on two different dates. Mr. O'Brien asked Dunn if he could explain why Mrs. Dunn would select these two particular evenings and this particular drugstore as a meeting place to talk over plans for reconciliation, when Redenbaugh was there. Dunn could not account for the coincidence.

O'Brien explained that Mrs. Dunn was hospitalized for a nervous condition after her separation. Dunn said that he never visited her while she was hospitalized. Dunn testified, in his final conclusion, that he knew nothing of the murder of his wife and that he was at a Knights of Columbus meeting the evening prior to her murder.

On June 29, the state prosecutors offered their final arguments. Mr. O'Brien told the jury that he had corroborating evidence that Dunn was the mover behind the murder. He talked about how the blackmailers were only successful because Dunn did in fact ask them to kill his wife. He spoke of the trip to Montana to hire killers, not to look for land. He pointed out the drugstore coincidence and that Dunn never visited his wife in the hospital. He did not send anything to his own wife's funeral, nor asked to attend. He did call an undertaker and told him he would spend a couple hundred dollars for her burial. But he had offered to pay $10,000 for her death.

Mr. Lawler spoke next for the defense. He called the investigation third rate. The reason Redenbaugh testified was to reduce his own sentence. Could you believe a couple of blackmailers? Are they the best the state can do? Who could trust notorious criminals' statements in a courtroom? Dunn loved his wife; otherwise, why would he try to win her back? The police made a huge investigation out of a couple of nervous burglars. The police let them get their stories straight before they testified. They all were thinking of saving themselves, not telling the truth.

Later that afternoon, the jury returned with a guilty verdict of first-degree murder. No one was surprised. Frank Dunn was sentenced to life in prison without parole.

Mike Moore's trial followed Dunn's. Redenbaugh was again the state's primary witness. Moore, known as the Fixer, was an ornery and heavyset man, not well groomed. Witnesses testified that they saw Dunn and Moore often talking at the bar. The accusations by Redenbaugh were collaborated.

Mike Moore, named as fixer in Dunn murder. Source: *St. Paul Pioneer Press*, May 16, 1917.

Mike Moore was found guilty of first-degree murder and sent to Stillwater Prison for life, never admitting to his participation in the murder of Alice Dunn. He said he would go to his deathbed without "squawking." Moore also never received the $1,000 Dunn had promised him. Dunn was in jail shortly after he gave Moore the money to pay the gunmen. When Moore went back to get his own money, it was too late.

Tacoma Johnny Doyle, a participant in the murder at the McQuillan home, went on the lam. You would think that anyone who calls himself Tacoma Johnny and has an arrest warrant for murder might stay away from Tacoma. Not Johnny. On July 31, 1920, Tacoma Johnny was arrested at a Tacoma tobacco store. Since the murder, he had married and fathered two sons. At the time of the marriage, his wife thought his name was O'Neil. She did not know his other name until after he was arrested. It was discovered that his birth name was Orrin Otis Shea. He waived extradition, and on October 23, 1920, Doyle's trial for first-degree murder commenced.

The trial was held in the courtroom of Ramsey County Judge Hascal R. Brill, with Richard O'Brien representing the state and Linus O'Mally and Harry Eweis representing the defense. I was the court reporter. Redenbaugh was scheduled to be the chief witness for the state prosecutors, but he changed his mind and refused to testify. I think the fact that the men he testified against would probably be living with him in the same building for the rest of his life discouraged his participation.[212]

The prosecution introduced a statement Redenbaugh gave to the police on May 22, 1917, that a third man was with them at the time of the shooting. Police proved Doyle arrived in St. Paul on April 10, 1917. His duties the night of the murder, described by Redenbaugh, were to stand at the top of the stairs to prevent any of the family members from interfering with the murder. Doyle was paid $985 by Moore for his participation in the murder.

The prosecution provided a letter that showed Doyle and Redenbaugh were friends: they agreed that if either was implicated in a crime, they would not turn evidence against the other. A hotel register with Doyle's name on it put him in St. Paul at the time of the murder.

Redenbaugh's wife, Pearl, testified that Doyle, McCool, and her husband left their apartment at 11:00 p.m. and returned at about one on the morning of the murder. She was not aware that the three men had murdered Alice Dunn until the later in the day.

Doyle's defense was that he was in William O'Connor's saloon the evening of the murder from about 10:00 p.m. to 1:00 a.m. The jury was

---

212 Redenbaugh was given six months in the county workhouse for his refusal to testify. The sentence was added on to his life sentence and would have to be served prior to parole.

out for twenty-four hours. Guilty of murder in the first degree was their verdict. Judge Brill gave him life.

This was the conclusion of a senseless and tragic conspiracy. The murderer, his two accomplices, the middleman, and the primary man were all roommates for life at the state prison. Dunn, Moore, and Doyle were there for the murder of Mrs. Dunn, and Redenbaugh and McCool for the murder of Officer Connery. I don't believe any of these men ever realized how much pain they brought to others because of their own greed. No one showed remorse of any kind. These were the most evil group of criminals I ever witnessed. God have mercy on them, for I can't.

I cannot let you go without telling some things that went on before, during, and after the Dunn trial.

Before the trial:

Remember Captain Arthur S. Gow, the man who was responsible for locating the body of Officer Connery? On Friday, May 18, 1917, Gow was involved in an automobile accident at Washington Avenue and Tenth Street Southeast Minneapolis. His automobile was hit by a car University of Minnesota football coach, Dr. H. L. Williams was driving. Gow was thrown from his car and received a life-threatening brain concussion. He was in a coma for about twenty-four hours. Gow was a cheerleader for Williams's 1913 University of Minnesota football team. He survived. Dr. Williams's name is still prominent at the University of Minnesota for the Gopher's basketball arena is named after him, Williams Arena. Evidentially Williams coached better than he drove.

During the trial:

This is so sad, but on Thursday evening, June 21, after court was completed for the day, Juror Frank B. Duford was notified that his eight-year-old daughter, Ruth, contracted meningitis and was given only a short time to live. He was told that the youngest of his five daughters was unconscious at that time. The last time Mr. Duford had seen his daughter was over a week prior when she arrived home from her second-grade class at the Harrison school.

Deputies Sheriff Court Herbert and Sam Marks allowed Duford to call home. He was not allowed to visit his daughter because of a court order sequestering him to the Ryan Hotel. Mrs. Duford sobbed as she and the rest of her family needed him at home to share in their grief. Judge Hanft called a meeting with the two attorneys and Mr. Duford the next morning. He explained that he could not allow Mr. Duford to leave, but if the child died, he would allow him to attend the funeral. Mr. Duford took his seat in the jury box, with tears in his eyes.

The following Saturday, June 23, 1917, at the noon recess, Judge Hanft called a meeting of juror Frank Duford, County Attorney O'Brien, Defense Attorney D. W. Lawler, and myself. The judge instructed me to bring my machine to record the communications. The judge looked at Mr. Duford and said, "I believe you have not heard of your daughter this morning. I am very sorry to have to tell you that she is dead." Mr. Duford wiped away his tears, as the others present expressed their sorrow for his daughter's death. This was a first in my long career as a court reporter and I hope it never happens again.

The Duford home, 1036 Simms, Street, St. Paul, was quarantined with two of his other daughters and his wife showing symptoms of the same illness. He had five daughters: Verl, age sixteen; Laura, age fourteen: Violet, age twelve; Evelyn, age ten; and Ruth, age eight. Mrs. Duford had a daughter from a previous marriage, Bernice, age seventeen. Mr. Duford was accompanied by Deputy R. J. Clark to the hospital and to make arrangements for the funeral. Judge Hanft explained to the public the reason for the recess of the trial. Mrs. McQuillan broke down in tears stating, "Oh that poor man. I know what it is like to lose a daughter."[213]

Mr. Duford went home and met with his family. They had a small ceremony and took their decreased child to Union cemetery in

213 *St. Paul Dispatch*, June 23, 1917.

Maplewood, Minnesota. They buried her in a temporary grave to be removed in eight days, July 1, to have a proper funeral. Mr. Duford returned to the Ryan Hotel the next day, Sunday, at five o'clock. This was the first time in Ramsey County Court history that anything like this ever happened.

AFTER THE TRIAL:

Interestingly enough Redenbaugh and Dunn met and spoke for the first time when they were in jail. Did Mr. O'Brien show conspiracy since Redenbaugh and Dunn never met or spoke to each other prior to the crime? The Minnesota Supreme Court affirmed the jury's decision.[214]

Whatever happened to . . . ?

George N. Hillman learned the Pitman system of shorthand and became a court reporter at the age of seventeen in Washington County, New York. He moved to St. Paul and became the head of Ramsey County court reporting from its beginning until 1929, when he retired after fifty-four years of service. According to the *St. Paul Dispatch* of July 7, 1934, at his retirement gathering he was honored by the bench and bar of St. Paul and by William Mitchell, then attorney general of the United States and other national figures. The Hillmans resided at 615 Lincoln in St. Paul. George died of pneumonia on June 12, 1950, at age eighty-two. His wife, two daughters, and a son survived him. He is remembered as the Dean of Court Reporters.

Sylvester C. Ferdig and **Albert F. Brown** returned to Montana, where they owned hotels. They were not arrested for blackmail because of their cooperation and testimony. It turns out that back in 1916 Ferdig had tried to tell someone about Dunn's plot to kill his wife. He had told his story to a prominent St. Paul attorney, Stan J. Donnelly. Donnelly thought it was a "crazy-sounding tale" but informed Warren McQuillan

---

214 140 Minn. 310; 168 *Northwestern Reporter* 2.

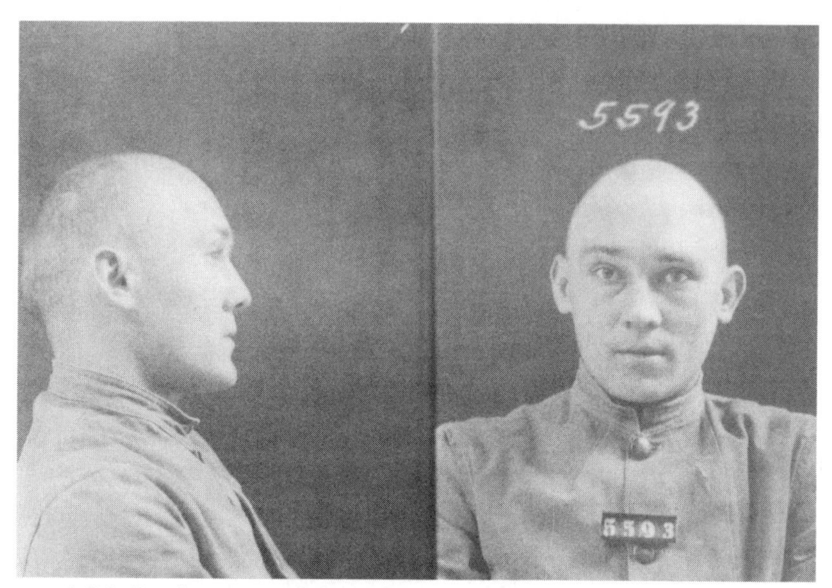

Frank McCool's mug shot from Stillwater Prison. Source: Minnesota Historical Society.

about what Ferdig knew and asked Warren, Alice's brother, to use his own judgment to decide which members of the family he should tell. Evidently Warren never shared the story with his sister.

Frank McCool was released from Stillwater Prison on November 17, 1937, and arrested the same day and tried for the murder of Mrs. Dunn. He was found guilty of third-degree murder and sentenced to another seven to thirty years in prison. He died at the St. Cloud Reformatory on August 25, 1943. He was fifty-two.

John Doyle, aka **Tacoma Johnny's** prison records indicate that he was twenty-eight years old, 5'4", a stocky 156 pounds, with chestnut hair, and a scar on right side of his neck. Doyle had a history of arrests before participating in the murder of Alice Dunn. He served time in Idaho and California prisons for burglaries. In 1916, he was sentenced to the Minneapolis workhouse for six months for vagrancy and attempting to sell fake jewelry. Also in 1916, he was held in Kansas City for questioning in a highway robbery. While incarcerated at Stillwater Prison, he

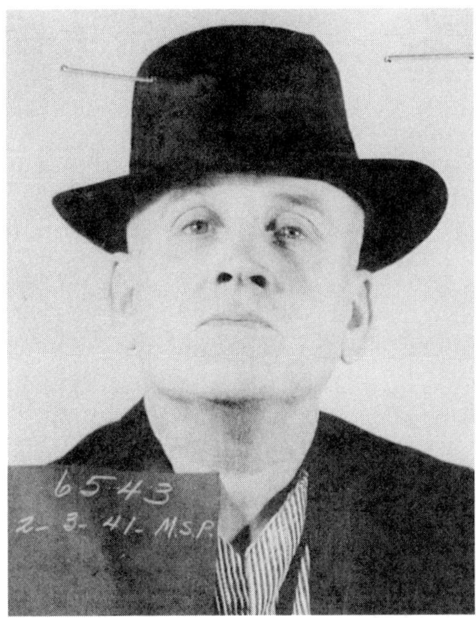

John Doyle in 1917 (left) and again in his Stillwater Prison mug shot in 1941. Source: Minnesota Historical Society.

was in and out of mental institutions. He died on September 19, 1960, at the state hospital in Hastings, Minnesota. He was seventy-seven. His wife divorced him in 1925, and he did not hear from any of his family in over seven years prior to his death.

Edward H. Hamilton aka **Joseph Redenbaugh** was sentenced to life in prison on May 25, 1917, for the murder of patrolman George Connery. In 1938 he pled guilty to third-degree murder in Ramsey District Court for the death of Mrs. Dunn. Again he was sentenced to life. He was assigned to the machine shop for work duty. On March 10, 1958, he appealed his sentence in a Writ of Habeas Corpus in Washington District Court. He contested his detention based on the following: (1) He was not guilty of the first-degree murder for which he was indicted. (2) He was ignorant of law and his rights so he had pleaded guilty. (3) He was not given opportunity to obtain counsel of his own choice nor given services of the court appointed attorney. (4) He was sentenced on the same day that he was arraigned and entered his plea of guilty.

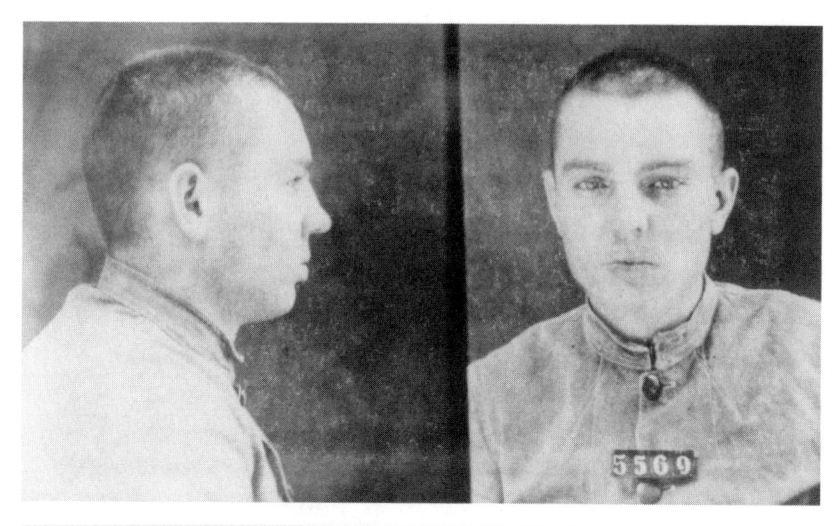

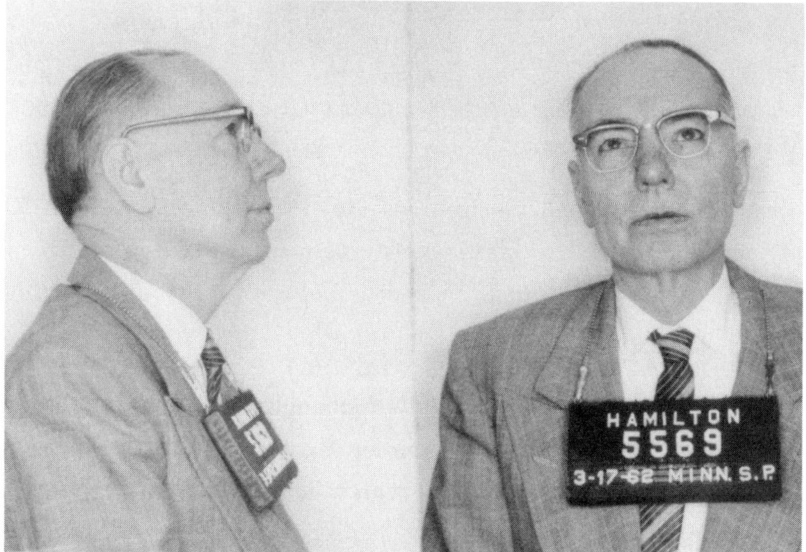

Edward H. Hamilton, who went by the alias Joseph Redenbaugh, posing for Stillwater Prison mug shots at age twenty (top) and age sixty-four (bottom). Source: Minnesota Historical Society.

(5) The accomplice received a thirty-year term. (6) He had not been advised by the Court of his constitutional rights. And 7) he was a minor. It was not upheld.

After serving forty-five years, Redenbaugh was up for parole in early 1962. In March 1962 Elmer C. Nordland, secretary to the Minneapolis Federation of Police Officers, wrote a letter to the Minnesota

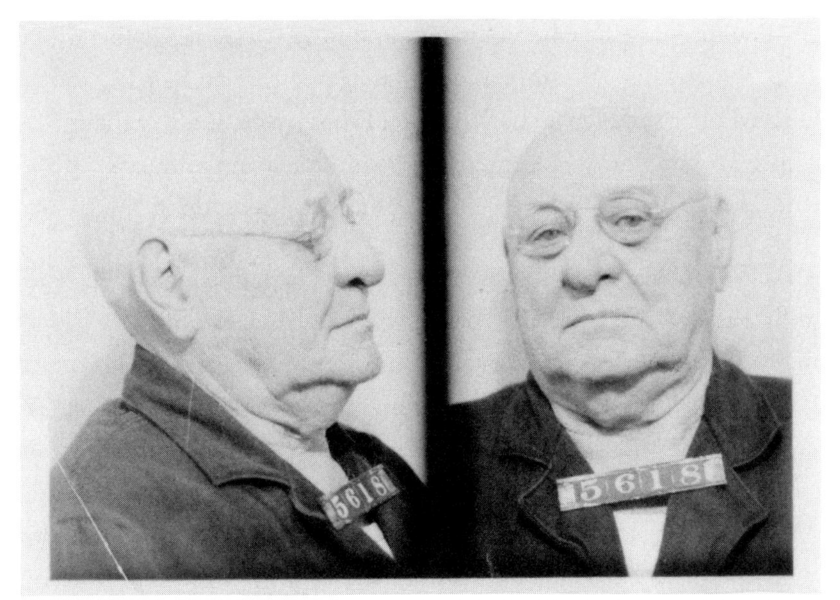

Frank Dunn's Stillwater Prison mug shot, shortly before his death at age eighty-four. Source: Minnesota Historical Society.

Department of Corrections opposing Redenbaugh's release. The chief of Minneapolis police, Pat Walling, and the chief of St. Paul police, Lester McAuliffe, both opposed releasing any murderer. A McQuillan family spokesperson, Dr. Phillip Soucheray, told the Department of Corrections' agent that the parole board should make the decision and the family did not want a voice in it.

Redenbaugh, now known as Hamilton, was released on May 9, 1962, at age sixty-four. He had not heard from his wife in twenty-five years. He traveled to Portland, Oregon, to live with his sister. He worked there at Tekronix, Inc. as a machinist. He died when he was in his late sixties.

Frank Dunn was sentenced to life in prison. Summary prison reports indicate that Dunn did not act as an inmate sentenced to life for murder. He was not a disciplinary problem and generally carried himself as a professional man.

Prison records state that Dunn was born on October 23, 1873. He was five feet five inches tall, with light gray hair, blue eyes and weighing

140 pounds when he entered prison on July 17, 1917, at age forty-four. Tests showed that Dunn had a mental age of 15.7 and an I.Q. of 97. He died in prison of arteriosclerosis on February 26, 1958, at the age of eighty-four. He never admitted any involvement in the murder of his wife. He was buried in St. Joseph Cemetery in Rosemount, Minnesota.

Mike Moore, forty-three, was sentenced to life in prison. Moore, born in St. Paul, had a criminal record that stated he was sent to St. Cloud Reformatory on three previous occasions for burglary before his arrest for murder. Prison records describe him at 210 pounds and five feet ten inches. He held his longest job as a bartender at Chickett's for fourteen continuous months prior to his arrest.

Moore was irritated with his sentencing and expressed profanity at the judge as he was escorted from the courtroom. By the time he arrived at Stillwater Prison on July 2, 1917, his disposition had not improved. He was placed in solitary confinement that afternoon at four o'clock because of being abusive to the guards and using insulting language to the deputy warden. Once adjusted, Moore was placed on the coal gang, where he shoveled coal from the trains every day for fifteen cents per hour.

On November 15, 1929, he was sent to St. Peter State Hospital for the criminally insane and returned to the prison on July 30, 1930. He was sent back to St. Peter on July 2, 1943. Dr. Royal C. Gray, a prison psychiatrist, wrote in Moore's prison file that Moore suffered from manic psychosis. He died at the asylum on November 19, 1945, at the age of seventy. Moore, like many other inmates of his era, was sent to the asylum for going "stir crazy."

Judge Hugo O. Hanft retired in the early 1940s. He lived at 1044 Portland in St. Paul.

Richard O'Brien became a district judge, and **Harry Peterson**, his assistant prosecutor, became a Minnesota Supreme Court Judge.

Mary McQuillan lived in her home on Selby for the rest of her life. She died in June of 1955 at the age of ninety-eight. She was buried at Calvary Cemetery.

Katherine McQuillan married Henry Kloman and resided in Mahtomedi, Minnesota. She died in March 1986 at the age of eighty-seven. She was survived by one daughter, two grandchildren, and two great-grandchildren. She is buried with her husband at Ft. Snelling National Cemetery.

Detective James A. "Burt" Weare was killed in the line of duty on February 7, 1919. He and Detective J. J. McGuire were attempting to apprehend Albert Gentz, a suspect in a number of armed robberies in Minneapolis. They disguised themselves as laborers and went to Gentz's sister's house at 52 Twenty-Second Avenue Northeast. Gentz's sister said he was not there. McGuire kept the lady busy while Weare started looking around the home. He was slowly opening a closed bedroom door when a shot rang out from inside the room. It hit Weare in the heart; he was killed instantly. Gentz ran to the backyard, and while attempting to scale a fence, he was shot and killed by McGuire.

Detective Weare, forty years old when killed, was survived by his wife and daughter. The Weare family resided at 2749 Polk Street Northeast in Minneapolis. Funeral services were at the Scottish Rite Temple at Franklin and Dupont, Minneapolis, with burial at Lakewood Cemetery.[215] Blessed are the peacemakers.

---

215 Miranda, *Killed in the Line of Duty.*

Acknowledgements

NINETY-FIVE PERCENT OF THE CONTENT in this book was found in the Minnesota History Center library. The staff there was extremely patient and kind to me, and their assistance was invaluable to the success of this transcript. I thank them for the use of their photos. A special thank-you to Nicholas Duncan, Eric Mortenson, and Steven Nielsen of the reference library.

Thank you to Betsy Kozullal; Jeremy, Sharon, and Steve Roth for their reviews and suggestions; Charlene Torkelson for her editing, illustrations, and enthusiastic support; Patricia Brennen for her extreme diligence in correcting grammar and spellings; Trio Books' Beth Wright, who conducted the first edit to this book.

Thanks to analysts Timothy O'Malley, Michael Campion, Peter Orput, Katie Jean Davey, and Larry Millett.

Hennepin, Anoka, Ramsey, Washington County Historical Societies; Allan and Darla Gephard and the Brown County Historical Society; Julia Dancken, Beltrami Historical Society; Rosella DePietro and Kristen and Kaalid Omar at the Hennepin County Library Special Collections; Traverse County Sheriff Don Montonye; and Stan Churchill, Traverse County historian. Thanks to Jodi Hofer from the Transverse County Recorders Office for her help.

Best to June Figura, niece to Arbogast sisters, of Maitland, Florida, and Mrs. Helen N. Carlton, daughter of Antonette Seidensticker, of Charlottesville, Virginia for their interviews and correspondence.

I'd like to acknowledge all those who would continue to ask me, "How's the book doing?" Especially Sean Corrigan, Greg Duffy, Brian Lingen, Jeremy Roth, Keith Simonette, John King, Jim Lemmer, Mark Ott, Father Goman, Ron Knutson, Vincent Carraher, Kent Yoshida, and many others.

Thanks to my sophomore high school English teacher Mr. John Sobodney. He treated his students with respect, which he received in return. I still remember him saying, "Keep writing. You can edit later."

To Lily Coyle, Alicia Ester, MacKenzie McCullum, Athena Currier, and Laurie Flanigan-Hegge, the great crew at Beaver's Pond Press for making this book possible.

I thank my children, Kelle and Casey, and their families, for their love and support during this endeavor. Finally, a huge thank-you to my best helper, a patient researcher and nicest person I know, my wife, Special K.

Where They Lived

All addresses are residential unless marked (O), denoting office.

CHAPTER 1: A WOMAN TO DIE FOR

Ezra Pabody	Juror	28 S. 13th St., Minneapolis
James Doyle	Chief of Police	2809 Dupont Ave. N., Minneapolis
Charles Francis	*Times* Editor	725 E. 16th St., Minneapolis
Frank Brooks	Judge	2729 Colfax Ave. S., Minneapolis
Frank Hamilton	Defendant	1317 4th Ave. S., Minneapolis
A. A. Ames	Mayor	627 Elwood Ave., Minneapolis
Ray Evans	Witness	903 3rd Ave. S., Minneapolis
Fred Boardman	County Attorney	Mt. Curve & Logan Ave. S., Minneapolis
A. J. Smith	Assistant County Attorney	1771 Irving Ave. S., Minneapolis
Frank Nye	Defense Attorney	2708 Pillsbury Ave. S., Minneapolis
R. L. Penny	Defense Attorney	800 5th St. SE, Minneapolis
Dr. J. W. Little	Witness	2300 Portland Ave. S., Minneapolis
Dr. C. A. Erdman	Witness	612 9th Ave. SE, Minneapolis
Thomas Rooney	Policeman	325 NE Broadway, Minneapolis
John Lind	Governor	651 Fairmount St., St. Paul
West Hotel		500-514 Hennepin Ave., Minneapolis
Golden West Hotel		301 Washington Ave. S., Minneapolis
Nicollet Hotel		Washington and Nicollet Ave., Minneapolis
Vendome Hotel		17-19 S. 4th St., Minneapolis
Starr's Saloon		46 S. 4th St., Minneapolis

CHAPTER 2: DID THE DENTIST DO IT?

Louis Gephardt	Victim	408 S. Broadway, New Ulm
Wm. J. Julius	Sheriff	Jail, New Ulm
F. H. Behnke	Witness	18 N. Broadway, New Ulm
Adolph Klause	Chief of Police	318 N. Broadway, New Ulm
Dr. L. A. Fritsch	Witness	200 S. Germany, (O) 2 N. Minnesota, New Ulm
A. J. Vogel	Witness	405 N. 2nd St., New Ulm
B. F. Webber	District Court Judge	324 S. Broadway, New Ulm

CHAPTER 3: THE MYSTERY OF THE MURDERED BUTCHER

John W. Finehout	Judge	595 Olive, St. Paul
Nicholas Lehmen	Chemist	367 Dayton, (O) 352 Robert, St. Paul
Anton Miesen	Sheriff	County jail: St. Peter & 4th St. SW corner
Stan Donnelly	Attorney	808 Laurel Ave., St. Paul
Hugo O. Hanft	Attorney	Buckingham Hotel, 9th St. and Smith corner, St. Paul
A.W. Miller	Coroner	White Bear Lake (O) 199 E. 7th St., St. Paul
Robert A. Smith	Mayor	Metropolitan Hotel, 4th Washington St., St. Paul
Phillip Martin	Deputy	293 Harrison Ave., St. Paul
Robt. C. Hine	Judge	Aberdeen Hotel, Virginia & Dayton corner, St. Paul
Asa A. Goodrich	Physician	256 Nelson, St. Paul

CHAPTER 4: NOT IN TRAVERSE COUNTY

Edward Rustad	County Attorney	Wheaton, MN
Seidensticker farm		Walls Township, Traverse County
Charley Teare's farmgate		Croke Township, Traverse County

CHAPTER 5: LAST OF THE ROPE DANCERS

Olin B. Lewis	Judge	23 W. Isabel, St. Paul
James Cormican	Attorney	570 Wabasha, St. Paul
Francis Clark	Attorney	1826 Charles, St. Paul
Thomas Kane	County Attorney	446 Dayton, St. Paul
John A. Johnson	Governor	Ryan Hotel, 6th and Robert NE corner, St. Paul
Frank Robert	Sheriff Deputy	549 Fuller, St. Paul
Justice Ohage	Physician	59 Irving, St. Paul

William Hanft	Lt. Police	783 E. Rose, St. Paul
Windsor Hotel		St. Peter and 5th St. SW corner, St. Paul
Schroeder's Undertaking Parlor		14 E. 6th St., St. Paul
St. Paul Police Station		83 W. 3rd St., St. Paul Paul

CHAPTER 6: NORTHERN HARDSHIPS

Marshall A. Spooner	District Court Judge	721 Lake Blvd., (O) 202 ½ 3rd St., Bemidji
Henry Funkley	County Attorney	1014 Doud Ave., Bemidji
C.W. Scrutchin	Attorney	818 Bemidji, (O) 214 2nd St., Bemidji
E. H. Marcum	Physician	8th and Bemidji, (O) 3rd and Minnesota corner, Bemidji
Herbert J. Loud	Witness	509 Bemidji, (O) Miles Block, Bemidji

CHAPTER 7: A DOUBLE HANGING

G. M. Torrance	Attorney	(O) 205 Beltrami Ave., Bemidji
J. F. Gibbons	Attorney	(O) 205 Beltrami Ave., Bemidji
Henry Funkley	County Attorney	(O) Miles Block, Bemidji

CHAPTER 8: FAMILY SILENCE

Michael Sweeney	Police	396 E. Curtice, St. Paul
J. J. Daly	Police	588 Olive, St. Paul
Charles J. Klabunde	Victim's employee	178 Maple, St. Paul
Belle Walrath	Physician	11 ½ E. 7th St., St. Paul
Arthur Sweeney	Physician	865 Fairmont Ave., St. Paul
William Manteuffel	Victim's friend	98 Garfield, St. Paul
William Mitchell	Attorney	521 Grand, St. Paul
Lawrence Ulmer	Victim's son-in-law	234 S. Exchange, St. Paul
Patrick J. McLaughlin	Attorney	853 Dayton, St. Paul
Richard D. O'Brien	County Attorney	941 Grand, St. Paul
Pierce Butler	Attorney	1347 Summit Ave., St. Paul
St. Luke's Hospital		Smith & Sherman NE corner, St. Paul
Sheriff William Gerber		County jail

CHAPTER 9: MR. FRIDLEY'S SORROW

George Armstrong	Attorney	Excelsior, MN
Fred Beckley	Physician	1840 Marshall, St. Paul
Louise (Wm.) Dye	Sister of Mary Fridley	1019 Knox Ave. S., Minneapolis
William E. Hale	Judge	1602 Laurel, Minneapolis
Carrie Olson	Girlfriend of Price	1002 Hawthorn, Minneapolis
Archie A. Buck	Deputy Sherriff	5020 Vincent Ave. S., Minneapolis
Michael Duffy	Detective	2313 Cedar Ave. S., Minneapolis
Daniel Fish	Judge	2303 3rd Ave. S., Minneapolis
M. C. Brady	Attorney	4037 Bryant Ave. S., Minneapolis
D. C. Cowles	Physician	2627 Park, Minneapolis
Metropolitan Theater		320 Marquette, Minneapolis
Midway Hospital		389 N. Snelling, St. Paul
Verdome Hotel		17-19 S. 4th, Minneapolis

CHAPTER 10: CAST OF KILLERS

Hugo O. Hanft	Judge	1044 Portland, Minneapolis
F. X. Kort	Police Officer	836 Broadway, Minneapolis
John O'Connor	St. Paul Chief of Police	114 West 4th St., St. Paul
Richard O'Brien	County Attorney	1740 Portland, St. Paul
Daniel W. Lawler	Attorney	552 Marshall, St. Paul
George Connery	Police Officer	3009 Taylor St., Minneapolis
Thomas Van Lear	Minneapolis Mayor	4717 Blaisdell Ave. S., Minneapolis
H. Lewis Harthill	Minneapolis Chief of Police	2800 17th Ave. S., Minneapolis
Knights of Columbus		150 N. Smith Ave., St. Paul
Charles F. Zielger	Police Officer	2314 Quincy St., Minneapolis
Frank W. Brunskill	Police Officer	3813 Park Ave., Minneapolis

Bibliography

CHAPTER 1: A WOMAN TO DIE FOR

Davison Minneapolis Directory, 1910.

Hennepin County Historical Society Magazine, 1997.

History and Biography of Minneapolis and Hennepin County Minnesota. Holcumbe, Mal, R. I. and Bingham, Wm. H, Henry Taylor & Co., Chicago, 1914 (Nye).

A History of the Municipal Building: The City of Minneapolis and the County of Hennepin 1897-1909. City Hall Commissioners, Fish, Daniel, Hahn and Harmon Co., Minneapolis 1910.

Lost Minnesota. El-Hai, Jack, University of Minnesota Press, 2000.

Minneapolis Courthouse and City Hall. Dworkin, Liza, Dworkin and Shulteis, Minneapolis, MN, 1974.

Minneapolis Journal, November 26, 1900: 1, 2 photo

Minneapolis Journal, November 27, 1900: 1 photo

Minneapolis Journal, February 2, 1901: 1 part II, photo

Minneapolis Journal, February 4, 1901: 1, 2

Minneapolis Journal, February 5, 1901:1

Minneapolis Journal, February 6, 1901: 1, 2

Minneapolis Journal, February 7, 1901: 1, 2 photo

Minneapolis Journal, February 8, 1901: 1, 2

Minneapolis Journal, February 9, 1901: 1, 2

Minneapolis Journal, February 11, 1901: 1, 2

Minneapolis Journal, February 12, 1901: 1, 2
Minneapolis Journal, February 13, 1901: 1, 2
Minneapolis Journal, February 14, 1901: 1, 2
Minneapolis Journal, February 15, 1901: 1, 2
Minneapolis Journal, February 16, 1901: 1, 2
Minneapolis Journal, February 18, 1901: 1, 2
Minneapolis Journal, February 19, 1901: 1, 2
Minneapolis Journal, February 20, 1901: 1, 2
Minneapolis Journal, February 21, 1901: 1
Minneapolis-St. Paul Then and Now. Richards, Hanje, Thunder Bay Press, San Diego, CA 2001
Minneapolis Times, November 25, 1900: 1
Minneapolis Times, November 26, 1900: 1, 2
Minneapolis Times, November 27, 1900: 1, 2
Minneapolis Times, February 5, 1901: 1 photo, 2
Minneapolis Times, February 6, 1901: 1, 2
Minneapolis Times, February 7, 1901: 1, photo, 2
Minneapolis Times, February 8, 1901: 1, 2
Minneapolis Times, February 9, 1901: 1 photo
Minneapolis Times, February 10, 1901: 1
Minneapolis Times, February 11, 1901: 1
Minneapolis Times, February 12, 1901: 1 photo, 2
Minneapolis Times, February 13, 1901: 1 photo, 2
Minneapolis Times, February 14, 1901: 1 photo, 2
Minneapolis Times, February 15, 1901: 1 photo, 2
Minneapolis Times, February 16, 1901: 1 photo, 2
Minneapolis Times, February 17, 1901: 1, 2
Minneapolis Times, February 18, 1901: 5
Minneapolis Times, February 19, 1901: 1
Minneapolis Times, February 20, 1901: 1, 2
Minneapolis Times, February 21, 1901: 1, 2
Minneapolis Tribune, November 25, 1900: 1
Minneapolis Tribune, November 26, 1900: 1 photo
Minneapolis Tribune, February 5, 1901: 1
Minneapolis Tribune, February 6, 1901: 1, 2
Minneapolis Tribune, February 7, 1901: 1, 2
Minneapolis Tribune, February 8, 1901: 1, 2
Minneapolis Tribune, February 9, 1901: 1, 2
Minneapolis Tribune, February 10, 1901: 1, 2 photo

Minneapolis Tribune, February 11, 1901: 1, 2, 3
Minneapolis Tribune, February 12, 1901: 1
Minneapolis Tribune, February 13, 1901: 1, 2
Minn*eapolis Tribune*, February 14, 1901: 1, photo, 2, 3, 4
Minneapolis Tribune, February 15, 1901: 1, 2, 3, 4
Minneapolis Tribune, February 16, 1901: 1, 2, 3
Minneapolis Tribune, February 17, 1901: 1, 2 photo, 3
Minneapolis Tribune, February 18, 1901: 1, 2
Minneapolis Tribune, February 19, 1901: 1
Minneapolis Tribune, February 20, 1901: 1
Minneapolis Tribune, February 21, 1901: 1, 2
Minneapolis Tribune, February 22, 1901: 1, 2
Mirror, July 1903. Stillwater Prison inmate publication.
Monument. Larson, Paul C., Municipal Building Commission, Minneapolis, Minnesota 1991
Trial Transcripts / Prison Case File, MHS/Hamilton.
The West Hotel. Staples, Loring M, Carlson Publishing Company, Minneapolis, MN 1979 *Municipal.*

CHAPTER 2: DID THE DENTIST DO IT?

Brown County History Center, Reference Library. New Ulm, MN
Brown County Journal, July 23, 1904: 3
Brown County Journal, November 5, 1904: 1
Brown County Journal, November 26, 1904: 1
Brown County Journal, December 17, 1904: 1
Brown County Journal, April 6, 1928.
Mankato Daily Free Press, July 26, 1905: 2
Minnesota Secretary of State, *Fifth Decennial of Minnesota*, 1905. Minnesota Historical Society.
New Ulm Review, November 2, 1904: 2
New Ulm Review, November 9, 1904: 1, 9
New Ulm Review, November 16, 1904: 1, 2
New Ulm Review, November 23, 1904: 1
New Ulm Review, December 7, 1904: 1
New Ulm Review, December 19, 1904: 1
New Ulm Review, December 21, 1904: 1, 2
New Ulm Review, December 28, 1904: 1
New Ulm Review, January 4, 1905: 1

New Ulm Review, January 11, 1905: 1, 4, 5, 8
New Ulm Review, January 18, 1905: 1, 5
New Ulm Review, January 25, 1905: 1
New Ulm Review, February 1, 1905: 1
New Ulm Review, February 8, 1905: 1
New Ulm Review, February 15, 1905: 1
New Ulm Review, February 22, 1905: 1
New Ulm Review, April 26, 1905: 1, 4. Supplement Section 1, 2, 3, 4 photo
New Ulm Review, May 3, 1905: 1. Supplement Section 1, 2, 3, 4, 5, 6 photo
New Ulm Review, May 10, 1905: 1. Supplement Section 1, 2, 3, 4, 5
New Ulm Review, May 17, 1905: 1. Supplement Section 1, 2, 3, 4, 5, 6, 7, 8
New Ulm Review, May 24, 1905: 1
New Ulm Review, August 2, 1905: 1, 3
New Ulm Review, August 9, 1905: 1
New Ulm Review, August 23, 1905: 1
St. Paul Dispatch, May 1, 1905: 1, photo
St. Paul Dispatch, May 2, 1905: 1, 4
St. Paul Dispatch, May 3, 1905: 1, 4
St. Paul Dispatch, May 4, 1905: 1, 4
St. Paul Dispatch May 5, 1905: 1, 6
St. Paul Dispatch May 6, 1905: 1
St. Paul Dispatch, May 8, 1905: 1, 3
St. Paul Dispatch, May 9, 1905: 1, 4
St. Paul Dispatch, May 10, 1905: 1, 5
St. Paul Dispatch, May 11, 1905: 1, 3
St. Paul Dispatch, May 12, 1905: 1, 20
St. Paul Dispatch, May 13, 1905: 1, 2, 3
St. Paul Dispatch, May 15, 1905: 1
St. Paul Dispatch, May 22, 1905: 1
St. Paul Dispatch, August 30, 1906.
St. Paul Pioneer Press, April 19, 1905: 1
St. Paul Pioneer Press, April 20, 1905: 1,
St. Paul Pioneer Press, April 21, 1905: 1, 5
St. Paul Pioneer Press, April 22, 1905: 1
St. Paul Pioneer Press, April 23, 1905: 1, 2
St. Paul Pioneer Press, April 24, 1905: 1, 8 photo
St. Paul Pioneer Press, April 26, 1905: 1, 6
St. Paul Pioneer Press, April 27, 1905: 1, 6
St. Paul Pioneer Press, April 28, 1905: 1, 5

St. Paul Pioneer Press, April 29, 1905: 1, 5
St. Paul Pioneer Press, April 30, 1905: 1, 2
St. Paul Pioneer Press, May 11, 1905: 3
St. Paul Pioneer Press, May 12, 1905: 1
St. Paul Pioneer Press, May 13, 1905: 1, 5
St. Paul Pioneer Press, May 14, 1905: 1, 2
St. Paul Pioneer Press, May 15, 1905: 1
St. Paul Pioneer Press, May 19, 1905: 10
St. Paul Pioneer Press, July 9, 1905: 1
St. Paul Pioneer Press, July 20, 1905: 1

CHAPTER 3: THE MYSTERY OF THE MURDERED BUTCHER

St. Paul Dispatch, July 20, 1905: 1
St. Paul Pioneer Press, February 19, 1905: 1, 4 photo, 6
St. Paul Pioneer Press, February 20, 1905: 1, 8
St. Paul Pioneer Press, February 21, 1905: 1, 2 photo
St. Paul Pioneer Press, February 23, 1905: 1
St. Paul Pioneer Press, February 25, 1905: 1
St. Paul Pioneer Press, February 26, 1905: 1, 6
St. Paul Pioneer Press, February 27, 1905: 1, 2
St. Paul Pioneer Press, February 28, 1905: 1, 2
St. Paul Pioneer Press, March 1, 1905: 1, 3
St. Paul Pioneer Press, March 2, 1905: 3
St. Paul Pioneer Press, March 3, 1905: 1
St. Paul Pioneer Press, March 4, 1905: 1, 2
St. Paul Pioneer Press, March 5, 1905: 1, Editorial
St. Paul Pioneer Press, March 9, 1905: 1, 9
St. Paul Pioneer Press, March 10, 1905: 2.
St. Paul Pioneer Press, March 16, 1905: 1, 5
St. Paul Pioneer Press, March 18, 1905: 1, 5
St. Paul Pioneer Press, March 19, 1905: 1
St. Paul Pioneer Press, March 21, 1905: 1, 5
St. Paul Pioneer Press, March 23, 1905: 1, 6
St. Paul Pioneer Press, April 15, 1905: 2
St. Paul Pioneer Press, May 8, 1905: 2
St. Paul Pioneer Press, May 9, 1905: 1, 4, 5, section 2, photos 4, 5
St. Paul Pioneer Press, May 11, 1905: 1
St. Paul Pioneer Press, May 12, 1905: 1, 3

St. Paul Pioneer Press, May 13, 1905: 3
St. Paul Pioneer Press, May 18, 1905: 6
St. Paul Pioneer Press, July 18, 1905: 2 photo
St. Paul Pioneer Press, July 19, 1905: 1, 2
St. Paul Pioneer Press, July 20, 1905: 1, 3 photo
St. Paul Pioneer Press, July 23, 1905: 1

CHAPTER 4: NOT IN TRAVERSE COUNTY

Minneapolis Journal, May 26, 1905: 1
Minneapolis Journal, June 30, 1905: 1
St. Paul Pioneer Press, July 1, 1905: 1
St. Paul Pioneer Press, July 4, 1905: 1
St. Paul Dispatch, June 20, 1905: 2
St. Paul Dispatch, July 1, 1905: 1
St. Paul Dispatch, July 4, 1905: 6
Traverse County Civil and Criminal Court Record, MHS
Traverse County Record's Office, Wheaton, MN
Trial Records: Minnesota Historical Society.
Weekly Foot Prints – Traverse County, June 30, 1905: 1
Weekly Foot Prints – Traverse County, July 7, 1905: 1
Wheaton Gazette-Reporter, May 26, 1905: 1
Wheaton Gazette-Reporter, June 2, 1905: 1
Wheaton Gazette-Reporter, June 30, 1905: 1, 5
Wheaton Gazette-Reporter, July 7, 1905: 1, 5
Wheaton Weekly Footprints, June 30, 1905:1

CHAPTER 5: LAST OF THE ROPE DANCERS

Legacy of Violence: Lynch Mobs and Executions in Minnesota. John D. Bessler. (Minneapolis: University of Minnesota Press, 2003): 4, 80, 87.
St. Paul Daily News, February 13, 1906: 1, 5, 6, 7 photo
St. Paul Dispatch, April 13, 1905: 1, 3 photo
St. Paul Dispatch, April 14, 1905: 1
St. Paul Dispatch, May 10, 1905: 4
St. Paul Dispatch, May 12, 1905: 1, 8
St. Paul Dispatch, May 17, 1905: 1, 2
St. Paul Dispatch, May 18, 1905: 1, 2

St. Paul Dispatch, May 19, 1905: 1, 5
St. Paul Dispatch, May 20, 1905: 2
St. Paul Dispatch, February 2, 1906: 1, 5
St. Paul Dispatch, February 5, 1906: 7
St. Paul Dispatch, February 10, 1906: 24
St. Paul Dispatch, February 12, 1906: 1, 3, 7 photo
St. Paul Dispatch, February 13, 1906: 3 photo
St. Paul Pioneer Press, April 13, 1905: 1
St. Paul Pioneer Press, April 14, 1905: 2
St. Paul Pioneer Press, April 15, 1905: 2
St. Paul Pioneer Press, April 25, 1905: 2
St. Paul Pioneer Press, May 12, 1905: 3
St. Paul Pioneer Press, May 13, 1905: 2
St. Paul Pioneer Press, May 18, 1905: 6
St. Paul Pioneer Press, May 19, 1905: 3
St. Paul Pioneer Press, May 20, 1905: 1, 5
St. Paul Pioneer Press, February 13, 1906: 1, 2

CHAPTER 6: NORTHERN HARDSHIPS

Beltrami County Court Transcripts: State Vs. Fournier, MHS
Bemidji Daily Pioneer, July 25, 1904: 4
Bemidji Daily Pioneer, July 26, 1904: 1
Bemidji Daily Pioneer, July 27, 1904: 4
Bemidji Daily Pioneer, July 28, 1904: 4
Bemidji Daily Pioneer, July 29, 1904: 4
Bemidji Daily Pioneer, July 30, 1904: 4
Bemidji Daily Pioneer, August 2, 1904: 4
Bemidji Daily Pioneer, August 9, 1904: 4
Bemidji Daily Pioneer, August 12, 1904: 4
Bemidji Daily Pioneer, August 15, 1904: 4
Bemidji Daily Pioneer, August 18, 1904: 4
Bemidji Daily Pioneer, August 19, 1904: 4
Bemidji Daily Pioneer, August 23, 1904: 4
Bemidji Daily Pioneer, August 25, 1904: 4
Bemidji Daily Pioneer, August 26, 1904: 4
Bemidji Daily Pioneer, August 31, 1904: 4
Bemidji Daily Pioneer, September 6, 1904: 4
Bemidji Daily Pioneer, March 28, 1907: 1, 4

Bemidji Daily Pioneer, March 29, 1907: 1, 4
Bemidji Daily Pioneer, March 30, 1907: 1, 4
Bemidji Daily Pioneer, April 1, 1907: 1, 4
Bemidji Daily Pioneer, April 2, 1907: 1, 4
Bemidji Daily Pioneer, April 3, 1907: 1, 4
Bemidji Daily Pioneer, April 4, 1907: 1, 4
Bemidji Daily Pioneer, April 5, 1907: 1, 4
Bemidji Daily Pioneer, April 6, 1907: 1
Bemidji Daily Pioneer, April 8, 1907: 1
Bemidji Daily Pioneer, April 9, 1907: 1, 4
Bemidji Daily Pioneer, April 10, 1907: 1
Bemidji Daily Pioneer, April 11, 1907: 1, 4
Bemidji Daily Pioneer, April 12, 1907: 1, 4
Bemidji Daily Pioneer, April 13, 1907: 1, 4
Bemidji Daily Pioneer, April 15, 1907: 1
Bemidji Daily Pioneer, December 17, 1909
For the Record, 150 Years of Law and Lawyers in Minnesota. Minnesota Bar Association, 1999.
Hoffbeck, Steven R., "Victories Yet to Win: Charles W. Scrutchin, Bemidji's Black Activist Attorney," *Minnesota History* 55, no. 2 (summer 1996): 66.
Minneapolis Tribune, March 30, 1907: 1
Mississippi Headwaters Region. Hagg, Harold T. (Bemidji, Minn.: Beltrami Historical Society, 1986). *State v. Fournier*, 108 Minn. 402, 122 N.W. 329 Criminal law.
State vs. Paul Fournier, Minnesota Supreme Court Library, July 16, 1909, NOS. 16, 070-(21).
Mississippi Headwaters Region. Hagg, Harold T. (Bemidji, Minn.: Beltrami Historical Society, 1986).

CHAPTER 7: A DOUBLE HANGING

Bemidji Daily Pioneer, September 23, 1907: 1
Bemidji Daily Pioneer, September 28, 1907: 1
Bemidji Daily Pioneer, October 3, 1907: 1 photo
Bemidji Daily Pioneer, October 5, 1907: 1, 4 photo
Bemidji Daily Pioneer, January 27, 1908: 1
The Book of Minnesotans, Marquis, Albert N., Marquis Publishing Co., Chicago, 1907
Brainerd Daily Dispatch, September 12, 1932: 1 photo
History of the Bench and Bar of Minnesota, Stevens, Hiram F., Legal Publishing and Engraving Co., Minneapolis, St. Paul, 1904

Minneapolis Journal, January 11, 1933: 1,4
Minneapolis Journal, January 12, 1933: 1, 15 photo
Minneapolis Star, January 12, 1933:5 photo
Minneapolis Tribune, January 12, 1933: 1 photo, 13 photo
Minnesota Historical Center, Reference Library
Stillwater State Prison inmate case files, MHS

CHAPTER 8: FAMILY SILENCE

Minneapolis Tribune, June 3, 1909: 1
St. Paul Daily News, May 13, 1909: 1, 2
St. Paul Daily News, May 14, 1909: 1
St. Paul Daily News, May 15, 1909: 1
St. Paul Daily News, May 16, 1909: 1, 2nd section
St. Paul Daily News, May 17, 1909: 1, 2
St. Paul Daily News, May 18, 1909: 1 photo
St. Paul Daily News, May 19, 1909: 1
St. Paul Daily News, May 20, 1909: 1, 2
St. Paul Daily News, May 21, 1909: 1
St. Paul Daily News, May 22, 1909: 1
St. Paul Daily News, May 23, 1909: 1, 2nd section
St. Paul Daily News, May 25, 1909: 1
St. Paul Daily News, May 26, 1909: 1
St. Paul Daily News, May 27, 1909: 1
St. Paul Daily News, May 28, 1909: 2
St. Paul Daily News, May 30, 1909: 1
St. Paul Daily News, June 1, 1909: 1
St. Paul Daily News, June 2, 1909: 1
St. Paul Daily News, June 3, 1909: 1
St. Paul Daily News, June 4, 1909: 1, 2 photo
St. Paul Daily News, June 5, 1909: 1
St. Paul Daily News, June 6, 1909: 1
St. Paul Daily News, June 7, 1909: 1
St. Paul Daily News, June 9, 1909: 1
St. Paul Daily News, June 10, 1909: 1
St. Paul Daily News, June 11, 1909: 2
St. Paul Daily News, June 12, 1909: 1
St. Paul Daily News, June 14, 1909: 1
St. Paul Daily News, October 21, 1909: 1

St. Paul Dispatch, May 13, 1909: 1, 2, 13 photo
St. Paul Dispatch, May 14, 1909: 1, 2 photo
St. Paul Dispatch, May 15, 1909: 1, 3 photo
St. Paul Dispatch, May 17, 1909: 1, 2
St. Paul Dispatch, May 18, 1909: 1
St. Paul Dispatch, May 19, 1909: 1
St. Paul Dispatch, May 20, 1909: 1, 2, 11
St. Paul Dispatch, May 21, 1909: 1, 2
St. Paul Dispatch, May 24, 1909: 1
St. Paul Dispatch, May 25, 1909: 1, 2
St. Paul Dispatch, May 26, 1909: 1
St. Paul Dispatch, May 28, 1909: 4
St. Paul Dispatch, May 29, 1909: 1
St. Paul Dispatch, June 4, 1909: 1
St. Paul Dispatch, October 19, 1909: 1
St. Paul Dispatch, October 20, 1909: 1
St. Paul Dispatch, October 21, 1909: 1
St. Paul Dispatch, October 22, 1909: 1
St. Paul Dispatch, October 23, 1909: 1
St. Paul Dispatch, October 24, 1909: 1
St. Paul Dispatch, October 26, 1909: 1
St. Paul Dispatch, October 28, 1909: 1
St. Paul Dispatch, October 29, 1909: 1
St. Paul Dispatch, October 30, 1909: 1
St. Paul Dispatch, November 2, 1909: 1
St. Paul Dispatch, November 3, 1909: 1, 17
St. Paul Dispatch, November 4, 1909: 1
St. Paul Dispatch, November 5, 1909: 1
St. Paul Pioneer Press, May 14, 1909: 1

CHAPTER 9: MR. FRIDLEY'S SORROW

Minneapolis Journal, November 29, 1914: 1 photo
Minneapolis Journal, December 1, 1915: 1
Minneapolis Journal, December 2, 1915: 1
Minneapolis Journal, December 7, 1915: 1, 2, 10 photo
Minneapolis Journal, December 8, 1915: 1, 2 photo
Minneapolis Journal, December 9, 1915: 1
Minneapolis Journal, December 10, 1915: 1, 28 photo

Minneapolis Journal, December 11, 1915: 1
Minneapolis Journal, December 13, 1915: 1, 2
Minneapolis Journal, December 14, 1915: 1, 2, 17 photo
Minneapolis Journal, December 15, 1915: 1
Minneapolis Journal, December 16, 1915: 10
Minneapolis Journal, December 17, 1915: 1
Minneapolis Journal, January 2, 1916: 1
Minneapolis Journal, January 4, 1916: 1, 2 photo
Minneapolis Journal, January 5, 1916: 1, 2, 8
Minneapolis Journal, January 6, 1916: 1, 2
Minneapolis Journal, January 7, 1916: 1, 15 photo
Minneapolis Journal, January 8, 1916: 1, 2
Minneapolis Journal, January 9, 1916: 1 City Section
Minneapolis Journal, January 10, 1916: 1, photo, 2, 16 photo
Minneapolis Journal, January 11, 1916: 1, photo, 2, 6 photo
Minneapolis Journal, January 12, 1916: 1, photo, 2, 8 photo, 16 photo
Minneapolis Journal, January 13, 1916: 1, 2, 7,
Minneapolis Journal, January 14, 1916: 1, 2
Minneapolis Journal, January 15, 1916: 1, 2
Minneapolis Journal, January 16, 1916: 1, 4 photo
Minneapolis Journal, March 26, 1926: 1
Minneapolis Tribune, December 2, 1915: 1
Minneapolis Tribune, December 7, 1915: 1, 2
Minneapolis Tribune, December 9, 1915: 2
Minneapolis Tribune, December 10, 1915: 2
Minneapolis Tribune, December 12, 1915: 2
Minneapolis Tribune, January 5, 1916: 1, 2
Minneapolis Tribune, January 6, 1916: 1
Minneapolis Tribune, January 7, 1916: 1 photo, 4, 5
Minneapolis Tribune, January 8, 1916: 1
Minneapolis Tribune, January 9, 1916: 6 photo
Minneapolis Tribune, January 12, 1916: 1
St. Paul Daily News, January 7, 1916: 2 photo

CHAPTER 10: CAST OF KILLERS

Dunn Murder Case, Hillman, George Nelson MHS
Killed in the Line of Duty, Miranda, Sgt. Tony, Minneapolis Police Officers Federation, 1998

Minneapolis Journal, April 30, 1917: 1
Minneapolis Journal, May 13, 1917: 1
Minneapolis Journal, May 14, 1917: 1
Minnesota History Society Magazine, 1933, Geo Hillman.
Reminiscences, Geo Hillman, MHS.
St. Paul Daily Press, April 27, 1917: 1 photo, 2
St. Paul Daily Press, April 28, 1917: 1, 2
St. Paul Daily Press, April 29, 1017: 1, 2
St. Paul Daily Press, April 30, 1917: 1
St. Paul Dispatch, May 5, 1917: 1
St. Paul Dispatch, June 2, 1917: 1
St. Paul Dispatch, June 7, 1917: 1, 12
St. Paul Dispatch, June 8, 1917: 1 photo, 16, 17, 18
St. Paul Dispatch, June 9, 1917: 1, 2
St. Paul Dispatch, June 11, 1917: 1 photo, 6
St. Paul Dispatch, June 14, 1917: 1, 2
St. Paul Dispatch, June 15, 1917: 1, 7
St. Paul Dispatch, June 16, 1917: 1, 2
St. Paul Dispatch, June 18, 1917: 1, 2
St. Paul Dispatch, June 19, 1917: 1, 12
St. Paul Dispatch, June 20, 1917: 1, 2, 6 photo
St. Paul Dispatch, June 21, 1917: 1 photo, 2
St. Paul Dispatch, June 22, 1917: 1, 2, 3
St. Paul Dispatch, June 23, 1917: 1 photo, 2
St. Paul Dispatch, June 25, 1917: 1, 2, 12
St. Paul Dispatch, June 26, 1917: 1, 2
St. Paul Dispatch, June 27, 1917: 1, 2
St. Paul Dispatch, June 28, 1917: 1, 2
St. Paul Dispatch, June 29, 1917: 1, 2
St. Paul Dispatch, June 30, 1917: 1, 2
St. Paul Dispatch, July 1, 1917: 1
St. Paul Pioneer Press, April 26, 1917: 1
St. Paul Pioneer Press, April 27, 1917: 1, 2
St. Paul Pioneer Press, April 28, 1917: 1
St. Paul Pioneer Press, April 29,1917: 1 2nd section
St. Paul Pioneer Press, April 30, 1917: 1
St. Paul Pioneer Press, May 1, 1917: 1
St. Paul Pioneer Press, May 2, 1917: 1, 11
St. Paul Pioneer Press, May 3, 1917: 1

St. Paul Pioneer Press, May 4, 1917: 1, 2, 3
St. Paul Pioneer Press, May 5, 1917: 1
St. Paul Pioneer Press, May 6, 1917; 1,2
St. Paul Pioneer Press, May 7, 1917: 1
St. Paul Pioneer Press, May 8, 1917: 1
St. Paul Pioneer Press, May 9, 1917: 1, 11
St. Paul Pioneer Press, May 10, 1917: 1
St. Paul Pioneer Press, May 12, 1917:1
St. Paul Pioneer Press, May 13, 1917:1
St. Paul Pioneer Press, May 14, 1917: 1, 2
St. Paul Pioneer Press, May 15, 1917: 1, 2
St. Paul Pioneer Press, May 16, 1917: 1, 11 photo
St. Paul Pioneer Press, May 17, 1917: 1
St. Paul Pioneer Press, May 21, 1917: 1
St. Paul Pioneer Press, May 22, 1917: 1
St. Paul Pioneer Press, May 23, 1917: 1, 2 photo
St. Paul Pioneer Press, May 24, 1917: 1
St. Paul Pioneer Press, May 25, 1917: 1
St. Paul Pioneer Press, May 26, 1917: 1, 2
St. Paul Pioneer Press, May 29, 1917: 1
St. Paul Pioneer Press, May 31, 1917: 1
St. Paul Pioneer Press, June 1, 1917: 1
St. Paul Pioneer Press, June 3, 1917: 9, 2nd section
St. Paul Pioneer Press, June 5, 1917: 1
St. Paul Pioneer Press, June 6, 1917: 12
St. Paul Pioneer Press, June 7, 1917: 1, 11
St. Paul Pioneer Press, June 8, 1917: 1, 2
St. Paul Pioneer Press, June 9, 1917: 1, 2
St. Paul Pioneer Press, June 10, 1917: 1, 2, 2nd section
St. Paul Pioneer Press, June 13, 1917: 1, 9
St. Paul Pioneer Press, June 15, 1917: 5
St. Paul Pioneer Press, June 16, 1917: 1, 3
St. Paul Pioneer Press, June 17, 1917: 1, 2nd section
St. Paul Pioneer Press, June 18, 1917: 8
St. Paul Pioneer Press, June 19, 1917: 1, 3
St. Paul Pioneer Press, June 20, 1917: 1, 2
St. Paul Pioneer Press, June 21, 1917: 1, 2
St. Paul Pioneer Press, June 22, 1917: 1, 2, 4
St. Paul Pioneer Press, June 23, 1917: 1, 2, 7

St. Paul Pioneer Press, June 24, 1917: 1, 2, 2nd section
St. Paul Pioneer Press, June 25, 1917: 1
St. Paul Pioneer Press, June 26, 1917: 1, 2, 3
St. Paul Pioneer Press, June 27, 1917: 1, 2, 11
St. Paul Pioneer Press, June 28, 1917: 1, 2, 3
St. Paul Pioneer Press, June 29, 1917: 1, 2, 3
St. Paul Pioneer Press, June 30, 1917: 1, 2, 3
Stillwater Prison inmate files, MHS